Program Arcade Games

Games

With Python and Pygame

Fourth Edition

■ ■ ■

Paul Vincent Craven

Apress®

Program Arcade Games: With Python and Pygame, Fourth Edition

ISBN-13 (pbk): 978-1-4842-1789-4

ISBN-13 (electronic): 978-1-4842-1790-0

Managing Director: Welmoed Spahr
Lead Editor: Steve Anglin
Editorial Board: Steve Anglin, Pramila Balan, Louise Corrigan, Jonathan Gennick, Robert Hutchinson, Celestin Suresh John, Michelle Lowman, James Markham, Susan McDermott, Matthew Moodie, Jeffrey Pepper, Douglas Pundick, Ben Renow-Clarke, Gwenan Spearing
Coordinating Editor: Mark Powers
Copy Editor: Karen Jameson
Compositor: SPi Global
Indexer: SPi Global
Artist: SPi Global

Distributed to the book trade worldwide by Springer Science+Business Media New York, 233 Spring Street, 6th Floor, New York, NY 10013. Phone 1-800-SPRINGER, fax (201) 348-4505, e-mail orders-ny@springer-sbm.com, or visit www.springeronline.com. Apress Media, LLC is a California LLC and the sole member (owner) is Springer Science + Business Media Finance Inc (SSBM Finance Inc). SSBM Finance Inc is a Delaware corporation

For information on translations, please e-mail rights@apress.com, or visit www.apress.com.

Apress and friends of ED books may be purchased in bulk for academic, corporate, or promotional use. eBook versions and licenses are also available for most titles. For more information, reference our Special Bulk Sales–eBook Licensing web page at www.apress.com/bulk-sales.

Any source code or other supplementary materials referenced by the author in this text is available to readers at www.apress.com/9781484217894. For detailed information about how to locate your book's source code, go to www.apress.com/source-code/. Readers can also access source code at SpringerLink in the Supplementary Material section for each chapter.

This book is dedicated to everyone who loves to learn.

Contents at a Glance

About the Author xix

Introduction xxi

■Chapter 1: Before Getting Started…... 1

■Chapter 2: Create a Custom Calculator 11

■Chapter 3: What Is a Computer Language? 33

■Chapter 4: Quiz Games and If Statements 41

■Chapter 5: Guessing Games with Random Numbers and Loops........................... 59

■Chapter 6: Introduction to Graphics 81

■Chapter 7: Back to Looping 107

■Chapter 8: Introduction to Lists.. 121

■Chapter 9: Introduction to Animation 137

■Chapter 10: Functions 153

■Chapter 11: Controllers and Graphics 179

■Chapter 12: Bitmapped Graphics and Sound... 205

■Chapter 13: Introduction to Classes 217

■Chapter 14: Introduction to Sprites... 247

■Chapter 15: Libraries and Modules 267

■Chapter 16: Searching... 273

■Chapter 17: Array-Backed Grids.. 287

■**Chapter 18: Sorting** **301**

■**Chapter 19: Exceptions** **311**

■**Chapter 20: Recursion** **319**

■**Chapter 21: Formatting** **335**

■**Chapter 22: Exercises** **347**

Index **389**

Contents

About the Author xix

Introduction xxi

■Chapter 1: Before Getting Started.. 1

Installing and Starting Python 1

Windows Installation 1

Mac Installation 3

Unix Installation 6

Optional Wing IDE 7

Viewing File Extensions.. 9

Learn to Make Games and Get Paid 9

Get the Most from This Book 10

Send Feedback 10

■Chapter 2: Create a Custom Calculator 11

Printing.. 12

Printing Text...12

Printing Results of Expressions 13

Printing Multiple Items 13

Escape Codes.. 14

Comments 15

Assignment Operators.. 16

Variables.. 18

Operators... 19

Operator Spacing..20

Order of Operations 20

Trig Functions 20

Custom Equation Calculators 21

Review 25

    Multiple Choice Quiz 25

    Short Answer Worksheet 28

    Exercise 31

■Chapter 3: What Is a Computer Language? 33

Short History of Programming 33

Review 38

    Multiple Choice Quiz 38

    Short Answer Worksheet 40

    Exercise 40

■Chapter 4: Quiz Games and If Statements 41

Basic Comparisons 41

Indentation 43

Using And/Or 44

Boolean Variables 44

Else and Else If 46

Text Comparisons 47

    Multiple Text Possibilities 48

    Case Insensitive Comparisons 48

Example if Statements 48

Review 51

    Multiple Choice Quiz 51

    Short Answer Worksheet 55

    Exercise 57

■Chapter 5: Guessing Games with Random Numbers and Loops.........................59

for Loops 63

    Counting by Numbers Other Than One 65

    Nesting Loops...66

    Keeping a Running Total 66

Example for Loops...68

while Loops 70

    Using Increment Operators...70

    Looping Until User Wants to Quit 71

    Common Problems with while Loops 72

Example while Loops 72

Random Numbers..74

    The randrange Function 74

    The random Function 74

Review..75

    Multiple Choice Quiz..75

    Short Answer Worksheet 78

    Exercise 79

■Chapter 6: Introduction to Graphics 81

Computer Coordinate Systems...82

Pygame Library 85

Colors 85

Open a Window 87

Interacting with the User...87

    The Event Processing Loop...88

    Processing Each Frame 89

Ending the Program..90

Clearing the Screen..90

Flipping the Screen 90

Open a Blank Window 90

Drawing Introduction 92

Drawing Lines 93

Drawing Lines with Loops and Offsets... 93

Drawing a Rectangle 95

Drawing an Ellipse 95

Drawing an Arc 96

Drawing a Polygon 96

Drawing Text.. 97

Full Program Listing 99

Review... 102

    Multiple Choice Quiz...102

    Short Answer Worksheet 105

    Exercise 106

■Chapter 7: Back to Looping 107

Print Statement End Characters.. 107

Advanced Looping Problems 108

Review... 115

    Multiple Choice Quiz...115

    Short Answer Worksheet 117

    Exercise 119

■Chapter 8: Introduction to Lists... 121

Working with Lists.. 122

Iterating through a List... 124

Adding to a List 125

Summing or Modifying a List 126

Slicing Strings 127

Secret Codes 128

Associative Arrays 131

Review...132

Multiple Choice Quiz..132

Short Answer Worksheet 135

Exercise 136

■Chapter 9: Introduction to Animation 137

Animating Snow 141

Code Explanation..141

Full Program Listing 143

3D Animation 145

Review...147

Multiple Choice Quiz..147

Short Answer Worksheet 151

Exercise 152

■Chapter 10: Functions 153

Function Parameters...154

Returning and Capturing Values..156

Returning Values...156

Capturing Returned Values 156

Improving the volume_cylinder Example 156

Documenting Functions 158

Variable Scope 158

Pass-by-copy 159

Functions Calling Functions 160

Main Functions and Globals 160

Short Examples 161

Mudball Game Example..165

Review 167

    Multiple Choice Quiz 167

    Short Answer Worksheet 171

    Correcting Code 175

    Exercise 178

■Chapter 11: Controllers and Graphics 179

Mouse 186

Keyboard 187

Game Controller 192

Review 201

    Multiple Choice Quiz 201

    Short Answer Worksheet 203

    Exercise 204

■Chapter 12: Bitmapped Graphics and Sound 205

Storing the Program in a Folder 205

Setting a Background Image 206

Moving an Image 208

Sounds 210

Full Listing 211

Review 213

    Multiple Choice Quiz 213

    Short Answer Worksheet 214

    Exercise 215

■Chapter 13: Introduction to Classes 217

Why Learn About Classes? 217

Defining and Creating Simple Classes 218

Adding Methods to Classes 223

    Example: Ball Class 225

References 226

    Functions and References 229

    Review Questions 231

Constructors 231

    Avoid This Mistake 232

    Review Questions 233

Inheritance 233

    Is-A and Has-A Relationships 237

Static Variables vs. Instance Variables 237

    Instance Variables Hiding Static Variables 239

Review 240

    Multiple Choice Quiz 240

    Short Answer Worksheet 244

    Exercise 246

■Chapter 14: Introduction to Sprites 247

Basic Sprites and Collisions 248

Moving Sprites 253

The Game Class 254

Other Examples 255

    Shooting things 255

    Walls 256

    Platforms 258

    Snake/Centipede 260

    Using Sprite Sheets 262

Review 262

    Multiple Choice Quiz 262

    Exercise 265

■Chapter 15: Libraries and Modules 267

Why Create a Library? 268

Creating Your Own Module/Library File: 268

Namespace 269

Third Party Libraries 270

Review 270

Multiple Choice Quiz 270

Short Answer Worksheet 271

Exercise 272

■Chapter 16: Searching 273

Reading from a File 274

Reading into an Array 275

Linear Search 276

Linear Search Algorithm 276

Variations on the Linear Search 276

Does at Least One Item Have a Property? 277

Do All Items Have a Property? 278

Create a List with All Items Matching a Property................................. 278

Binary Search 279

Review 281

Multiple Choice Quiz 281

Short Answer Worksheet Linear Search Review.................................. 283

Binary Search Review 284

Challenge Question.. 285

Exercise 285

■Chapter 17: Array-Backed Grids.. 287

Application 289

Drawing the Grid.. 290

Populating the Grid 293

Final Program 296

Review...298

    Multiple Choice Quiz..298

    Short Answer Worksheet...299

■Chapter 18: Sorting 301

Swapping Values 301

Selection Sort..303

Insertion Sort..305

Review..306

    Multiple Choice Quiz..306

    Short Answer Worksheet...308

■Chapter 19: Exceptions...311

Vocabulary...311

Exception Handling..311

Example: Saving High Score..313

Exception Objects..314

Exception Generating 315

Proper Exception Use 315

Review..315

    Multiple Choice Quiz..315

    Short Answer Worksheet...317

■Chapter 20: Recursion 319

Where Is Recursion Used? 319

How Is Recursion Coded?...321

Controlling Recursion Depth...321

Recursion Factorial Calculation..322

Recursive Rectangles...324

Fractals 327

Recursive Binary Search 332

Review... 333

    Short Answer Worksheet 333

■**Chapter 21: Formatting** **335**

Decimal Numbers.. 335

Strings... 338

Leading Zeros.. 339

Floating-Point Numbers 340

Printing Dollars and Cents.. 342

Use in Pygame... 345

Review... 345

    Short Answer Worksheet 345

■**Chapter 22: Exercises**.. **347**

Exercise 1: Custom Calculators.. 348

    Program A.. 348

    Program B.. 349

    Program C.. 349

Exercise 2: Create-a-Quiz... 350

    Description 350

    Example Run.. 351

Exercise 3: Camel.. 352

    Description of the Camel Game 352

    Sample Run of Camel 353

    Programming Guide... 354

    Hints 356

Exercise 4: Create-a-Picture 357

    Description 357

Exercise 5: Loopy Lab...362

    Part 1...362

    Part 2...362

    Part 3...363

    Part 4...363

Exercise 6: Adventure!...365

    Description of the Adventure Game...365

    Sample Run..365

    Creating Your Dungeon..366

    Step-by-step Instructions...367

Exercise 7: Animation 369

    Requirements 369

Exercise 8: Functions 369

Exercise 9: User Control 372

Exercise 10: Bitmapped Graphics and User Control 372

Exercise 11: Classes and Graphics...373

    Instructions..373

Exercise 12: Sprite Collecting...379

Exercise 13: Sprite Moving..381

Exercise 14: Spell Check 383

    Requirements 383

    Steps to Complete: 383

    Example Run...385

Exercise 15: Final Exercise...386

    Video Game Option 386

    Text Adventure Option..387

Index..389

About the Author

Paul Vincent Craven is a Computer Science professor at Simpson College in Indianola, Iowa. He worked in the IT industry for several years before switching to teaching full-time. He has a Ph.D. from the University of Idaho, a M.S. from Missouri University of Science and Technology, and B.A. from Simpson College.

Introduction

It all started in 1983 when my dad, who was also a teacher, bought an Apple //e computer for our use at home. Since it was to be "dad's computer" for educational purposes only, my brother and I were not allowed to purchase any games. So, at the local library I found two programming books by David H. Ahl: *BASIC Computer Games* and *More BASIC Computer Games*. These books had code I could use to type in and run my own games. This was the beginning of my creative outlet with computers.

As a computer science professor, I have found getting other people to program their own games as a great way to foster interest in computer science. Unfortunately, back when I started teaching students this way, the type of book I started with in the 1980s did not seem to be available any longer. I wanted to help others learn to program the same way I started. To provide a textbook for my students, I began to write my own programming book.

I started the website ProgramArcadeGames.com in 2009. The book you have in your hand morphed from the materials on that website and from student input from my beginning computer programming classes.

I would like to acknowledge and thank everyone who took time to give feedback, no matter how large or small. This book is the product of hundreds of students I have worked with personally, and the feedback of hundreds of people on-line. I continue to develop the website and use this book to share my love of programming with others.

CHAPTER 1

■ ■ ■

Before Getting Started...

This introductory chapter has two parts:

- Getting your computer set up to write games.

- Job and career prospects in technology.

Installing and Starting Python

To get started, two programs need to be installed: Python and Pygame. Python is the computer language we will program in, and Pygame is a library of commands that will help make writing games easier.

Windows Installation

If you are working with a computer that already has Python and Pygame set up on it, you can skip this step. But if you want to set up Python and Pygame on your own Windows computer, don't worry. It is very easy.

1. Run the Python installer downloaded from
   `http://ProgramArcadeGames.com/python-3.4.3.msi`

2. Run the Pygame installer downloaded from
   `http://ProgramArcadeGames.com/pygame-1.9.2a0.win32-py3.4.msi`

Once everything has been installed, start Python up by selecting the Integrated Development Environment (IDLE) as shown in the figure.

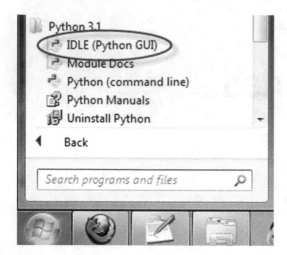

Starting Python

The files provided above come from the Python download page at http://www.python.org/download/ and the Pygame file originally comes from https://bitbucket.org/pygame/pygame/downloads.

■ **Note**   There are many versions of Python and Pygame. It can be complicated to get the correct versions and get them to work together. I recommend using the links on ProgramArcadeGames.com rather than downloading them from the Python and Pygame web sites.

If you must use a different version of Python than what is listed here, find a matching version of Pygame at this website: www.lfd.uci.edu/~gohlke/pythonlibs/#pygame.

Mac Installation

The installation for the Mac is a bit involved, but it isn't too bad. Here are the steps.

1. Open up a terminal window. Click on "Finder" then "Applications" and then open "Utilities."

Starting a terminal window

2. Double-click on "Terminal."

Starting a terminal window

3. We can issue commands to the Mac in the old-school style by typing them rather than pointing and clicking. We are going to start by typing in a command you probably don't have yet. This command is gcc. Type this and hit the Enter key. Your Mac will recognize that you don't have this command and offer to install it for you. Go ahead and do this. (If instead it says error: no input files you already have gcc, so go on to the next step.)

Starting a terminal window

4. Install XQuartz from: http://xquartz.macosforge.org.

5. Line by line, copy and paste the following items into your terminal window:

```
ruby -e "$(curl -fsSL https://raw.githubusercontent.com/Homebrew/install/master/install)"
sudo brew doctor
brew update
brew install python3
brew install sdl sdl_image sdl_mixer sdl_ttf portmidi mercurial
```

6. If you want support for MP3s and movies, you can try adding smpeg. I've found support for this to be kind of spotty, so my recommendation is to skip this and use Ogg Vorbis files instead. But if you'd like to try, use these commands:

```
brew install --HEAD https://raw.github.com/Homebrew/homebrew-
headonly/master/smpeg.rb
```

7. Now you have all the supporting libraries. Let's finally install Pygame. Replace YourName with your account name. If you don't know what your account name is, type ls /Users to see all the user accounts on your computer.

```
cd /Users/YourName/Downloads
hg clone https://bitbucket.org/pygame/pygame
cd pygame
cd src
pip3 install /Users/YourName/Downloads/pygame
```

At this point, Pygame and Python should be up and running on your system. Python does not come with a way to edit files, so you will need to download an IDE like Wing IDE (http://wingware.com/downloads) or PyCharm (https://www.jetbrains.com/pycharm/download/), or some other editor.

Unix Installation

Unix and Unix-like distributions may come with a Pygame package or the ability to easily get one. If you want to compile from source, this is what I've used on Linux Mint (http://www.linuxmint.com/):

```
# Load required packages
sudo apt-get install mercurial libsdl1.2-dev
sudo apt-get install libasound2-doc libglib2.0-doc python3-dev
sudo apt-get install libsdl-ttf2.0-dev  libsdl-image1.2-dev
sudo apt-get install libsdl-mixer1.2-dev libportmidi-dev
sudo apt-get install libavformat-dev libswscale-dev
sudo apt-get install libfreetype6-dev
sudo apt-get install libsmpeg-dev

# Use mercurial to clone current code
hg clone https://bitbucket.org/pygame/pygame

# Build and install
cd pygame
sudo python3 setup.py
```

The biggest risk on UNIX platforms is that your default Python version might be in the 2.x series, and that code won't work with the code examples here in the book. Make sure you have and are using Python 3.x.

Optional Wing IDE

Python comes with an editor and an environment to develop code in. Unfortunately it isn't very good. Here are two issues you might run into when using Python's default editor:

Issue 1. When working with multiple files it is difficult to keep track of the all the open files. It is easy to forget to save a file before running the program. When this happens the program runs with the old code that was saved rather than the new code. This is very confusing.

Issue 2. If there is an error in a program that does graphics the Python program will crash and hang. Once the program has crashed it is difficult to shut down. The error message that describes why it crashed is often buried and difficult to find. See the following figure.

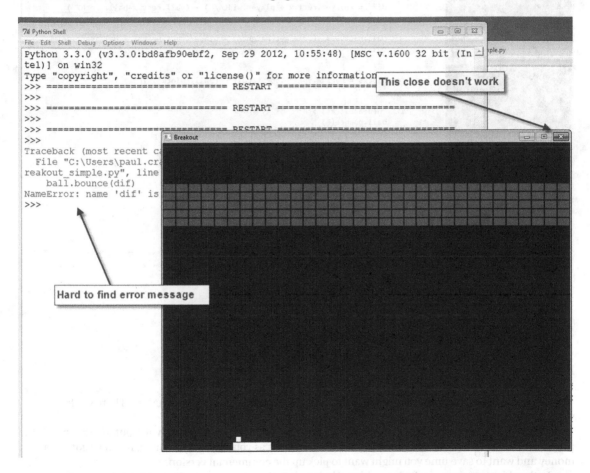

Python Program Hanging in IDLE

The Wing editor solves issue 1 by using an editor with a tab for each file. It will also prompt to save all files before running a program. A program run under the Wing debugger does not hang as described in issue 2; instead the editor will immediately take the user to the line of code that caused the error. See the following figure.

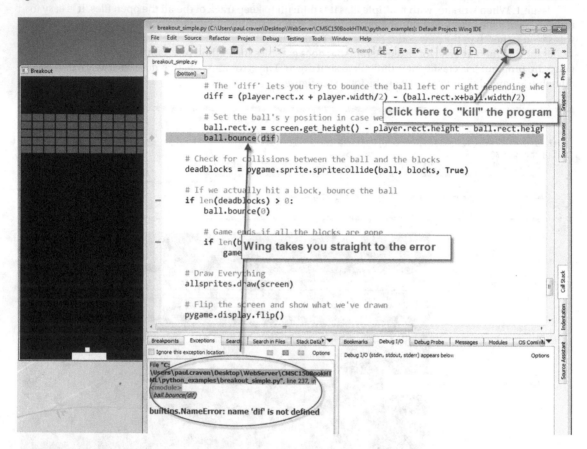

Python Program Hanging in Wing IDE

Therefore, while it is yet a third thing to install, I recommend using the Wing editor. There is a free version called Wing IDE 101 at wingware.com/downloads/wingide-101/.

There is no need for all the bells and whistles the commercial version comes with, but they are nice. The program will often help you by auto-filling in variable names as you start to type them. If you've got extra money and want to save time you might want to pick up the commercial version.

In the videos on the web site I use either the default Python editor or the Wing editor. There are many other editors that can be used as well:

- PyCharm (http://www.jetbrains.com/pycharm/)

- Sublime (http://www.sublimetext.com/)

- PyDev on Eclipse (http://pydev.org/)

- Komodo Edit (http://www.activestate.com/komodo-edit)

- Notepad++ (http://notepad-plus-plus.org/)

Among some developers, discussing "which is the best editor?" is similar to getting a group of people together and discussing "which is the best religion?". It is best to pick your own favorite and then avoid this topic with other people.

Viewing File Extensions

It is a great idea to change your windows configuration to show file extensions. A file usually has a name like Book report.docx where the .docx tells the computer it is a Microsoft Word compatible document. By default Windows hides the .docx extension if there is a program installed to handle it. If you are programming, this hiding part of the file name can be annoying.

For Windows 7, to show file extensions, open up your computer's control panel. Find the selection for "Folder Options." Click the "View" tab, and then unselect the option for "Hide extensions for known file types."

For Windows 8, bring up a file explorer by hitting the Windows-E key. Then click the "view" tab and make sure "File name extensions" has been checked.

Learn to Make Games and Get Paid

As you start to learn to program, you might soon find that it looks like *work*. We all know we'd rather skip work and go farming for gold in World of Warcraft or Eve Online or some other game, right? So why learn to program? What does a person get out of it?

Bags of money

Learn how to make games and get paid? Ok, *I* won't pay you, but if you learn to program, there are plenty of people that *will* pay you. Here's how to profit:

1. Learn to program games.

2. Have fun making your own games.

3. Select a favorite job offer.

4. Profit.

Look, no ??? in this plan!

Think about it. You can *play* games, but anyone can do that. Being great at a video game really isn't much of an accomplishment in life if you think about it. Or you can learn to *create* games. People care about that.

Get the Most from This Book

Great basketball players practice. So do great programmers.

Looking to make your time here worthwhile? Answer the chapter questions! Don't skip them. They are necessary to understand the material.

Do the exercises! This is even more important. Learning by only reading the material is about as useful as trying to become an expert basketball player only by reading a book.

Practice! You might see other people that don't have to practice. It isn't fair. Or, you might be smarter than other people, and they start doing better than you because they work at it and you don't. That's not fair either. That's life. Get used to it. Practice.

Are you reading this book as part of a class? Great! Did you know you can save time and *copy* the answers and exercises from the Internet? You can also buy yourself a gym membership and send someone else to work out for you. It makes about as much sense.

Seriously, what on earth are you thinking copying from someone else? If you aren't going to do the work, stop reading now and start filling out McDonald's applications.

You *can't* learn without doing the work. Do the reading. Do the exercises.

Send Feedback

If you notice any errors or omissions in the book, please send me an e-mail. I'd like this to be the best resource possible.

Dr. Paul Vincent Craven
Department Head, Computer Science Department
Simpson College, Indianola, Iowa, 50125 USA
paul.craven@simpson.edu

CHAPTER 2

■ ■ ■

Create a Custom Calculator

One of the simplest things that can be done with Python is to use it as a fancy calculator. Wait, a calculator isn't a game. Why are we talking about calculators? Boring....

Hey, to calculate objects dropping, bullets flying, and high scores, we need calculations. Plus, any true geek will consider a calculator a toy rather than a torture device! Let's start our game education with calculators. Don't worry, we'll start graphics by Chapter 6.

A simple calculator program can be used to ask the user for information and then calculate boring things like mortgage payments, or more exciting things like the trajectory of mud balls as they are flung through the air.

The figure below shows an example program that calculates kinetic energy, something we might need to do as part of a game physics engine.

```
7⁄6 Python Shell                                                    ─ ▣ ✕
File  Edit  Shell  Debug  Options  Windows  Help
Python 3.1.2 (r312:79149, Mar 21 2010, 00:41:52) [MSC v.1500 32 bit (Intel)] on
win32
Type "copyright", "credits" or "license()" for more information.
>>> ============================= RESTART ==================================
>>>
This program calculates the kinetic energy of a moving object.
Enter the object's mass in kilograms: 5
Enter the object's speed in meters per second: 10
The object has 250.0 joules of energy.
>>> |
                                                                  Ln: 9 Col: 4
```

Using Python to calculate kinetic energy

The best thing about doing this as a program is the ability to hide the complexities of an equation. All the user needs to do is supply the information, and he or she can get the result in an easy-to-understand format. Any similar custom calculator could run on a smart phone, allowing a person to easily perform the calculation on the go.

Printing
Printing Text

How does a program print something to the screen? The code is simple. Just one line is required:

```
print("Hello World.")
```

This program prints out "Hello World" to the screen. Go ahead and enter it into IDLE prompt and see how it works. Try printing other words and phrases as well. The computer will happily print out just about anything you like, true or not.

What does the "Hello World" program look like in other computer programming languages? Check out Wikipedia. They keep a nice set of "Hello World" programs written in many different computer programming languages: http://en.wikipedia.org/wiki/Hello_world_program_examples.

It is interesting to see how many different computer languages there are. You can get an idea how complex a language is by how easy the "Hello World" program is.

Remember, the command for printing in Python is easy. Just use print. After the print command are a set of parentheses ( ). Inside these parentheses is what should be printed to the screen. Using parentheses to pass information to a function is standard practice in math and computer languages.

Math students learn to use parentheses evaluating expressions like $sin(\theta)=cos(\frac{\pi}{2}-\theta)$. sin and cos are functions. Data passed to these functions is inside the parentheses. What is different in our case is that the information being passed is text.

Notice that there are *double quotes* around the text to be printed. If a print statement has quotes around text, the computer will print it out just as it is written. For example, this program will print 2+3:

```
print("2 + 3")
```

Printing Results of Expressions

This next program does not have quotes around $2+3$, and the computer will evaluate it as a *mathematical expression*. It will print 5 rather than 2+3.

```
print(2 + 3)
```

The code below will generate an error because the computer will try to evaluate "Hello World" as a mathematical expression, and that doesn't work at all:

```
print(Hello World)
```

The code above will print out an error `SyntaxError: invalid syntax`, which is computer speak for not knowing what "Hello" and "World" mean.

Also, please keep in mind that this is a single quote: ' and this is a double quote: ". If I ask for a double quote, it is a common mistake to write "", which is really a double, double quote.

Printing Multiple Items

A `print` statement can output multiple things at once, each item separated by a comma. For example, this code will print out `Your new score is 1040`:

```
print("Your new score is", 1030 + 10)
```

The next line of code will print out `Your new score is 1030+10`. The numbers are not added together because they are inside the quotes. Anything inside quotes, the computer treats as text. Anything outside the computer thinks is a mathematical statement or computer code.

```
print("Your new score is", "1030 + 10")
```

Does a comma go inside or outside the quotes?

This next code example doesn't work at all. This is because there is no comma separating the text between the quotes and the 1030+10. At first, it may appear that there is a comma, but the comma is *inside* the quotes. The comma that separates the terms to be printed must be *outside* the quotes. If the programmer wants a comma to be printed, then it must be inside the quotes:

```
print("Your new score is," 1030 + 10)
```

This next example does work, because there is a comma separating the terms. It prints:

```
Your new score is, 1040
```

Note that only one comma prints out. Commas outside the quotes separate terms, commas inside the quotes are printed. The first comma is printed; the second is used to separate terms.

```
print("Your new score is,", 1030 + 10)
```

Escape Codes

If quotes are used to tell the computer the start and end of the string of text you wish to print, how does a program print out a set of double quotes? For example:

```
print("I want to print a double quote " for some reason.")
```

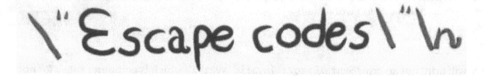

This code doesn't work. The computer looks at the quote in the middle of the string and thinks that is the end of the text. Then it has no idea what to do with the commands for some reason, and the quote and the end of the string confuses the computer even further.

It is necessary to tell the computer that we want to treat that middle double quote as text, not as a quote ending the string. This is easy: just prepend a backslash in front of quotes to tell the computer it is part of a string, not a character that terminates a string. For example:

```
print("I want to print a double quote \" for some reason.")
```

This combination of the two characters \" is called an *escape code*. Almost every language has them. Because the backslash is used as part of an escape code, the backslash itself must be escaped. For example, this code does not work correctly:

```
print("The file is stored in C:\new folder")
```

Why? Because \n is an escape code. To print the backslash it is necessary to escape it like so:

```
print("The file is stored in C:\\new folder")
```

There are a few other important escape codes to know. Here is a table of the important escape codes:

Escape code	Description
\'	Single Quote
\"	Double Quote
\t	Tab
\r	CR: Carriage Return (move to the left)
\n	LF: Linefeed (move down)

What is a carriage return and what is a linefeed? Try this example:

```
print("This\nis\nmy\nsample.")
```

The output from this command is:

```
This
is
my
sample.
```

The \n is a linefeed. It moves the cursor where the computer will print text down one line. The computer stores all text in one big long line. It knows to display the text on different lines because of the placement of \n characters.

To make matters more complex, different operating systems have different standards on what makes a line ending.

Escape codes	Description
\r\n	CR+LF: Microsoft Windows
\n	LF: UNIX-based systems, and newer Macs
\r	CR: Older Mac-based systems

Usually your text editor will take care of this for you. Microsoft Notepad doesn't though, and UNIX files opened in notepad look terrible because the line endings don't show up at all, or show up as black boxes. Every programmer should have a good text editor installed on their computer. I recommend Sublime (www.sublimetext.com/) or Notepad++ (http://notepad-plus-plus.org/).

Comments

Comments are important (even if the computer ignores them)!

Sometimes code needs some extra explanation to the person reading it. To do this, we add comments to the code. The comments are meant for the human reading the code, and not for the computer.

There are two ways to create a comment. The first is to use the # symbol. The computer will ignore any text in a Python program that occurs after the #. For example:

```
# This is a comment, it begins with a # sign
# and the computer will ignore it.

print("This is not a comment, the computer will")
print("run this and print it out.")
```

If a program has the # sign between quotes it is not treated as a comment. A programmer can disable a line of code by putting a # sign in front of it. It is also possible to put a comment in at the end of a line.

```
print("A # sign between quotes is not a comment.")

# print("This is a comment, even if it is computer code.")

print("Hi") # This is an end-of-line comment
```

It is possible to comment out multiple lines of code using three single quotes in a row to delimit the comments.

```
print("Hi")
'''
This is
a
multi
line
comment. Nothing
Will run in between these quotes.
print("There")
'''
print("Done")
```

Most professional Python programmers will only use this type of multiline comment for something called *docstrings*. Docstrings allow documentation to be written alongside the code and later be automatically pulled out into printed documentation, web sites, and Integrated Development Environments (IDEs). For general comments, the # tag works best.

Even if you are going to be the only one reading the code that you write, comments can help save time. Adding a comment that says "Handle alien bombs" will allow you to quickly remember what that section of code does without having to read and decipher it.

Assignment Operators

How do we store the score in our game? Or keep track of the health of the enemy? What we need to do this is the *assignment operator*.

An *operator* is a symbol like + or -. An assignment operator is the = symbol. It stores a value into a *variable* to be used later on. The code below will assign 10 to the variable x and then print the value stored in x.

Look at the example below.

```
# Create a variable x
# Store the value 10 into it.
x = 10

# This prints the value stored in x.
print(x)

# This prints the letter x, but not the value in x
print("x")

# This prints "x= 10"
print("x=", x)
```

Variables go outside the quotes, not inside.

■ **Note** The listing above also demonstrates the difference between printing an x *inside* quotes and an x *outside* quotes. If an x is inside quotation marks, then the computer prints x. If an x is outside the quotation marks then the computer will print the value of x. Getting confused on the "inside or outside of quotes" question is very common for those learning to program.

pi=3.14159

An assignment statement (a line of code using the = operator) is different than the algebraic equality your learned about in math. Do not think of them as the same. On the left side of an assignment operator must be exactly one variable. Nothing else may be there.

On the right of the equals sign/assignment operator is an *expression*. An expression is anything that evaluates to a value. Examine the code below.

```
x = x + 1
```

The code above obviously can't be an algebraic equality. But it is valid to the computer because it is an assignment statement. Mathematical equations are different than assignment statements even if they have variables, numbers, and an equals sign.

The code above the statement takes the current value of x, adds one to it, and stores the result back into x.

Expanding our example, the statement below will print the number 6.

```
x = 5
x = x + 1
print(x)
```

Statements are run sequentially. The computer does not look ahead. In the code below, the computer will print out 5 on line 2, and then line 4 will print out a 6. This is because on line 2, the code to add one to x has not been run yet.

```
x = 5
print(x) # Prints 5
x = x + 1
print(x) # Prints 6
```

The next statement is valid and will run, but it is pointless. The computer will add one to x, but the result is never stored or printed.

```
x + 1
```

The code below will print 5 rather than 6 because the programmer forgot to store the result of x + 1 back into the variable x.

```
x = 5
x + 1
print(x)
```

The statement below is not valid because on the left of the equals sign is more than just a variable:

```
x + 1 = x
```

Python has other types of assignment operators. They allow a programmer to modify a variable easily. For example:

```
x += 1
```

The above statement is equivalent to writing the code below:

```
x = x + 1
```

There are also assignment operators for addition, subtraction, multiplication, and division.

Variables

Variables start with a lowercase letter.

Variables *should* start with a lowercase letter. Variables *can* start with an uppercase letter or an underscore, but those are special cases and should not be done on a normal basis. After the first lowercase letter, the variable may include uppercase and lowercase letters, along with numbers and underscores. Variables may not include spaces.

Variables are case sensitive. This can be confusing if a programmer is not expecting it. In the code below, the output will be 6 rather than 5 because there are two different variables, x and X.

```
x = 6
X = 5
print(x)
```

The official style guide for Python (yes, programmers really wrote a book on style) says that multiword variable names in Python should be separated by underscores. For example, use hair_style and not hairStyle. Personally, I don't care about this rule too much because the next language we introduce, Java, has the exact opposite style rule. I used to try teaching Java-style rules in chapters like this, but then I started getting hate mail from Python lovers. These people came by my web site and were shocked, *shocked* I tell you, about my poor style.

Joan Rivers has nothing on these people, so I gave up and try to use proper style guides now.

Here are some example variable names that are ok and not ok to use:

Legal variable names	Illegal variable names	Legal, but not proper
first_name	first name	FirstName
distance	9ds	firstName
ds9	%correct	X

All uppercase variable names like MAX_SPEED are allowed only in circumstances where the variable's value should *never* change. A variable that isn't variable is called a *constant*.

Operators

For more complex mathematical operations, common mathematical operators are available. Along with some not-so-common ones:

operator	operation	example equation	example code
+	addition	$3 + 2$	a = 3 + 2
-	subtraction	3 - 2$	a = 3 - 2
*	multiplication	$3 \cdot 2$	a = 3 * 2
/	division	$\dfrac{10}{2}$	a = 10 / 2
//	floor division	N/A	a = 10 // 3
**	power	2^3	a = 2 ** 3
%	modulus	N/A	a = 8 % 3

Floor division will always round the answer down to the nearest integer. For example, 11//2 will be 5, not 5.5, and 99//100 will equal 0.

Multiplication by juxtaposition does not work in Python. The following two lines of code will not work:

```
# These do not work
x = 5y
x = 5(3/2)
```

It is necessary to use the multiplication operator to get these lines of code to work:

```
# These do work
x = 5 * y
x = 5 * (3 / 2)
```

Operator Spacing

There can be any number of spaces before and after an operator, and the computer will understand it just fine. For example, each of these three lines is equivalent:

```
x=5*(3/2)
x = 5 * (3 / 2)
x       =5      *(    3/   2)
```

The official style guide for Python says that there should be a space before and after each operator. (You've been dying to know, right? Ok, the official style guide for python code is called PEP-8 (http://www.python.org/dev/peps/pep-0008/). Look it up for more excitement). Of the three lines of code above, the most stylish one would be line 2.

Order of Operations

Python will evaluate expressions using the same order of operations that are expected in standard mathematical expressions. For example this equation does not correctly calculate the average:

```
average = 90 + 86 + 71 + 100 + 98 / 5
```

The first operation done is 98/5. The computer calculates:

$$90 + 86 + 71 + 100 + \frac{98}{5}$$ rather than the desired:

$$\frac{90 + 86 + 71 + 100 + 98}{5}$$ By using parentheses this problem can be fixed:

```
average = (90 + 86 + 71 + 100 + 98) / 5
```

Trig Functions

Trigonometric functions are used to calculate sine and cosine in equations. By default, Python does not know how to calculate sine and cosine, but it can once the proper library has been imported. Units are in radians.

```
# Import the math library
# This line is done only once, and at the very top
# of the program.
from math import *

# Calculate x using sine and cosine
x = sin(0) + cos(0)
```

Custom Equation Calculators

A program can use Python to calculate the mileage of a car that drove 294 miles on 10.5 gallons of gas.

```
m = 294 / 10.5
print(m)
```

This program can be improved by using variables. This allows the values to easily be changed in the code without modifying the equation.

```
m = 294
g = 10.5
m2 = m / g # This uses variables instead
print(m2)
```

Good variable names are important.

By itself, this program is actually difficult to understand. The variables m and g don't mean a lot without some context. The program can be made easier to understand by using appropriately named variables:

```
miles_driven = 294
gallons_used = 10.5
mpg = miles_driven / gallons_used
print(mpg)
```

Now, even a non-programmer can probably look at the program and have a good idea of what it does. Another example of good versus bad variable naming:

```
# Hard to understand
ir = 0.12
b = 12123.34
i = ir * b

# Easy to understand
interest_rate = 0.12
account_balance = 12123.34
interest_amount = interest_rate * account_balance
```

In the IDLE editor it is possible to edit a prior line without retyping it. Do this by moving the cursor to that line and hitting the enter key. It will be copied to the current line.

Entering Python code at the >>> prompt is slow and can only be done one line at a time. It is also not possible to save the code so that another person can run it. Thankfully, there is an even better way to enter Python code.

Python code can be entered using a script. A script is a series of lines of Python code that will be executed all at once. To create a script, open up a new window as shown in the figure below.

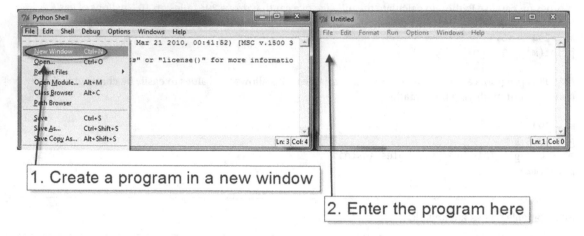

1. Create a program in a new window

2. Enter the program here

Entering a script

You may wish to use a different program to create your script, like the Wing IDE or PyCharm. These programs are easier and more powerful than the IDLE program that comes with Python.

Enter the Python program for calculating gas mileage, and then save the file. Save the file to a flash drive, network drive, or some other location of your choice. Python programs should always end with .py. See the figure below.

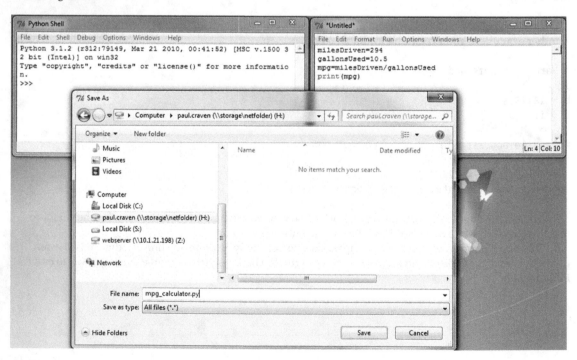

Saving a script

Run the program typed in by clicking on the Run menu and selecting Run Module. Try updating the program to different values for miles driven and gallons used.

Caution, common mistake!

From this point forward, almost all code entered should be in a script/module. Do *not* type your program out on the IDLE >>> prompt. Code typed here is not saved. If this happens, it will be necessary to start over. This is a very common mistake for new programmers.

This program would be even more useful if it would interact with the user and ask the user for the miles driven and gallons used. This can be done with the input statement. See the code below:

```
# This code almost works
miles_driven = input("Enter miles driven:")
gallons_used = input("Enter gallons used:")
mpg = miles_driven / gallons_used
print("Miles per gallon:", mpg)
```

Running this program will ask the user for miles and gallons, but it generates a strange error as shown in the figure below.

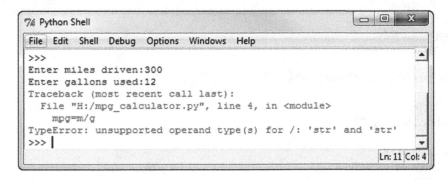

Error running MPG program

The reason for this error can be demonstrated by changing the program a bit:

```
miles_driven = input("Enter miles driven:")
gallons_used = input("Enter gallons used:")
x = miles_driven + gallons_used
print("Sum of m + g:", x)
```

23

Running the program above results in the output shown below.

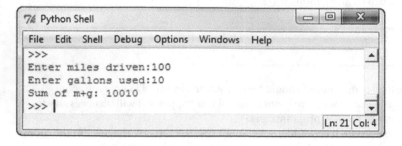

Incorrect Addition

The program doesn't add the two numbers together: it just puts one right after the other. This is because the program does not know the user will be entering numbers. The user might enter Bob and Mary, and adding those two variables together would be BobMary, which would make more sense.

To tell the computer these are numbers, it is necessary to surround the input function with an int( ) or a float( ). Use the former for integers, and the latter for floating point numbers.

The final working program:

```
# Sample Python/Pygame Programs
# Simpson College Computer Science
# http://programarcadegames.com/
# http://simpson.edu/computer-science/

# Explanation video: http://youtu.be/JK5ht5_m6Mk

# Calculate Miles Per Gallon
print("This program calculates mpg.")

# Get miles driven from the user
miles_driven = input("Enter miles driven:")
# Convert text entered to a
# floating point number
miles_driven = float(miles_driven)

# Get gallons used from the user
gallons_used = input("Enter gallons used:")
# Convert text entered to a
# floating point number
gallons_used = float(gallons_used)

# Calculate and print the answer
mpg = miles_driven / gallons_used
print("Miles per gallon:", mpg)
```

And another example, calculating the kinetic energy of an object:

```
# Sample Python/Pygame Programs
# Simpson College Computer Science
# http://programarcadegames.com/
# http://simpson.edu/computer-science/

# Calculate Kinetic Energy

print("This program calculates the kinetic energy of a moving object.")
m_string = input("Enter the object's mass in kilograms: ")
m = float(m_string)
v_string = input("Enter the object's speed in meters per second: ")
v = float(v_string)

e = 0.5 * m * v * v
print("The object has " + str(e) + " joules of energy.")
```

To shorten a program, it is possible to nest the input statement into the float statement. For example, these lines of code:

```
milesDriven = input("Enter miles driven:")
milesDriven = float(milesDriven)
```

perform the same as this line:

```
milesDriven = float(input("Enter miles driven:"))
```

In this case, the output of the input function is directly fed into the float function. Either one works, and it is a matter of programmer's preference which to choose. It is important, however, to be able to understand both forms.

Review

Multiple Choice Quiz

1. What is the correct code to print out the words 'Hello World' to the screen?

   a. `print (Hello World)`

   b. `print 'Hello World'`

   c. `print {'Hello World'}`

   d. `print Hello World`

   e. `print ['Hello World']`

   f. `print ("Hello World")`

   g. `print {'Hello World'}`

2. What does this code output?

```
a = 1
b = 3
print(a + b)
```

a. A+B

b. a+b

c. "a+b"

d. 4

e. 1+3

f. Nothing, the code is invalid.

3. What does this code output?

```
a = 1
b = 3
print("a+b")
```

a. A+B

b. a+b

c. "a+b"

d. The values of a and b added together.

e. 10

f. Nothing, the code is invalid.

4. What does this code output?

```
print("The answer to 10+10 is," 10+10)
```

a. The answer to 10+10 is 10+10

b. The answer to 10+10 is 20

c. The answer to 10+10 is10+10

d. The answer to 10+10 is20

e. The answer to 10+10 is,10+10

f. The answer to 10+10 is,20

g. Nothing, the code is invalid.

5. What does this code output?

    ```
    # print("Hello")
    ```

    a. Hello

    b. "Hello"

    c. Nothing, there is an error in the code.

    d. Nothing, the code is commented out.

6. What does this code output?

    ```
    x = 10
    print("x")
    ```

    a. "x"

    b. x

    c. 10

    d. Nothing

7. What does this code output?

    ```
    x = 10
    x + 1
    print(x)
    ```

    a. 10

    b. 11

    c. "x"

    d. x

    e. Nothing

8. What does this code output?

    ```
    x = 10 + 6 / 2
    x = x + 1
    print(x)
    ```

    a. 8

    b. 9

    c. 13

    d. 14

    e. Nothing

9. What does this code output?

```
x = input("Enter a value:")
print(x / 2)
```

a. 10

b. 0

c. The value the user entered.

d. The value the user entered divided by two.

e. An error because the value was not converted to a number.

10. What does this code output?

```
print("Have a "great" day!")
```

a. "Have a "great" day!"

b. Have a "great" day!

c. Have a great day!

d. Nothing, the double quotes make for a syntax error.

11. What does this code output?

```
print("Save in c:\new folder")
```

a. Save in c:\new folder

b. Save in c:

ew folder

c. Save in c:ew folder

d. Nothing, the escape code makes for a syntax error.

Short Answer Worksheet

1. Write a line of code that will print your name.

2. How do you enter a comment in a program?

3. What do the following lines of code output? ALSO: Why do they give a different answer?

```
print(2 / 3)
print(2 // 3)
```

4. Write a line of code that creates a variable called pi and sets it to an appropriate value.

5. Why does this code not work?

    ```
    A = 22
    print(a)
    ```

6. All of the variable names below can be used. But which ONE of these is the *better*
    variable name to use?

    ```
    a
    A
    Area
    AREA
    area
    area_of_rectangle
    Area_Of_Rectangle
    ```

7. Which of these variables names are not allowed in Python? (More than one
    might be wrong. Also, this question is not asking about improper names, just
    names that aren't allowed. Test them if you aren't sure.)

    ```
    apple
    Apple
    APPLE
    Apple2
    1Apple
    account number
    account_number
    account.number
    accountNumber
    account#
    pi
    PI
    fred
    Fred
    GreatBigVariable
    greatBigVariable
    great_big_variable
    great.big.variable
    2x
    x2x
    total%
    #left
    ```

8. Why does this code not work?

    ```
    print(a)
    a = 45
    ```

9. Explain the mistake in this code:

```
pi = float(3.14)
```

10. This program runs, but the code still could be better. Explain what is wrong with the code.

```
radius = float(input("Radius:"))
x = 3.14
pi = x
area = pi  * radius ** 2
print(area)
```

11. Explain the mistake in the following code:

```
x = 4
y = 5
a = ((x) * (y))
print(a)
```

12. Explain the mistake in the following code:

```
x = 4
y = 5
a = 3(x + y)
print(a)
```

13. Explain the mistake in the following code:

```
radius = input(float("Enter the radius:"))
```

14. Do all these print the same value? Which one is better to use and why?

```
print(2/3+4)
print(2 / 3 + 4)
print(   2 /    3+   4 )
```

15. What is a *constant*?

16. How are variable names for constants different than other variable names?

17. What is a single quote and what is a double quote? Give and label an example of both.

18. Write a Python program that will use escape codes to print a double quote and a new line using the Window's standard. (Note: I'm asking for the Window's standard here. Look it up out of Chapter 1.)

19. Can a Python program print text to the screen using single quotes instead of double quotes?

20. Why does this code not calculate the average?

```
print(3 + 4 + 5 / 3)
```

21.   What is an operator in Python?

22.   What does the following program print out?

```
x = 3
x + 1
print(x)
```

23.   Correct the following code:

```
user_name = input("Enter your name: )"
```

24.   Correct the following code:

```
value = int(input(print("Enter your age")))
```

Exercise

Check the appendix for the exercise that goes along with this chapter.

CHAPTER 3

■ ■ ■

What Is a Computer Language?

What makes a computer language? Why do computers have them? Why are there so many different computer languages?

It isn't necessary to understand the answer to these questions to do basic programming, just like understanding how an engine works isn't necessary to drive a car. However, to *progress* to an advanced level it is. This chapter provides a brief explanation to help you get started.

Short History of Programming

Computers are electronic, and they are *digital*. To a computer everything is in terms of no voltage potential along a wire or some voltage available. No voltage means a zero to the computer, and some voltage means a one. Computers can't actually count higher than that without combining multiple ones and zeros.

In the early days, switches were used to load ones or zeros into computer memory. The figure below, courtesy of Wikimedia Commons (http://en.wikipedia.org/wiki/File:Altair_Computer_Front_Panel.jpg), shows an Altair 8800. The front panel switches were used to load in the program. The lights showed the output. There was no monitor.

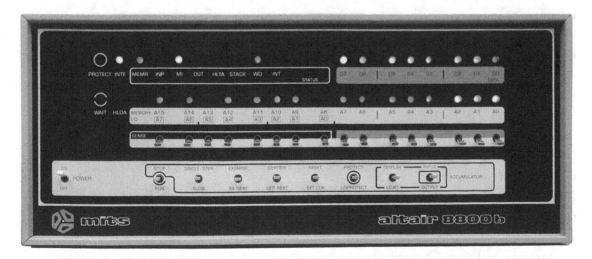

Altair 8800

Each set of on/off switches represented a number. Each number would represent data or an instruction for the computer to perform. This system of only using ones and zeros to represent numbers is called the binary number system. This type of computer language is called a 1GL (First Generation Language). Note: there isn't a language called 1GL, it is just an abbreviation for First Generation Language. 1GL is the same thing as the machine's native language (machine language) where numbers represent the commands and data for the program.

Binary numbers are usually represented in groups of four. For example:

```
1010 0010 0011
```

Both data and computer instructions are stored in binary. Machine languages are the binary numbers representing instructions that the computer interprets. Not all binary data is machine language, however. Data such as documents, databases, and financial figures are also stored in binary on the computer. This data is, of course, is not intended to be run by the computer.

An improvement over entering programs via switches was the use of hexadecimal codes. The decimal numbers used by most people use the digits 0–9. Hexadecimal uses the numbers 0–9 and A–F to represent a set of four switches, or the numbers 0–15. See the table below for an idea of how binary, decimal, and hexadecimal relate.

Binary	Decimal	Hexadecimal
0	0	0
1	1	1
10	2	2
11	3	3
100	4	4
101	5	5
110	6	6
111	7	7
1000	8	8
1001	9	9
1010	10	A
1011	11	B
1100	12	C
1101	13	D
1110	14	E
1111	15	F
1 0000	16	10
1 0001	17	11

In order to make entering programs easier, later computers allowed users to enter programs using *assembly language*. Each command used a mnemonic, and a program called a compiler would change the mnemonics into the numbers that represented the commands. Assembly Language is also called a 2GL language, or Second Generation Language.

The figure below shows part of an example assembly language program, also courtesy of the Wikimedia Commons (http://en.wikipedia.org/wiki/File:Altair_Computer_Front_Panel.jpg).

```
MONITOR FOR 6802 1.4          9-14-80  TSC ASSEMBLER   PAGE    2


C000                     ORG    ROM+$0000 BEGIN MONITOR
C000 8E 00 70  START     LDS    #STACK

               *****************************************
               * FUNCTION: INITA - Initialize ACIA
               * INPUT: none
               * OUTPUT: none
               * CALLS: none
               * DESTROYS: acc A

0013           RESETA    EQU    %00010011
0011           CTLREG    EQU    %00010001

C003 86 13     INITA     LDA A  #RESETA    RESET ACIA
C005 B7 80 04            STA A  ACIA
C008 86 11               LDA A  #CTLREG    SET 8 BITS AND 2 STOP
C00A B7 80 04            STA A  ACIA

C00D 7E C0 F1            JMP    SIGNON     GO TO START OF MONITOR

               *****************************************
               * FUNCTION: INCH - Input character
               * INPUT: none
               * OUTPUT: char in acc A
               * DESTROYS: acc A
               * CALLS: none
               * DESCRIPTION: Gets 1 character from terminal

C010 B6 80 04  INCH      LDA A  ACIA       GET STATUS
C013 47                  ASR A             SHIFT RDRF FLAG INTO CARRY
C014 24 FA               BCC    INCH       RECIEVE NOT READY
C016 B6 80 05            LDA A  ACIA+1     GET CHAR
C019 84 7F               AND A  #$7F       MASK PARITY
C01B 7E C0 79            JMP    OUTCH      ECHO & RTS

               *****************************************
               * FUNCTION: INHEX - INPUT HEX DIGIT
               * INPUT: none
               * OUTPUT: Digit in acc A
               * CALLS: INCH
               * DESTROYS: acc A
               * Returns to monitor if not HEX input

C01E 8D F0     INHEX     BSR    INCH       GET A CHAR
C020 81 30               CMP A  #'0        ZERO
C022 2B 11               BMI    HEXERR     NOT HEX
C024 81 39               CMP A  #'9        NINE
C026 2F 0A               BLE    HEXRTS     GOOD HEX
C028 81 41               CMP A  #'A
C02A 2B 09               BMI    HEXERR     NOT HEX
C02C 81 46               CMP A  #'F
C02E 2E 05               BGT    HEXERR
C030 80 07               SUB A  #7         FIX A-F
C032 84 0F     HEXRTS    AND A  #$0F       CONVERT ASCII TO DIGIT
C034 39                  RTS

C035 7E C0 AF  HEXERR    JMP    CTRL       RETURN TO CONTROL LOOP
```

Example assembly language

While this was an improvement, it still wasn't very easy to program. The next generation of languages allowed for higher-level abstractions. The first of the third generation languages (COBOL, FORTRAN, and LISP) were a lot easier to understand and program.

The second and third generation languages used a program called a *compiler*. A compiler takes the program typed in by the user (called *source code*) and turns it into machine code. The programmer then runs the machine code. The original source code is not run.

If there are several pieces of source code in a program, they can be linked together into one program with the use of a program called a *linker*. The linker is run on the machine code generated by the compiler to generate a final program. This final program is what the user runs, and the original source code is not needed.

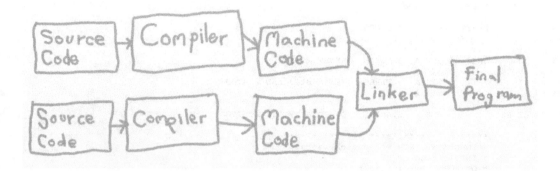

Compilers and linkers

A disadvantage of compiling to machine language is that the program only works for that particular type of machine. Programs compiled for Windows computers do not work on Apple Macintosh computers or Linux computers.

Because the whole compile and link steps could be complex for new programmers, some languages instead ran using *interpreters*. These programs look at the source code and interpret it to machine language instructions on the fly. It also allows the same programs to run on Windows, Mac, and Unix computers, provided there is an interpreter available for each platform.

The drawback of using interpreters is that it is slower to operate through an interpreter than in the machine's native language.

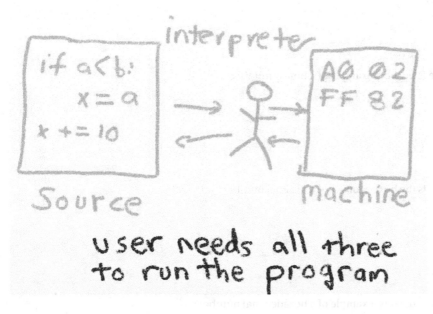

Interpreter

Python is an example of an interpreted language. It is easier to develop in Python than C, but Python runs slower and must have a Python interpreter to work.

Languages such as Java use a system where programs are compiled to machine code that runs on a Java Virtual Machine (JVM), rather than the actual machine. Another popular language that does this is C#, a Common Language Infrastructure (CLI) language that runs on the Virtual Execution System (VES) virtual machine. A full discussion of these is beyond the scope of this book, but feel free to read up on them.

There are many different computer languages today. Because computers perform so many types of tasks, different languages have been developed that specialize in these tasks. Languages such as C are good for operating systems and small embedded computers. Other languages like PHP specialize in creating web pages. Python is a general purpose language that specializes in being easy-to-use.

The company Tiobe keeps track of the popularity of various programming language in their index that is updated each month. It is a good idea to look here, and at job placement boards like DICE (http://www. dice.com/) to keep up to date with what languages are popular.

Thankfully almost all languages share the same common elements, and once one language has been learned, the same theories will apply to the other languages.

For an entertaining history of computing, I recommend watching *Triumph of the Nerds* by Robert X Cringely, a three-part series on the origins of computing. The movies are entertaining enough that your entire family might enjoy them. I also recommend the book *Accidental Empires* if you are more into reading than video.

What happens after those videos? They don't even cover the birth of the Internet! To learn more about that, check out the video series Nerds 2.0.1 also by Robert X Cringely.

Review

Multiple Choice Quiz

1. Which of these is the best example of a binary number

    a. 101101

    b. 82

    c. 3FA

    d. GAF

2. Which of these is the best example of a decimal number?

    a. 101101

    b. 82

    c. 3FA

    d. GAF

3. Which of these is the best example of a hexadecimal number?

    a. 101101

    b. 82

    c. 3FA

    d. GAF

4. What is the decimal number equivalent to the binary number "100"?

    a. 1

    b. 2

    c. 3

    d. 4

    e. 8

    f. None of the above

5. What is source code?

    a. Runs source code directly, without compiling

    b. The machine code the computer runs

    c. Converts source code to machine code

    d. The program the developer types into the computer

    e. Links machine code together into one big program

6. What is machine code?

    a. Runs source code directly, without compiling

    b. Converts source code to machine code

    c. The native code the computer runs

    d. The program the developer types into the computer

    e. Links machine code together into one big program

7. What is a compiler?

    a. The machine code the computer runs

    b. Converts source code to machine code

    c. The program the developer types into the computer

    d. Links machine code together into one big program

    e. Runs source code directly, without compiling

8. What is an interpreter?

    a. Converts source code to machine code

    b. Runs source code directly, without compiling

    c. The program the developer types into the computer

    d. The machine code the computer runs

    e. Links machine code together into one big program

9. What is a linker?

    a. Links machine code together into one big program

    b. Converts source code to machine code

    c. The program the developer types into the computer

    d. The machine code the computer runs

    e. Runs source code directly, without compiling

10. What is a first generation language (1GL)?

    a. Assembly language

    b. Language like Python or C that has logical structures

    c. Machine language

    d. A language built for a specific purpose

11. What is a second generation language (2GL)?

    a.   Language like Python or C that has logical structures

    b.   Assembly language

    c.   Machine language

    d.   A language built for a specific purpose

12. What is a third generation language (3GL)?

    a.   A language built for a specific purpose

    b.   Assembly language

    c.   Machine language

    d.   Language like Python or C that has logical structures

Short Answer Worksheet

1. Give an example of a binary number. (While a number such as 1 can be a binary, decimal, and hexadecimal number, try coming up with an example that better illustrates the differences between the different bases of numbers.)

2. Give an example of a decimal number.

3. Give an example of a hexadecimal number.

4. Convert the numbers 1, 10, 100, 1000, and 10000 from binary to decimal.

5. What is a compiler?

6. What is source code?

7. What is machine language? (Don't just say binary. That's not correct.)

8. What is a first generation language? (Don't just say binary. That's not correct.)

9. What is a second generation language?

10. What is a third generation language? (Explain, don't just give one example.)

11. What is an interpreter and how does it differ from a compiler?

12. Search the Web and find some of the most popular programming languages. List the web site(s) you got the information from and what the languages are.

13. Look at the job boards and see what languages people are looking for. List the languages and the job board you looked at.

14. What is the difference between the syntax and semantics of a language?

15. Pick a piece of technology, other than a computer you use regularly. Briefly describe the hardware and software that run on it.

Exercise

Check the appendix for the exercise that goes along with this chapter.

CHAPTER 4

■ ■ ■

Quiz Games and If Statements

How do we tell if a player has beaten the high score? How can we tell if he has run out of lives? How can we tell if she has the key required to open the locked door?

What we need is the if statement. The if statement is also known as a *conditional statement*. (You can use the term conditional statement when you want to impress everyone how smart you are.) The if statement allows a computer to make a decision. Is it hot outside? Has the spaceship reached the edge of the screen? Has too much money been withdrawn from the account? A program can test for these conditions with the if statement.

Basic Comparisons

Here are a few examples of if statements. The first section sets up two variables (a and b) for use in the if statements. Then two if statements show how to compare the variables to see if one is greater than the other.

```
# Variables used in the example if statements
a = 4
b = 5

# Basic comparisons
if a < b:
    print("a is less than b")

if a > b:
    print("a is greater than b")

print("Done")
```

Since a is less than b, the first statement will print out if this code is run. If the variables a and b were both equal to 4, then neither of the two if statements above would print anything out. The number 4 is not greater than 4, so the if statement would fail.

To show the flow of a program a *flowchart* may be used. Most people can follow a flowchart even without an introduction to programming. See how well you can understand the following figure.

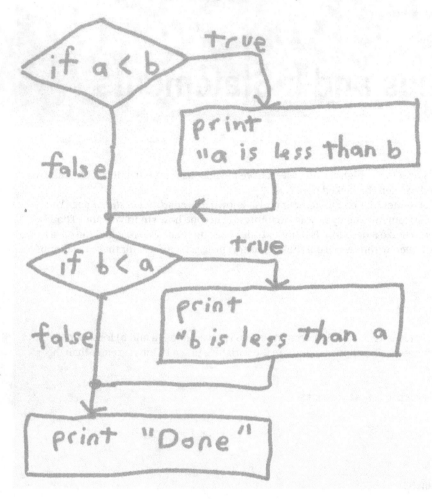

Flowchart

This book skips an in-depth look at flowcharting because it is boring. But if you want to be a superstar programmer, please read more about it at: http://en.wikipedia.org/wiki/Flowchart.

The prior example checked for greater than or less than. Numbers that were equal would not pass the test. To check for a values greater than *or equal*, the following examples show how to do this:

```
if a <= b:
    print("a is less than or equal to b")

if a >= b:
    print("a is greater than or equal to b")
```

The <= and >= symbols must be used in order, and there may not be a space between them. For example, =< will not work, nor will < =.

When writing these statements out, some people like to use the ≤ symbol. For example:

```
if a ≤ b:
```

This ≤ symbol doesn't actually work in a program. Plus most people don't know how to easily type it on the keyboard. (Just in case you are curious, to type it hold down the 'alt' key while typing 243 on the number pad.) So when writing out code, remember that it is <= and not ≤.

The next set of code checks to see if two items are equal or not. The operator for equal is == and the operator for not equal is !=. Here they are in action.

```
# Equal
if a == b:
    print("a is equal to b")

# Not equal
if a != b:
    print("a and b are not equal")
```

Learn when to use = and ==.

It is very easy to mix up when to use == and =. Use == if you are asking if they are equal, use = if you are assigning a value.

The two most common mistakes in mixing the = and == operators are demonstrated below:

```
# This is wrong
a == 1

# This is also wrong
if a = 1:
    print("A is one")
```

Stop! Please take a moment to go back and carefully study the last two code examples. Save time later by making sure you understand when to use = and ==. Don't guess.

Indentation

Indentation matters. Each line under the if statement that is indented will only be executed if the statement is true:

```
if a == 1:
    print("If a is one, this will print.")
    print("So will this.")
    print("And this.")

print("This will always print because it is not indented.")
```

Indentation must be the same. This code doesn't work.

```
if a == 1:
  print("Indented two spaces.")
    print("Indented four. This will generate an error.")
  print("The computer will want you to make up your mind.")
```

Once an if statement has been finished, it is not possible to re-indent to go back to it. The test has to be performed again.

```
if a == 1:
    print("If a is one, this will print.")
    print("So will this.")

print("This will always print because it is not indented.")
    print("This will generate an error. Why it is indented?")
```

Using And/Or

An if statement can check multiple conditions by chaining together comparisons with and and or. These are also considered to be *operators* just like + or - are.

```
# And
if a < b and a < c:
    print("a is less than b and c")

# Non-exclusive or
if a < b or a < c:
    print("a is less than either b or c (or both)")
```

Repeat yourself please.

A common mistake is to omit a variable when checking it against multiple conditions. The code below does not work because the computer does not know what to check against the variable c. It will not assume to check it against a.

```
# This is not correct
if a < b or < c:
    print("a is less than b and c")
```

Boolean Variables

Python supports Boolean variables. What are Boolean variables? Boolean variables can store either a True or a value of False. Boolean algebra was developed by George Boole back in 1854. If only he knew how important his work would become as the basis for modern computer logic!

CHAPTER 4 ■ QUIZ GAMES AND IF STATEMENTS

An if statement needs an expression to evaluate to True or False. What may seem odd is that it does not actually need to do any comparisons if a variable already evaluates to True or False.

```
# Boolean data type. This is legal!
a = True
if a:
    print("a is true")
```

Back when I was in school it was popular to say some false statement. Wait three seconds, then shout "NOT!" Well, even your computer thinks that is lame. If you are going to do that, you have to start with the not operator. The following code uses the not to flip the value of a between true and false.

```
# How to use the not function
if not(a):
    print("a is false")
```

Because not is an operator and not a function, the parentheses aren't necessary. This is also legal:

```
# How to use the not function
if not a:
    print("a is false")
```

It is also possible to use Boolean variables with and and or operators.

```
a = True
b = False

if a and b:
    print("a and b are both true")
```

Who knew True/False could be hard?

It is also possible to assign a variable to the result of a comparison. In the code below, the variables a and b are compared. If they are equal, c will be True; otherwise c will be False.

```
a = 3
b = 3
# This next line is strange-looking, but legal.
# c will be true or false, depending if
# a and b are equal.
c = a == b
# Prints value of c, in this case True
print(c)
```

Zero means False. Everything else is True.

It is possible to create an if statement with a condition that does not evaluate to true or false. This is not usually desired, but it is important to understand how the computer handles these values when searching for problems. The statement below is legal and will cause the text to be printed out because the values in the if statement are nonzero:

```
if 1:
        print("1")
if "A":
        print("A")
```

The code below will not print out anything because the value in the if statement is zero, which is treated as False. Any value other than zero is considered true.

```
if 0:
        print("Zero")
```

In the code below, the first if statement appears to work. The problem is that it will always trigger as true even if the variable a is not equal to b. This is because b by itself is considered true.

```
a = "c"
if a == "B" or "b":
        print("a is equal to b. Maybe.")

# This is a better way to do the if statement.
if a == "B" or a == "b":
        print("a is equal to b.")
```

Else and Else If

Below is code that will get the temperature from the user and print if it is hot.

```
temperature = int(input("What is the temperature in Fahrenheit? "))
if temperature > 90:
    print("It is hot outside")
print("Done")
```

If the programmer wants code to be executed if it is not hot, she can use the else statement. Notice how the else is lined up with the i in the if statement, and how it is followed by a colon just like the if statement.

In the case of an if...else statement, one block of code will always be executed. The first block will be executed if the statement evaluates to True, the second block if it evaluates to False.

```
temperature = int(input("What is the temperature in Fahrenheit? "))
if temperature > 90:
    print("It is hot outside")
else:
    print("It is not hot outside")
print("Done")
```

It is possible to chain several if statements together using the else...if statement. Python abbreviates this as elif.

```
temperature = int(input("What is the temperature in Fahrenheit? "))
if temperature > 90:
    print("It is hot outside")
elif temperature < 30:
    print("It is cold outside")
else:
    print("It is not hot outside")
print("Done")
```

In the code below, the program will output "It is hot outside" even if the user types in 120 degrees. Why? How can the code be fixed?

```
temperature = int(input("What is the temperature in Fahrenheit? "))
if temperature > 90:
    print("It is hot outside")
elif temperature > 110:
    print("Oh man, you could fry eggs on the pavement!")
elif temperature < 30:
    print("It is cold outside")
else:
    print("It is ok outside")
print("Done")
```

Text Comparisons

It is possible to use an if statement to check text.

```
user_name = input("What is your name? ")
if user_name == "Paul":
    print("You have a nice name.")
else:
    print("Your name is ok.")
```

The prior example will only match if the user enters "Paul". It will not work if the user enters "paul" or "PAUL".

A common mistake is to forget the quotes around the string being compared. In the example below, the computer will think that Paul is a variable that stores a value. It will flag an error because it has no idea what is stored in the variable Paul.

```
user_name = input("What is your name? ")
if user_name == Paul: # This does not work because quotes are missing
    print("You have a nice name.")
else:
    print("Your name is ok.")
```

Multiple Text Possibilities

When comparing a variable to multiple possible strings of text, it is important to remember that the comparison must include the variable. For example:

```
# This does not work! It will always be true
if user_name == "Paul" or "Mary":
```

Instead, the code should read:

```
# This does work
if user_name == "Paul" or user_name == "Mary":
```

This is because any value other than zero, the computer assumes to mean True. So to the computer "Mary" is the same thing as True and so it will run the code in the if statement.

Case Insensitive Comparisons

If the program needs to match regardless as to the case of the text entered, the easiest way to do that is to convert everything to lowercase. This can be done with the lower command.

Learn to be insensitive.

The example below will take whatever the user enters, convert it to lower case, and then do the comparison. Important: Don't compare it against a string that has uppercase. If the user input is converted to lowercase, then compared against uppercase letters, there is no way a match can occur.

```
user_name = input("What is your name? ")
if user_name.lower() == "paul":
    print("You have a nice name.")
else:
    print("Your name is ok.")
```

Example if Statements

The next set of example code below runs through all the concepts talked about earlier.

```
# Sample Python/Pygame Programs
# Simpson College Computer Science
# http://programarcadegames.com/
# http://simpson.edu/computer-science/

# Explanation video: http://youtu.be/pDpNSck2aXQ

# Variables used in the example if statements
a = 4
b = 5
c = 6
```

```python
# Basic comparisons
if a < b:
    print("a is less than b")

if a > b:
    print("a is greater than than b")

if a <= b:
    print("a is less than or equal to b")

if a >= b:
    print("a is greater than or equal to b")

# NOTE: It is very easy to mix when to use == and =.
# Use == if you are asking if they are equal, use =
# if you are assigning a value.
if a == b:
    print("a is equal to b")

# Not equal
if a != b:
    print("a and b are not equal")

# And
if a < b and a < c:
    print("a is less than b and c")

# Non-exclusive or
if a < b or a < c:
    print("a is less than either a or b (or both)")

# Boolean data type. This is legal!
a = True
if a:
    print("a is true")

if not a:
    print("a is false")

a = True
b = False

if a and b:
    print("a and b are both true")

a = 3
b = 3
c = a == b
print(c)
```

```python
# These are also legal and will trigger as being true because
# the values are not zero:
if 1:
    print("1")
if "A":
    print("A")

# This will not trigger as true because it is zero.
if 0:
    print("Zero")

# Comparing variables to multiple values.
# The first if statement appears to work, but it will always
# trigger as true even if the variable a is not equal to b.
# This is because "b" by itself is considered true.
a = "c"
if a == "B" or "b":
    print("a is equal to b. Maybe.")

# This is the proper way to do the if statement.
if a == "B" or a == "b":
    print("a is equal to b.")

# Example 1: If statement
temperature = int(input("What is the temperature in Fahrenheit? "))
if temperature > 90:
    print("It is hot outside")
print("Done")

# Example 2: Else statement
temperature = int(input("What is the temperature in Fahrenheit? "))
if temperature > 90:
    print("It is hot outside")
else:
    print("It is not hot outside")
print("Done")

# Example 3: Else if statement
temperature = int(input("What is the temperature in Fahrenheit? "))
if temperature > 90:
    print("It is hot outside")
elif temperature < 30:
    print("It is cold outside")
else:
    print("It is not hot outside")
print("Done")

# Example 4: Ordering of statements
# Something with this is wrong. What?
temperature = int(input("What is the temperature in Fahrenheit? "))
```

```
if temperature > 90:
    print("It is hot outside")
elif temperature > 110:
    print("Oh man, you could fry eggs on the pavement!")
elif temperature < 30:
    print("It is cold outside")
else:
    print("It is ok outside")
print("Done")

# Comparisons using string/text
# Note, this example does not work when running under Eclipse
# because the input will contain an extra carriage return at the
# end. It works fine under IDLE.
userName = input("What is your name? ")
if userName == "Paul":
    print("You have a nice name.")
else:
    print("Your name is ok.")
```

Review

Multiple Choice Quiz

1. Which statement will check if a is less than b?

   a. `if a less than b:`

   b. `if a < b`

   c. `if a > b`

   d. `if a < b:`

   e. `if (a < b)`

   f. `if a >= b`

   g. `if a <= b:`

2. Which statement will check if a is equal to b?

   a. `if a equals b:`

   b. `if a = b`

   c. `if a = b:`

   d. `if a == b:`

   e. `if a == b`

   f. `if a === b`

   g. `if a === b:`

3.   Which statement will check if a is less than or equal to b?

   a.   `if a < or = b:`

   b.   `if a <= b:`

   c.   `if a < = b:`

   d.   `if a >= b:`

   e.   `if a =< b:`

   f.   `if a < b or == b:`

   g.   `if a <== b:`

4.   Which statement will check if a is less b and less than c?

   a.   `if a < b and < c:`

   b.   `if a < b & c:`

   c.   `if a < b and a < c:`

   d.   `if a < b and c:`

5.   What will this code print?

```
if 3 < 4:
    print("A")
else:
    print("B")
    print("C")
```

   a.   A

   b.   A
        B

   c.   B

   d.   B
        C

   e.   A
        C

   f.   A
        B
        C

   g.   Nothing, the code won't run.

6. What will this code print?

```
if 3 < 4:
    print("A")
else:
    print("B")
print("C")
```

a. A

b. A
   B

c. B

d. B
   C

e. A
   C

f. A
   B
   C

g. Nothing, the code won't run.

7. What will this code print?

```
a = True
if a:
    print("A")
else:
    print("B")
print("C")
```

a. A

b. A
   B

c. B

d. B
   C

e. A
   C

f. A
   B
   C

g. Nothing, the code won't run.

8. What will this code print?

```
a = True
if not(a):
    print("A")
else:
    print("B")
print("C")
```

a. A

b. A
   B

c. B

d. B
   C

e. A
   C

f. A
   B
   C

g. Nothing, the code won't run.

9. What will this code print?

```
if 4 < 4:
    print("A")
elif 3 < 4:
    print("B")
else:
    print("C")
print("D")
```

a. A

b. A
   B

c. B

d. B
   D

e. A
   D

f. A
   C

g. Nothing, the code won't run.

Short Answer Worksheet

1. What is missing from this code?

```python
temperature = float(input("Temperature: "))
if temperature > 90:
    print("It is hot outside.")
else:
    print("It is not hot out.")
```

2. Write a Python program that will take in a number from the user and print if it is positive, negative, or zero. Use a proper if/elif/else chain; don't just use three if statements.

3. Write a Python program that will take in a number from a user and print out Success if it is greater than -10 and less than 10, inclusive.

4. This runs, but there is something wrong. What is it?

```python
user_input = input("A cherry is a: ")
print("A. Dessert topping")
print("B. Desert topping")
if user_input.upper() == "A":
    print("Correct!")
else:
    print("Incorrect.")
```

5. There are two things wrong with this code that tests if x is set to a positive value. One prevents it from running, and the other is subtle. Make sure the if statement works no matter what x is set to. Identify both issues.

```python
x == 4
if x >= 0:
    print("x is positive.")
else:
    print("x is not positive.")
```

6. What three things are wrong with the following code?

```python
x = input("Enter a number: ")
if x = 3
    print("You entered 3")
```

7. There are four things wrong with this code. Identify all four issues.

```python
answer = input("What is the name of Dr. Bunsen Honeydew's assistant? ")
if a = "Beaker":
    print("Correct!")
    else
    print("Incorrect! It is Beaker.")
```

8. This program doesn't work correctly. What is wrong?

```
x = input("How are you today?")
if x == "Happy" or "Glad":
    print("That is good to hear!")
```

9. Look at the code below. Write you best guess here on what it will print. Next, run the code and see if you are correct. Clearly label your guess and the actual answer. Also, if this or any other example results in an error, make sure to state that an error occurred. While you don't need to write an explanation, make sure you understand why the computer prints what it does. Don't get caught flat-footed when you need to know later.

```
x = 5
y = x == 6
z = x == 5
print("x=", x)
print("y=", y)
print("z=", z)
if y:
    print("Fizz")
if z:
    print("Buzz")
```

10. Look at the code below. Write you best guess on what it will print. Next, run the code and see if you are correct.

```
x = 5
y = 10
z = 10
print(x < y)
print(y < z)
print(x == 5)
print(not x == 5)
print(x != 5)
print(not x != 5)
print(x == "5")
print(5 == x + 0.00000000001)
print(x == 5 and y == 10)
print(x == 5 and y == 5)
print(x == 5 or y == 5)
```

11. Look at the code below. Write you best guess on what it will print. Next, run the code and see if you are correct.

```
print("3" == "3")
print(" 3" == "3")
print(3 < 4)
print(3 < 10)
print("3" < "4")
print("3" < "10")
print( (2 == 2) == "True" )
print( (2 == 2) == True )
print(3 < "3")
```

12. What things are wrong with this section of code? The programmer wants to set the money variable according to the initial occupation the user selects.

```
print("Welcome to Oregon Trail!")

print("A. Banker")
print("B. Carpenter")
print("C. Farmer")

user_input = input("What is your occupation?")

if user_input = A:
    money = 100
else if user_input = B:
    money = 70
else if user_input = C:
    money = 50
```

Exercise

Find Exercise 3 "Create-a-Quiz" in the appendix.

CHAPTER 5

Guessing Games with Random Numbers and Loops

The last step before we start with graphics is learning how to loop a section of code. Most games loop. They repeat the same code over and over. For example, the number guessing game below loops for each guess that the user makes:

```
Hi! I'm thinking of a random number between 1 and 100.
--- Attempt 1
Guess what number I am thinking of: 50
Too high.
--- Attempt 2
Guess what number I am thinking of: 25
Too high.
--- Attempt 3
Guess what number I am thinking of: 17
Too high.
--- Attempt 4
Guess what number I am thinking of: 9
Too low.
--- Attempt 5
Guess what number I am thinking of: 14
Too high.
--- Attempt 6
Guess what number I am thinking of: 12
Too high.
--- Attempt 7
Guess what number I am thinking of: 10
Too low.
Aw, you ran out of tries. The number was 11.
```

Wait, what does this have to do with graphics and video games? A lot. Each *frame* the game displays is one time through a loop. You may be familiar with the frames-per-second (FPS) statistic that games show. The FPS represents the number of times the computer updates the screen each second. The higher the rate, the smoother the game. (Although an FPS rate past 60 is faster than most screens can update, so there isn't much point to push it past that.) The figure below shows the game Eve Online and a graph showing how many frames per second the computer is able to display.

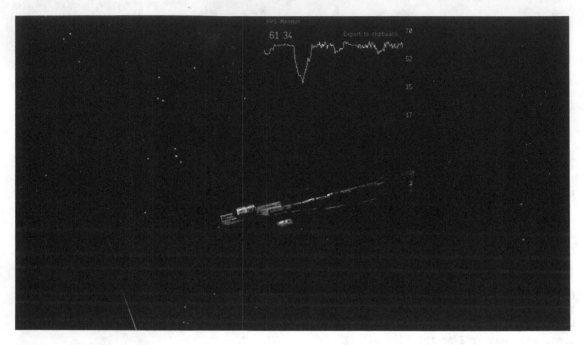

FPS in video games

The loop in these games works like the flowchart in the following figure. Despite the complexities of modern games, the inside of this loop is similar to the calculator program we did in Chapter 2. Get user input. Perform calculations. Output the result. In a video game, we try to repeat this up to 60 times per second.

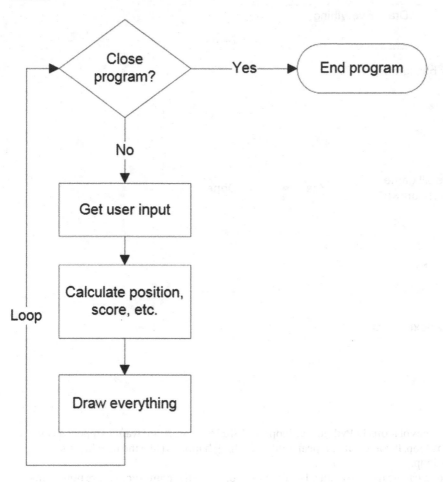

Game loop

There can even be loops inside of other loops. A real "loop the loop." Take a look at the "Draw Everything" box in the next figure. This set of code loops through and draws each object in the game. That loop is inside of the larger loop that draws each frame of the game, which looks like this figure.

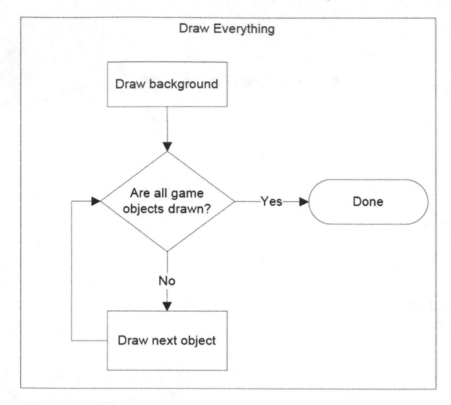

Draw everything loop

There are two major types of loops in Python: for loops and while loops. If you want to repeat a certain number of times, use a for loop. If you want to repeat until something happens (like the user hits the quit button), then use a while loop.

For example, a for loop can be used to print all student records since the computer knows how many students there are. A while loop would need to be used to check for when a user hits the mouse button since the computer has no idea how long it will have to wait.

for Loops

The for loop example below runs the print statement five times. It could just as easily run 100 or 1,000,000 times just by changing the 5 to the desired number of times to loop. Note the similarities of how the for loop is written to the if statement. Both end in a colon, and both use indentation to specify which lines are affected by the statement.

```
for i in range(5):
    print("I will not chew gum in class.")

I will not chew gum in class.
I will not chew gum in class.
I will not chew gum in class.
I will not chew gum in class.
I will not chew gum in class.
```

The i on line 1 is a variable that keeps track of how many times the program has looped. It is a new variable and can be named any legal variable name. Programmers often use i as for the variable name, because the i is short for *increment*. This variable helps track when the loop should end.

The range function controls how many times the code in the loop is run. In this case, five times.

The next example code will print "Please," five times and "Can I go to the mall?" only once. "Can I go to the mall?" is not indented so it is not part of the for loop and will not print until the for loop completes.

```
for i in range(5):
    print("Please,")
print("Can I go to the mall?")

Please,
Please,
Please,
Please,
Please,
Can I go to the mall?
```

This next code example takes the prior example and indents line 3. This change will cause the program to print "Please," and "Can I go to the mall?" five times. Since the statement has been indented "Can I go to the mall?" is now part of the for loop and will repeat five times just like the word "Please,".

```
for i in range(5):
    print("Please,")
    print("Can I go to the mall?")

Please,
Can I go to the mall?
Please,
Can I go to the mall?
Please,
Can I go to the mall?
Please,
Can I go to the mall?
Please,
Can I go to the mall?
```

The code below will print the numbers 0 to 9. Notice that the loop starts at 0 and does not include the number 10. It is natural to assume that range(10) would include 10, but it stops just short of it.

```
for i in range(10):
    print(i)
```

```
0
1
2
3
4
5
6
7
8
9
```

A program does not need to name the variable i; it could be named something else. For example, a programmer might use line_number if she was processing a text file.

If a programmer wants to go from 1 to 10 instead of 0 to 9, there are a couple of ways to do it. The first way is to send the range function two numbers instead of one. The first number is the starting value; the second is just beyond the ending value.

It does take some practice to get used to the idea that the for loop will include the first number, but not the second number listed. The example below specifies a range of (1,11), and the numbers 1 to 10 are printed. The starting number 1 is included, but not the ending number of 11.

```
for i in range(1, 11):
    print(i)
```

```
1
2
3
4
5
6
7
8
9
10
```

Another way to print the numbers 1 to 10 is to still use range(10) and have the variable i go from 0 to 9. But just before printing out the variable the programmer adds one to it. This also works to print the numbers 1 to 10. Either method works just fine.

```
# Print the numbers 1 to 10.
for i in range(10):
    print(i + 1)
```

Counting by Numbers Other Than One

If the program needs to count by 2s or use some other increment, this is easy. Just like before there are two ways to do it. The easiest is to supply a third number to the range function that tells it to count by 2s. The second way to do it is to go ahead and count by 1's but multiply the variable by 2. The code example below shows both methods.

```python
# Two ways to print the even numbers 2 to 10
for i in range(2,12,2):
    print(i)

for i in range(5):
    print((i + 1) * 2)
```

```
2
4
6
8
10
2
4
6
8
10
```

It is also possible to count backwards down towards zero by giving the range function a negative step. In the example below, start at 10, go down to but not including 0, and do it by -1 increments. The hardest part of creating these loops is to accidentally switch the start and end numbers. The program starts at the larger value, so it goes first. Normal for loops that count up start with the smallest value listed first in the range function.

```python
for i in range(10, 0, -1):
    print(i)
```

```
10
9
8
7
6
5
4
3
2
1
```

If the numbers that a program needs to iterate through don't form an easy pattern, it is possible to pull numbers out of a list. (A full discussion of lists is covered in Chapter 8. This is just a preview of what you can do.)

```
for i in [2,6,4,2,4,6,7,4]:
    print(i)
```

This prints:

```
2
6
4
2
4
6
7
4
```

Nesting Loops

Try to predict what the code below will print. Then enter the code and see if you are correct.

```
# What does this print? Why?
for i in range(3):
    print("a")
for j in range(3):
        print("b")
```

This next block of code is almost identical to the one above. The second for loop has been indented one tab stop so that it is now *nested* inside of the first for loop. This changes how the code runs significantly. Try it and see.

```
# What does this print? Why?
for i in range(3):
    print("a")
    for j in range(3):
        print("b")

print("Done")
```

I'm not going to tell you what the code does; go to a computer and see.

Keeping a Running Total

A common operation in working with loops is to keep a running total. This "running total" code pattern is used a lot in this book. Keep a running total of a score, total a person's account transactions, use a total to find an average, etc. You might want to bookmark this code listing because we'll refer back to it several times. In the code below, the user enters five numbers and the code totals up their values.

```
total = 0
for i in range(5):
    new_number = int(input("Enter a number: " ))
    total += new_number
print("The total is: ", total)
```

Note that line 1 creates the variable `total` and sets it to an initial amount of zero. It is easy to forget the need to create and initialize the variable to zero. Without it the computer will complain when it hits line 4. It doesn't know how to add `new_number` to `total` because `total` hasn't been given a value yet.

A common mistake is to use i to `total` instead of `new_number`. Remember, we are keeping a running total of the values entered by the user, not a running total of the current loop count.

Speaking of the current loop count, we can use the loop count value to solve some mathematical operations. For example:

$$\sum_{n=1}^{100} n$$

If you aren't familiar with this type of formula, it is just a fancy way of stating:

$$s = 1 + 2 + 3 + 4 + 5 \ldots 98 + 99 + 100$$

The code below adds all the numbers from 1 to 100. It demonstrates a common pattern where a running total is kept inside of a loop. This also uses a separate variable sum to track the running total.

```
# What is the value of sum?
sum = 0
for i in range(1, 101):
    sum = sum + i
print(sum)
```

Here's a different variation. This takes five numbers from the user and counts the number of times the user enters a zero:

```
total = 0
for i in range(5):
    new_number = int(input( "Enter a number: "))
    if new_number == 0:
        total += 1
print("You entered a total of", total, "zeros")
```

A programmer that understands the nested for loops and running totals should be able to predict the output of the code below.

```
# What is the value of a?
a = 0
for i in range(10):
    a = a + 1
print(a)
```

```
# What is the value of a?
a = 0
for i in range(10):
    a = a + 1
for j in range(10):
    a = a + 1
print(a)

# What is the value of a?
a = 0
for i in range(10):
    a = a + 1
    for j in range(10):
        a = a + 1
print(a)
```

Don't go over this section too fast. Give it a try and predict the output of the code above. Then copy it into a Python program and run it to see if you are right. If you aren't, figure out why.

Example for Loops

This example code covers common for loops and shows how they work.

```
# Sample Python/Pygame Programs
# http://programarcadegames.com/

# Print 'Hi' 10 times
for i in range(10):
    print("Hi")

# Print 'Hello' 5 times and 'There' once
for i in range(5):
    print("Hello")
print("There")

# Print 'Hello' 'There' 5 times
for i in range(5):
    print("Hello")
    print("There")

# Print the numbers 0 to 9
for i in range(10):
    print(i)

# Two ways to print the numbers 1 to 10
for i in range(1, 11):
    print(i)
```

```
for i in range(10):
    print(i + 1)

# Two ways to print the even numbers 2 to 10
for i in range(2, 12, 2):
    print(i)

for i in range(5):
    print((i + 1) * 2)

# Count down from 10 down to 1 (not zero)
for i in range(10, 0, -1):
    print(i)

# Print numbers out of a list
for i in [2, 6, 4, 2, 4, 6, 7, 4]:
    print(i)

# What does this print? Why?
for i in range(3):
    print("a")
    for j in range(3):
        print("b")

# What is the value of a?
a = 0
for i in range(10):
    a = a + 1
print(a)

# What is the value of a?
a = 0
for i in range(10):
    a = a + 1
for j in range(10):
    a = a + 1
print(a)

# What is the value of a?
a = 0
for i in range(10):
    a = a + 1
    for j in range(10):
        a = a + 1
print(a)

# What is the value of sum?
sum = 0
for i in range(1, 101):
    sum = sum + i
```

while Loops

A for loop is used when a program knows it needs to repeat a block of code for a certain number of times. A while loop is used when a program needs to loop until a particular condition occurs.

Oddly enough, a while loop can be used anywhere a for loop is used. It can be used to loop until an increment variable reaches a certain value. Why have a for loop if a while loop can do everything? The for loop is simpler to use and code. A for loop that looks like this:

```
for i in range(10):
    print(i)
```

...can be done with a while loop that looks like this:

```
i = 0
while i < 10:
    print(i)
    i = i + 1
```

Line 1 of the while loop sets up a "sentinel" variable that will be used to count the number of times the loop has been executed. This happens automatically in a for loop eliminating one line of code. Line 2 contains the actual while loop. The format of the while loop is very similar to the if statement. If the condition holds, the code in the loop will repeat. Line 4 adds to the increment value. In a for loop this happens automatically, eliminating another line of code. As one can see from the code, the for loop is more compact than a while loop and is easier to read. Otherwise, programs would do everything with a while loop.

A common mistake is to confuse the for loop and the while loop. The code below shows a programmer that can't quite make up his/her mind between a for loop or a while loop.

```
while range(10):
    print(i)
```

Don't use range with a while loop!
The range function only works with the for loop. Do not use it with the while loop!

Using Increment Operators

Increment operators are often used with while loops. It is possible to shorthand the code:

```
i = i + 1
```

With the following:

```
i += 1
```

In the while loop it would look like:

```
i = 0
while i < 10:
    print(i)
    i += 1
```

This can be done with subtraction and multiplication as well. For example:

```
i *= 2
```

Is the same as:

```
i = i * 2
```

See if you can figure out what would this print:

```
i = 1
while i <= 2 ** 32:
    print(i)
    i *= 2
```

Looping Until User Wants to Quit

A very common operation is to loop until the user performs a request to quit:

```
quit = "n"
while quit == "n":
    quit = input("Do you want to quit? ")
```

There may be several ways for a loop to quit. Using a Boolean variable to trigger the event is a way of handling that. Here's an example:

```
done = False
while not done:
    quit = input("Do you want to quit? ")
    if quit == "y":
        done = True

    attack = input("Does your elf attack the dragon? ")
    if attack == "y":
        print("Bad choice, you died.")
        done = True
```

This isn't perfect though, because if the user says she wants to quit, the code will still ask if she wants to attack the dragon. How could you fix this?

Here is an example of using a while loop where the code repeats until the value gets close enough to zero:

```
value = 0
increment = 0.5
while value < 0.999:
    value += increment
    increment *= 0.5
    print(value)
```

Common Problems with while Loops

The programmer wants to count down from 10. What is wrong and how can it be fixed?

```
i = 10
while i == 0:
    print(i)
    i -= 1
```

What is wrong with this loop that tries to count to 10? What will happen when it is run? How should it be fixed?

```
i = 1
while i < 10:
    print(i)
```

Example while Loops

Here's a program that covers the different uses of the while loop that we just talked about.

```
# Sample Python/Pygame Programs
# http://programarcadegames.com/

# A while loop can be used anywhere a for loop is used:
i = 0
while i < 10:
    print(i)
    i = i + 1

# This is the same as:
for i in range(10):
    print(i)

# It is possible to short hand the code:
# i = i + 1
# With the following:
# i += 1
# This can be done with subtraction, and multiplication as well.
i = 0
while i < 10:
    print(i)
    i += 1

# What would this print?
i = 1
while i <= 2**32:
    print(i)
    i *= 2
```

```
# A very common operation is to loop until the user performs
# a request to quit
quit = "n"
while quit == "n":
    quit = input("Do you want to quit? ")

# There may be several ways for a loop to quit. Using a boolean
# to trigger the event is a way of handling that.
done = False
while not done:
    quit = input("Do you want to quit? ")
    if quit == "y":
        done = True

    attack = input("Does your elf attach the dragon? ")
    if attack == "y":
        print("Bad choice, you died.")
        done = True

value = 0
increment = 0.5
while value < 0.999:
    value += increment
    increment *= 0.5
    print(value)

# -- Common problems with while loops --

# The programmer wants to count down from 10
# What is wrong and how to fix it?
i = 10
while i == 0:
    print(i)
    i -= 1

# What is wrong with this loop that tries
# to count to 10? What will happen when it is run?
i = 1
while i < 10:
    print(i)
```

Random Numbers

Random numbers are heavily used in computer science for programs that involve games or simulations.

The randrange Function

By default, Python does not know how to make random numbers. It is necessary to have Python import a code library that can create random numbers. So to use random numbers, the first thing that should appear at the top of the program is an `import` statement:

```
import random
```

Just like with pygame, it is important not to create a file with the same name as what is being imported. Creating a file called `random.py` will cause Python to start importing that file instead of the system library that creates random numbers.

After this, random numbers can be created with the `randrange` function. For example, this code creates random numbers from 0 to 49. By default the lower bound is 0.

```
my_number = random.randrange(50)
```

The next code example generates random numbers from 100 to 200. Just like the range function the second parameter specifies an upper bound that is not inclusive. Therefore if you want random numbers up to and including 200, specify 201.

```
my_number = random.randrange(100, 201)
```

What if you don't want a number, but a random item? That requires a list. We don't cover lists in detail until Chapter 8, but to give you preview of what selecting a random item out of a list would look like, see below:

```
my_list = ["rock", "paper", "scissors"]
random_index = random.randrange(3)
print(my_list[random_index])
```

The random Function

All of the prior code generates integer numbers. If a floating-point number is desired, a programmer may use the `random` function.

The code below generates a random number from 0 to 1 such as 0.4355991106620656.

```
my_number = random.random()
```

With some simple math, this number can be adjusted. For example, the code below generates a random floating-point number between 10 and 15:

```
my_number = random.random() * 5 + 10
```

Review

Multiple Choice Quiz

1. What does this code print?

```
for x in range(4):
    print("Hello")
```

   a. The word Hello 3 times

   b. The word Hello 4 times

   c. The word Hello 5 times

   d. It will print nothing

   e. It will print Hello forever

   f. Nothing, it won't run

2. What does this code print?

```
for y in range(4):
    print("y")
```

   a. The numbers 0 to 3

   b. The numbers 0 to 4

   c. The numbers 1 to 3

   d. The numbers 1 to 4

   e. It will print "y" four times

   f. Nothing, it won't run

3. What does this code print?

```
for y in range(4):
    print(y)
```

   a. The numbers 0 to 3

   b. The numbers 0 to 4

   c. The numbers 1 to 3

   d. The numbers 1 to 4

   e. It will print "y" four times

   f. Nothing, it won't run

4. What does this code print?

```
for y in range(1, 11):
        print(y)
```

   a. The numbers 0 to 11

   b. The numbers 1 to 11

   c. The numbers 1 to 10

   d. The numbers 0 to 10

   e. Nothing, it won't run

5. What does this code print?

```
for y in range(2, 12, 2):
        print(y + 1)
```

   a. The even numbers 2 to 12

   b. The even numbers 2 to 10

   c. The odd numbers 3 to 11

   d. The odd numbers 3 to 13

   e. Nothing, it won't run

6. What does this code print?

```
a=0
for i in range(10):
    a += 1
print(a)
```

   a. 9

   b. 10

   c. 11

   d. Nothing, it won't run

7. What does this code print?

```
a = 0
for i in range(10):
    a += 1
for j in range(10):
        a += 1
print(a)
```

   a. 10

   b. 20

   c. 18

   d. 100

   e. Nothing, it won't run

8. What does this code print?

```
a = 0
for i in range(10):
        for j in range(10):
                a += 1
print(a)
```

a. 10

b. 20

c. 110

d. 100

e. Nothing, it won't run

9. What does this code print?

```
a = 0
for i in range(10):
        a += 1
        for j in range(10):
                a += 1
print(a)
```

a. 10

b. 20

c. 110

d. 100

e. Nothing, it won't run

10. When should a programmer use a for loop instead of a while loop?

a. for loops are used to when there is a set number of loops

b. for loops are used to loop until a condition is true

c. while loops should always be used

d. for loops should always be used

11. What does this do?

```
x = random.randrange(50)
```

a. The number 50

b. A random integer 0 to 49 (inclusive)

c. A random integer 1 to 50 (inclusive)

d. A random integer 1 to 49 (inclusive)

e. A random integer 0 to 50 (inclusive)

f. A random integer 1 to 51 (inclusive)

12. What does this do?

    ```
    x = random.randrange(1, 50)
    The number 50
    ```

    a. A random integer 0 to 49 (inclusive)

    b. A random integer 1 to 50 (inclusive)

    c. A random integer 1 to 49 (inclusive)

    d. A random integer 0 to 50 (inclusive)

    e. A random integer 1 to 51 (inclusive)

13. What does this do?

    ```
    x = random.random() * 10
    ```

    a. A random floating-point number from 0 to 10

    b. A random integer from 0 to 10

    c. A random integer from 0 to 9

    d. A random integer from 0 to 1

Short Answer Worksheet

Note: Don't create a loop that only loops once. That doesn't make sense. Python runs the code once by default anyway. Avoid loops like this:

```
for i in range(1):
    # Do something.
```

1. Write a Python program that will use a for loop to print your name 10 times, and then the word "Done" at the end.

2. Write a Python program that will use a for loop to print "Red" and then "Gold" 20 times. (Red Gold Red Gold Red Gold... all on separate lines. Don't use \n.)

3. Write a Python program that will use a for loop to print the even numbers from 2 to 100, inclusive.

4. Write a Python program that will use a while loop to count from 10 down to, and including, 0. Then print the words "Blast off!" Remember, use a WHILE loop, don't use a FOR loop.

5. There are three things wrong with this program. List each.

    ```
    print("This program takes three numbers and returns the sum.")
    total = 0

    for i in range(3):
        x = input("Enter a number: ")
        total = total + i
    print("The total is:", x)
    ```

6. Write a program that prints a random integer from 1 to 10 (inclusive).

7. Write a program that prints a random floating-point number somewhere between 1 and 10 (inclusive). Do not make the mistake of generating a random number from 0 to 10 instead of 1 to 10.

8. Write a Python program that will:

   - Ask the user for seven numbers

   - Print the total sum of the numbers

   - Print the count of the positive entries, the number of entries equal to zero, and the number of negative entries. Use an if, elif, else chain, not just three if statements.

9. Coin flip tosser:

   - Create a program that will print a random 0 or 1.

   - Instead of 0 or 1, print heads or tails. Do this using if statements. Don't select from a list, as shown in the chapter.

   - Add a loop so that the program does this 50 times.

   - Create a running total for the number of heads flipped and the number of tails.

10. Write a program that plays rock, paper, scissors:

    - Create a program that randomly prints 0, 1, or 2.

    - Expand the program so it randomly prints rock, paper, or scissors using if statements. Don't select from a list, as shown in the chapter.

    - Add to the program so it first asks the user their choice.

    - (It will be easier if you have them enter 1, 2, or 3.)

    - Add a conditional statement to figure out who wins.

Exercise

Check the appendix for the exercise "Camel" that goes along with this chapter.

CHAPTER 6

■■■

Introduction to Graphics

Now that you can create loops, it is time to move on to learning how to create graphics. This chapter covers:

- How the computer handles x, y coordinates. It isn't like the coordinate system you learned in math class.

- How to specify colors. With millions of colors to choose from, telling the computer what color to use isn't as easy as just saying "red."

- How to open a blank window for drawing. Every artist needs a canvas.

- How to draw lines, rectangles, ellipses, and arcs.

Computer Coordinate Systems

The Cartesian coordinate system, shown in the figure below (`https://commons.wikimedia.org/wiki/File:Cartesian_coordinates_2D.svg`), is the system most people are used to when plotting graphics. This is the system taught in school. The computer uses a similar, but somewhat different, coordinate system. Understanding why it is different requires a quick bit of computer history.

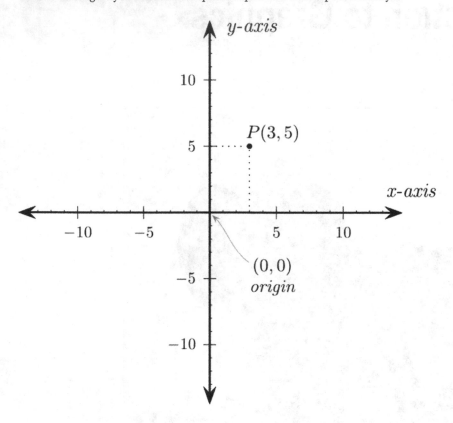

Cartesian coordinate system

During the early '80s, most computer systems were text-based and did not support graphics. The next figure (`https://en.wikipedia.org/wiki/File:Visicalc.png`) shows an early spreadsheet program run on an Apple][computer that was popular in the '80s. When positioning text on the screen, programmers started at the top, calling it line 1. The screen continued down for 24 lines and across for 40 characters.

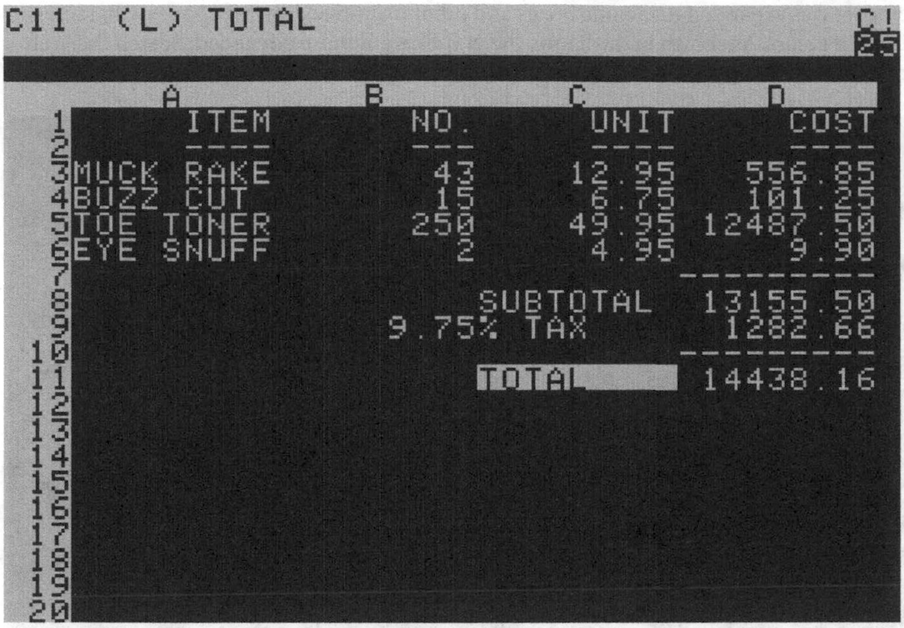

Early Apple text screen

Even with plain text, it was possible to make rudimentary graphics by just using characters on the keyboard. See this kitten shown in the next figure and look carefully at how it is drawn. When making this art, characters were still positioned starting with line 1 at the top.

Text screen

Later the character set was expanded to include boxes and other primitive drawing shapes. Characters could be drawn in different colors. As shown in the figure, the graphics got more advanced. Search the Web for "ASCII art," and many more examples can be found.

Spaceware text screen

Once computers moved to being able to control individual pixels for graphics, the text-based coordinate system stuck.

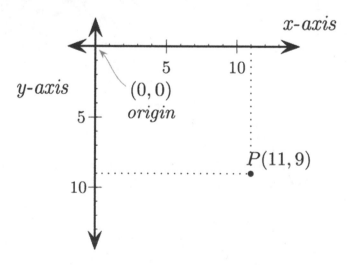

Computer coordinate system

The x coordinates work the same as the Cartesian coordinates system. But the y coordinates are reversed. Rather than the zero y coordinate at the bottom of the graph like in Cartesian graphics, the zero y coordinate is at the top of the screen with the computer. As the y values go up, the computer coordinate position moved down the screen, just like lines of text rather than standard Cartesian graphics. See the figure above.

Also, note the screen covers the lower-right quadrant, where the Cartesian coordinate system usually focuses on the upper-right quadrant. It is possible to draw items at negative coordinates, but they will be drawn offscreen. This can be useful when part of a shape is off screen. The computer figures out what is offscreen, and the programmer does not need to worry too much about it.

Pygame Library

To make graphics easier to work with, we'll use "Pygame." Pygame is a library of code that other people have written and makes it simple to:

- Draw graphic shapes

- Display bitmapped images

- Animate

- Interact with the keyboard, mouse, and gamepad

- Play sound

- Detect when objects collide

The first code a Pygame program needs to do is load and initialize the Pygame library. Every program that uses Pygame should start with these lines:

```
# Import a library of functions called 'pygame'
import pygame
# Initialize the game engine
pygame.init()
```

If you haven't installed Pygame yet, directions for installing Pygame are available in the "before you begin" section. If Pygame is not installed on your computer, you will get an error when trying to run import pygame.

Important: The import pygame looks for a library file named pygame. If a programmer creates a new program named pygame.py, the computer will import that file instead! This will prevent any pygame programs from working until that pygame.py file is deleted.

Colors

Next, we need to add variables that define our program's colors. Colors are defined in a list of three colors: red, green, and blue. Have you ever heard of an RGB monitor? This is where the term comes. Red-Green-Blue. With older monitors, you could sit really close to the monitor and make out the individual RGB colors. At least before your mom told you not to sit so close to the TV. This is hard to do with today's high resolution monitors.

Each element of the RGB triad is a number ranging from 0 to 255. Zero means there is none of the color, and 255 tells the monitor to display as much of the color as possible. The colors combine in an additive way, so if all three colors are specified, the color on the monitor appears white. (This is different than how ink and paint work.)

Lists in Python are surrounded by either square brackets or parentheses. (Chapter 8 covers lists in detail and the difference between the two types.) Individual numbers in the list are separated by commas. Below is an example that creates variables and sets them equal to lists of three numbers. These lists will be used later to specify colors.

```
# Define some colors
BLACK   = (   0,   0,   0)
WHITE   = ( 255, 255, 255)
GREEN   = (   0, 255,   0)
RED     = ( 255,   0,   0)
```

Why are these variables in uppercase? Remember back from Chapter 2, a variable that doesn't change is called a *constant*. We don't expect the color of black to change; it is a constant. We signify that variables are constants by naming them with all uppercase letters. If we expect a color to change, like if we have sky_color that changes as the sun sets, then that variable would be in all lowercase letters.

Using the interactive shell in IDLE, try defining these variables and printing them out. If the five colors above aren't the colors you are looking for, you can define your own. To pick a color, find an online "color picker" like the one shown in the figure below. One such color picker is at: http://www.colorpicker.com/

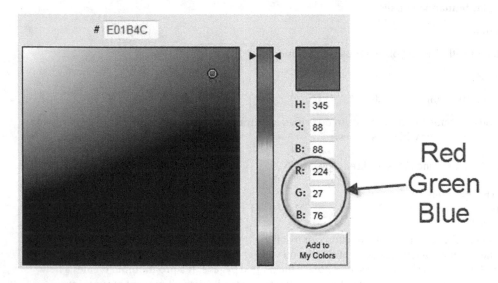

Color picker

Extra: Some color pickers specify colors in hexadecimal. You can enter hexadecimal numbers if you start them with 0x. For example:

```
WHITE = (0xFF, 0xFF, 0xFF)
```

Eventually the program will need to use the value of π when drawing arcs, so this is a good time in our program to define a variable that contains the value of π. (It is also possible to import this from the math library as math.pi.)

```
PI = 3.141592653
```

Open a Window

So far, the programs we have created only printed text out to the screen. Those programs did not open any windows like most modern programs do. The code to open a window is not complex. Below is the required code, which creates a window sized to a width of 700 pixels and a height of 500:

```
size = (700, 500)
screen = pygame.display.set_mode(size)
```

Why set_mode? Why not open_window? The reason is that this command can actually do a lot more than open a window. It can also create games that run in a full-screen mode. This removes the start menu, title bars, and gives the game control of everything on the screen. Because this mode is slightly more complex to use, and most people prefer windowed games anyway, we'll skip a detailed discussion on full-screen games. But if you want to find out more about full-screen games, check out the documentation on pygame's display command.

Also, why size = (700, 500) and not size = 700, 500? The same reason why we put parentheses around the color definitions. Python can't normally store two numbers (a height and width) into one variable. The only way it can is if the numbers are stored as a list. Lists need either parentheses or square brackets. (Technically, parentheses surrounding a set of numbers is more accurately called a *tuple* or an *immutable list*. Lists surrounded by square brackets are just called lists. An experienced Python developer would cringe at calling a list of numbers surrounded by parentheses a list rather than a tuple. Also you *can* actually say size = 700, 500, and it will default to a tuple but I prefer to use parentheses.) Lists are covered in detail in Chapter 8.

To set the title of the window (which is shown in the title bar), use the following line of code:

```
pygame.display.set_caption("Professor Craven's Cool Game")
```

Interacting with the User

With just the code written so far, the program would create a window and immediately hang. The user can't interact with the window, even to close it. All of this needs to be programmed. Code needs to be added so that the program waits in a loop until the user clicks "exit."

This is the most complex parts of the program, and a complete understanding of it isn't needed yet. But it is necessary to have an *idea* of what it does, so spend some time studying it and asking questions.

```
# Loop until the user clicks the close button.
done = False

# Used to manage how fast the screen updates
clock = pygame.time.Clock()

# -------- Main Program Loop -----------
while not done:
    # --- Main event loop
    for event in pygame.event.get(): # User did something
        if event.type == pygame.QUIT: # If user clicked close
            done = True # Flag that we are done so we exit this loop
```

```
# --- Game logic should go here

# --- Drawing code should go here

# First, clear the screen to white. Don't put other drawing commands
# above this, or they will be erased with this command.
screen.fill(WHITE)

# --- Go ahead and update the screen with what we've drawn.
pygame.display.flip()

# --- Limit to 60 frames per second
clock.tick(60)
```

Eventually we will add code to handle the keyboard and mouse clicks. That code will go below the comment for main event loop on line 9. Code for determining when bullets are fired and how objects move will go below the comment for game logic on line 14. We'll talk about that in later chapters. Code to draw will go in below where the screen is filled with white on line 20.

The Event Processing Loop

Alert! One of the most frustrating problems programmers have is to mess up the event processing loop. This "event processing" code handles all the keystrokes, mouse button clicks, and several other types of events. For example, your loop might look like:

```
for event in pygame.event.get():
    if event.type == pygame.QUIT:
        print("User asked to quit.")
    elif event.type == pygame.KEYDOWN:
        print("User pressed a key.")
    elif event.type == pygame.KEYUP:
        print("User let go of a key.")
    elif event.type == pygame.MOUSEBUTTONDOWN:
        print("User pressed a mouse button")
```

The events (like pressing keys) all go together in a list. The program uses a for loop to loop through each event. Using a chain of if statements the code figures out what type of event occurred, and the code to handle that event goes in the if statement.

All the if statements should go together, in one for loop. A common mistake when doing copy and pasting of code is to not merge loops from two programs, but to have two event loops.

```
# Here is one event loop
for event in pygame.event.get():
    if event.type == pygame.QUIT:
        print("User asked to quit.")
    elif event.type == pygame.KEYDOWN:
        print("User pressed a key.")
    elif event.type == pygame.KEYUP:
        print("User let go of a key.")
```

```
# Here the programmer has copied another event loop
# into the program. This is BAD. The events were already
# processed.
for event in pygame.event.get():
    if event.type == pygame.QUIT:
        print("User asked to quit.")
    elif event.type == pygame.MOUSEBUTTONDOWN:
        print("User pressed a mouse button")
```

The for loop on line 2 grabbed all of the user events. The for loop on line 13 won't grab any events because they were already processed in the prior loop.

Another typical problem is to start drawing and then try to finish the event loop:

```
for event in pygame.event.get():
    if event.type == pygame.QUIT:
        print("User asked to quit.")
    elif event.type == pygame.KEYDOWN:
        print("User pressed a key.")

pygame.draw.rect(screen, GREEN, [50,50,100,100])

# This is code that processes events. But it is not in the
# 'for' loop that processes events. It will not act reliably.
if event.type == pygame.KEYUP:
    print("User let go of a key.")
elif event.type == pygame.MOUSEBUTTONDOWN:
    print("User pressed a mouse button")
```

This will cause the program to ignore some keyboard and mouse commands. Why? The for loop processes all the events in a list. So if there are two keys that are hit, the for loop will process both. In the example above, the if statements are not in the for loop. If there are multiple events, the if statements will only run for the last event, rather than all events.

Processing Each Frame

The basic logic and order for each frame of the game:

- While not done:
  - For each event (keypress, mouse click, etc.):
    - Use a chain of if statements to run code to handle each event.
- Run calculations to determine where objects move, what happens when objects collide, etc.
- Clear the screen.
- Draw everything.

It makes the program easier to read and understand if these steps aren't mixed together. Don't do some calculations, some drawing, some more calculations, some more drawing. Also, see how this is similar to the calculator done in Chapter 2. Get user input, run calculations, and output the answer. That same pattern applies here.

The code for drawing the image to the screen happens inside the while loop. With the clock tick set at 10, the contents of the window will be drawn 10 times per second. If it happens too fast the computer is sluggish because all of its time is spent updating the screen. If it isn't in the loop at all, the screen won't redraw properly. If the drawing is outside the loop, the screen may initially show the graphics, but the graphics won't reappear if the window is minimized, or if another window is placed in front.

Ending the Program

Right now, clicking the "close" button of a window while running this Pygame program in IDLE will still cause the program to crash. This is a hassle because it requires a lot of clicking to close a crashed program.

The problem is, even though the loop has exited, the program hasn't told the computer to close the window. By calling the command below, the program will close any open windows and exit as desired.

```
pygame.quit()
```

Clearing the Screen

The following code clears whatever might be in the window with a white background. Remember that the variable WHITE was defined earlier as a list of three RGB values.

```
# Clear the screen and set the screen background
screen.fill(WHITE)
```

This should be done before any drawing command is issued. Clearing the screen *after* the program draws graphics results in the user only seeing a blank screen.

When a window is first created it has a black background. It is still important to clear the screen because there are several things that could occur to keep this window from starting out cleared. A program should not assume it has a blank canvas to draw on.

Flipping the Screen

Very important! You must flip the display after you draw. The computer will not display the graphics as you draw them because it would cause the screen to flicker. This waits to display the screen until the program has finished drawing. The command below "flips" the graphics to the screen.

Failure to include this command will mean the program just shows a blank screen. Any drawing code after this flip will not display.

```
# Go ahead and update the screen with what we've drawn.
pygame.display.flip()
```

Open a Blank Window

Let's bring everything we've talked about into one full program. This code can be used as a base template for a Pygame program. It opens up a blank window and waits for the user to press the close button.

On the web site, if you click the "Examples" button you can select "graphics examples" and then you will find this file as pygame_base_template.py.

```
"""
 Pygame base template for opening a window

 Sample Python/Pygame Programs
 Simpson College Computer Science
 http://programarcadegames.com/
 http://simpson.edu/computer-science/

 Explanation video: http://youtu.be/vRB_983kUMc
"""

import pygame

# Define some colors
BLACK = (0, 0, 0)
WHITE = (255, 255, 255)
GREEN = (0, 255, 0)
RED = (255, 0, 0)

pygame.init()

# Set the width and height of the screen [width, height]
size = (700, 500)
screen = pygame.display.set_mode(size)

pygame.display.set_caption("My Game")

# Loop until the user clicks the close button.
done = False

# Used to manage how fast the screen updates
clock = pygame.time.Clock()

# -------- Main Program Loop -----------
while not done:
    # --- Main event loop
    for event in pygame.event.get():
        if event.type == pygame.QUIT:
            done = True

    # --- Game logic should go here

    # --- Drawing code should go here

    # First, clear the screen to white. Don't put other drawing commands
    # above this, or they will be erased with this command.
    screen.fill(WHITE)
```

```
    # --- Go ahead and update the screen with what we've drawn.
    pygame.display.flip()

    # --- Limit to 60 frames per second
    clock.tick(60)

# Close the window and quit.
# If you forget this line, the program will 'hang'
# on exit if running from IDLE.
pygame.quit()
```

Drawing Introduction

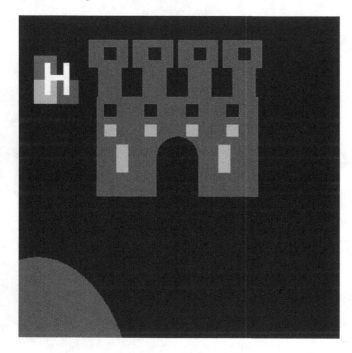

Here is a list of things that you can draw: http://www.pygame.org/docs/ref/draw.html

A program can draw things such as rectangles, polygons, circles, ellipses, arcs, and lines. We will also cover how to display text with graphics. Bitmapped graphics such as images are covered in Chapter 12. If you decide to look at that pygame reference, you might see a function definition like this:

```
pygame.draw.rect(Surface, color, Rect, width=0): return Rect
```

A frequent cause of confusion is the part of the line that says width=0. What this means is that if you do not supply a width, it will default to zero. Thus, this function call:

```
pygame.draw.rect(screen, RED, [55, 50, 20, 25])
```

Is the same as this function call:

```
pygame.draw.rect(screen, RED, [55, 50, 20, 25], 0)
```

The : return Rect is telling you that the function returns a rectangle, the same one that was passed in. You can just ignore this part.

What will not work, is attempting to copy the line and put width = 0 in the parentheses.

```
# This fails and the error the computer gives you is
# really hard to understand.
pygame.draw.rect(screen, RED, [55, 50, 20, 25], width=0)
```

Drawing Lines

The code example below shows how to draw a line on the screen. It will draw on the screen a green line from (0, 0) to (100, 100) that is 5 pixels wide. Remember that GREEN is a variable that was defined earlier as a list of three RGB values.

```
# Draw on the screen a green line from (0, 0) to (100, 100)
# that is 5 pixels wide.
pygame.draw.line(screen, GREEN, [0, 0], [100, 100], 5)
```

Use the base template from the prior example and add the code to draw lines. Read the comments to figure out exactly where to put the code. Try drawing lines with different thicknesses, colors, and locations. Draw several lines.

Drawing Lines with Loops and Offsets

Programs can repeat things over and over. The next code example draws a line over and over using a loop. Programs can use this technique to do multiple lines and even draw an entire car.

Putting a line drawing command inside a loop will cause multiple lines being drawn to the screen. But here's the catch. If each line has the same starting and ending coordinates, then each line will draw *on top* of the other line. It will look like only one line was drawn.

To get around this, it is necessary to offset the coordinates each time through the loop. So the first time through the loop the variable y_offset is zero. The line in the code below is drawn from (0,10) to (100, 110). The next time through the loop y_offset increased by 10. This causes the next line to be drawn to have new coordinates of (0, 20) and (100, 120). This continues each time through the loop shifting the coordinates of each line down by 10 pixels.

```
# Draw on the screen several lines from (0, 10) to (100, 110)
# 5 pixels wide using a while loop
y_offset = 0
while y_offset < 100:
    pygame.draw.line(screen,RED,[0,10+y_offset],[100,110+y_offset],5)
    y_offset = y_offset + 10
```

This same code could be done even more easily with a for loop:

```
# Draw on the screen several lines from (0,10) to (100,110)
# 5 pixels wide using a for loop
for y_offset in range(0, 100, 10):
    pygame.draw.line(screen,RED,[0,10+y_offset],[100,110+y_offset],5)
```

Run this code and try using different changes to the offset. Try creating an offset with different values. Experiment with different values until exactly how this works is obvious.

For example, here is a loop that uses sine and cosine to create a more complex set of offsets and produces the image shown in the figure below.

```
for i in range(200):

        radians_x = i / 20
        radians_y = i / 6

        x = int(75 * math.sin(radians_x)) + 200
        y = int(75 * math.cos(radians_y)) + 200

    pygame.draw.line(screen, BLACK, [x,y], [x+5,y], 5)
```

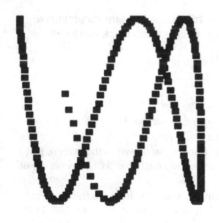

Complex Offsets

Multiple elements can be drawn in one for loop, such as this code that draws the multiple X's shown in the next figure.

```
for x_offset in range(30, 300, 30):
    pygame.draw.line(screen,BLACK,[x_offset,100],[x_offset-10,90],2)
    pygame.draw.line(screen,BLACK,[x_offset,90],[x_offset-10,100],2)
```

✕ ✕ ✕ ✕ ✕ ✕ ✕ ✕ ✕

Multiple X's

Drawing a Rectangle

When drawing a rectangle, the computer needs coordinates for the upper-left rectangle corner (the origin), and a height and width.

This figure shows a rectangle (and an ellipse, which will be explained later) with the origin at (20, 20), a width of 250, and a height of 100. When specifying a rectangle, the computer needs a list of these four numbers in the order of (x, y, width, height).

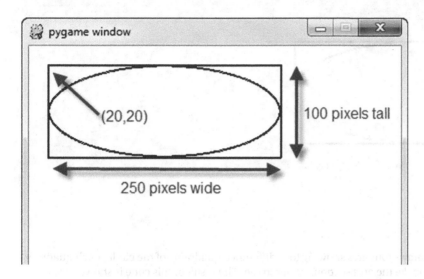

Drawing an Ellipse

The next code example draws this rectangle. The first two numbers in the list define the upper left corner at (20, 20). The next two numbers specify first the width of 250 pixels, and then the height of 100 pixels.

The 2 at the end specifies a line width of 2 pixels. The larger the number, the thicker the line around the rectangle. If this number is 0, then there will not be a border around the rectangle. Instead it will be filled in with the color specified.

```
# Draw a rectangle
pygame.draw.rect(screen,BLACK,[20,20,250,100],2)
```

Drawing an Ellipse

An ellipse is drawn just like a rectangle. The boundaries of a rectangle are specified, and the computer draws an ellipse inside those boundaries.

The most common mistake in working with an ellipse is to think that the starting point specifies the center of the ellipse. In reality, nothing is drawn at the starting point. It is the upper left of a rectangle that contains the ellipse.

Looking back at the figure one can see an ellipse 250 pixels wide and 100 pixels tall. The upper left corner of the 250x100 rectangle that contains it is at (20, 20). Note that nothing is actually drawn at (20, 20). With both drawn on top of each other it is easier to see how the ellipse is specified.

```
# Draw an ellipse, using a rectangle as the outside boundaries
pygame.draw.ellipse(screen, BLACK, [20,20,250,100], 2)
```

Drawing an Arc

What if a program only needs to draw part of an ellipse? That can be done with the `arc` command. This command is similar to the `ellipse` command, but it includes start and end angles for the arc to be drawn. The angles are in radians. See the figure below.

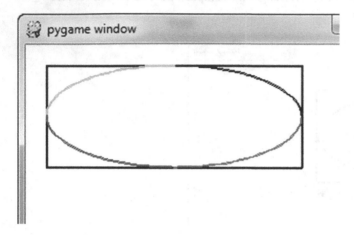

Arcs

The code example below draws four arcs showing four difference quadrants of the circle. Each quadrant is drawn in a different color to make the arcs sections easier to see. The result of this code is shown in the figure above.

```
# Draw an arc as part of an ellipse. Use radians to determine what
# angle to draw.
pygame.draw.arc(screen, GREEN, [100,100,250,200],  PI/2,    PI, 2)
pygame.draw.arc(screen, BLACK, [100,100,250,200],    0,  PI/2, 2)
pygame.draw.arc(screen, RED,   [100,100,250,200],3*PI/2,  2*PI, 2)
pygame.draw.arc(screen, BLUE,  [100,100,250,200],   PI, 3*PI/2, 2)
```

Drawing a Polygon

The next line of code draws a polygon. The triangle shape is defined with three points at (100, 100) (0, 200) and (200, 200). It is possible to list as many points as desired. Note how the points are listed. Each point is a list of two numbers, and the points themselves are nested in another list that holds all the points. This code draws what can be seen in the following figure.

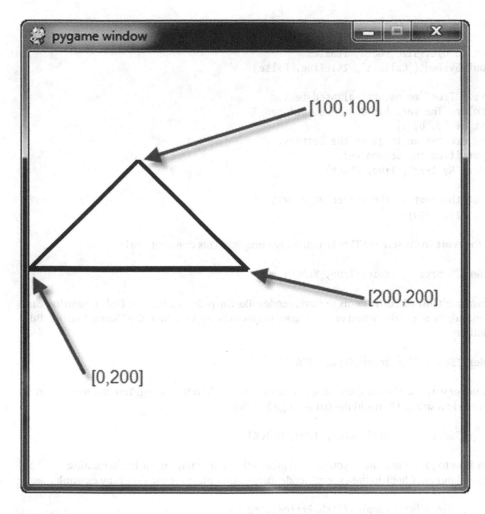

Polygon

```
# This draws a triangle using the polygon command
pygame.draw.polygon(screen, BLACK, [[100,100], [0,200], [200,200]], 5)
```

Drawing Text

Text is slightly more complex. There are three things that need to be done. First, the program creates a variable that holds information about the font to be used, such as what typeface and how big.

Second, the program creates an image of the text. One way to think of it is that the program carves out a "stamp" with the required letters that is ready to be dipped in ink and stamped on the paper.

The third thing that is done is the program tells where this image of the text should be stamped (or "blit'ed") to the screen.

Here's an example:

```
# Select the font to use, size, bold, italics
font = pygame.font.SysFont('Calibri', 25, True, False)

# Render the text. "True" means anti-aliased text.
# Black is the color. The variable BLACK was defined
# above as a list of [0, 0, 0]
# Note: This line creates an image of the letters,
# but does not put it on the screen yet.
text = font.render("My text", True, BLACK)

# Put the image of the text on the screen at 250x250
screen.blit(text, [250, 250])
```

Want to print the score to the screen? That is a bit more complex. This does not work:

```
text = font.render("Score: ", score, True, BLACK)
```

Why? A program can't just add extra items to font.render like the print statement. Only one string can be sent to the command; therefore the actual value of score needs to be appended to the "Score: " string. But this doesn't work either:

```
text = font.render("Score: " + score, True, BLACK)
```

If score is an integer variable, the computer doesn't know how to add it to a string. You, the programmer, must convert the score to a string. Then add the strings together like this:

```
text = font.render("Score: " + str(score), True, BLACK)
```

Now you know how to print the score. If you want to print a timer, that requires print formatting, discussed in a chapter later on. Check in the example code for section online for the timer.py example:

```
ProgramArcadeGames.com/python_examples/f.php?file=timer.py
```

Full Program Listing

This is a full listing of the program discussed in this chapter. This program, along with other programs, may be downloaded from:

ProgramArcadeGames.com/index.php?chapter=example_code

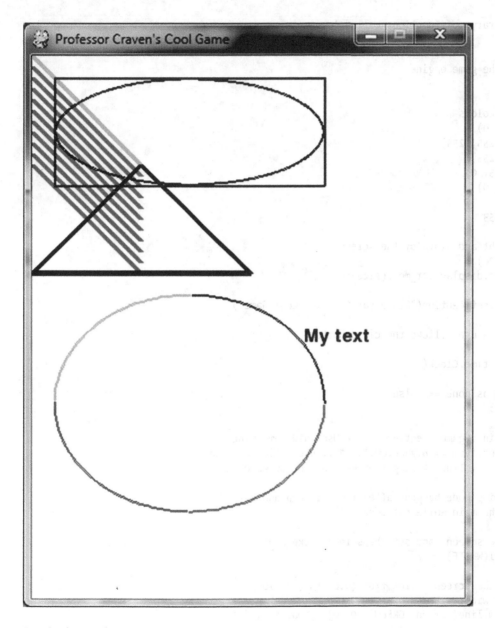

Result of example program

```
"""
 Simple graphics demo

 Sample Python/Pygame Programs
 http://programarcadegames.com/

"""

# Import a library  of functions called 'pygame'
import pygame

# Initialize the game engine
pygame.init()

# Define some colors
BLACK = (0, 0, 0)
WHITE = (255, 255, 255)
BLUE = (0, 0, 255)
GREEN = (0, 255, 0)
RED = (255, 0, 0)

PI = 3.141592653

# Set the height and width of the screen
size = (400, 500)
screen = pygame.display.set_mode(size)

pygame.display.set_caption("Professor Craven's Cool Game")

# Loop until the user clicks the close button.
done = False
clock = pygame.time.Clock()

# Loop as long as done == False
while not done:

    for event in pygame.event.get():  # User did something
        if event.type == pygame.QUIT:  # If user clicked close
            done = True  # Flag that we are done so we exit this loop

    # All drawing code happens after the for loop and but
    # inside the main while not done loop.

    # Clear the screen  and set the screen background
    screen.fill(WHITE)

    # Draw on the screen a line from (0,0) to (100,100)
    # 5 pixels wide.
    pygame.draw.line(screen, GREEN, [0, 0], [100, 100], 5)
```

```python
    # Draw on the screen several lines from (0,10) to (100,110)
    # 5 pixels wide using a loop
    for y_offset in range(0, 100, 10):
        pygame.draw.line(screen, RED, [0, 10 + y_offset], [100, 110 + y_offset], 5)

    # Draw a rectangle
    pygame.draw.rect(screen, BLACK, [20, 20, 250, 100], 2)

    # Draw an ellipse, using a rectangle as the outside boundaries
    pygame.draw.ellipse(screen, BLACK, [20, 20, 250, 100], 2)

    # Draw an arc as part of an ellipse.
    # Use radians to determine what angle to draw.
    pygame.draw.arc(screen, BLACK, [20, 220, 250, 200], 0, PI / 2, 2)
    pygame.draw.arc(screen, GREEN, [20, 220, 250, 200], PI / 2, PI, 2)
    pygame.draw.arc(screen, BLUE, [20, 220, 250, 200], PI, 3 * PI / 2, 2)
    pygame.draw.arc(screen, RED, [20, 220, 250, 200], 3 * PI / 2, 2 * PI, 2)

    # This draws a triangle using the polygon command
    pygame.draw.polygon(screen, BLACK, [[100, 100], [0, 200], [200, 200]], 5)

    # Select the font to use, size, bold, italics
    font = pygame.font.SysFont('Calibri', 25, True, False)

    # Render the text. "True" means anti-aliased text.
    # Black is the color. This creates an image of the
    # letters, but does not put it on the screen
    text = font.render("My text", True, BLACK)

    # Put the image of the text on the screen at 250x250
    screen.blit(text, [250, 250])

    # Go ahead and update the screen with what we've drawn.
    # This MUST happen after all the other drawing commands.
    pygame.display.flip()

    # This  limits the while loop to a max of 60 times per second.
    # Leave this out and we will use all CPU we can.
    clock.tick(60)

# Be IDLE friendly
pygame.quit()
```

Review

Multiple Choice Quiz

1. If a box is drawn starting at (x,y) coordinate (0,0), where will it be on the screen?

    a. Upper left

    b. Lower left

    c. Upper right

    d. Lower right

    e. Center

    f. It won't display

2. If the screen width and height are both 400 pixels, and a rectangle is drawn starting at (0,400), where will it display?

    a. Upper left

    b. Lower left

    c. Upper right

    d. Lower right

    e. Center

    f. It won't display

3. In computer graphics, as x and y coordinates increase in value, a point will move:

    a. Down and to the right

    b. Up and to the right

    c. Down and to the left

    d. Up and to the left

    e. Nowhere

4. What color would be defined by (0, 0, 0)?

    a. Black

    b. Red

    c. Green

    d. Blue

    e. White

5. What color would be defined by (0, 255, 0)?

    a. Black

    b. Red

    c. Green

    d. Blue

    e. White

6. What color would be defined by (255, 255, 255)?

    a. Black

    b. Red

    c. Green

    d. Blue

    e. White

7. What code will open up a window 400 pixels high and 800 pixels wide?

    a. ```
        size = [800, 400]
        screen = pygame.display.set_mode(size)
        ```

    b.  ```
        size = [400, 800]
        screen = pygame.display.set_mode(size)
        ```

    c. ```
        size = 800,400
        screen = pygame.display.set_mode(size)
        ```

    d.  ```
        size = 400,800
        screen = pygame.display.set_mode(size)
        ```

    e. ```
        screen = pygame.display.open_window(800, 400)
        ```

    f.  ```
        screen = pygame.display.open_window(400, 800)
        ```

8. What is the main program loop?

    a. It processes user input, updates objects, and draws the screen in each frame of the game.

    b. It runs once for the entire game.

    c. It loops once for each life that the player has.

    d. It loops once for each level of the game.

9. Where does this code go?

    ```
    clock = pygame.time.Clock()
    ```

    a. The code is placed after the main program loop.

    b. The code is placed inside the main program loop.

    c. This code is placed before the main program loop.

10.   Where does this code go, and what does it do?

```
clock.tick(20)
```

   a.   The code is place after the main program loop and pauses 20 milliseconds.

   b.   The code is place after the main program loop and limits the game to 20 frames per second.

   c.   The code is placed inside the main program loop and limits the game to 20 frames per second.

   d.   This code is placed before the main program loop and limits the game to 20 frames per second.

   e.   The code is placed inside the main program loop and pauses 20 milliseconds.

11.   Changing this code from 20 to 30 will cause what to happen?

```
clock.tick(20)
```

   a.   Nothing.

   b.   The game will run faster.

   c.   The game will run slower.

12.   What does this code do?

```
pygame.display.flip()
```

   a.   Nothing.

   b.   Clears the screen.

   c.   Displays everything that has been drawn so far.

   d.   Flips the screen from left to right.

   e.   Flips the screen from top to bottom.

13.   What code will draw a line from x, y coordinates (0, 0) to (100, 100)?

   a.   `pygame.draw.line(screen, GREEN, [0,0,100,100], 5)`

   b.   `pygame.draw.line(screen, GREEN, 0, 0, 100, 100, 5)`

   c.   `pygame.draw.line(screen, GREEN, [0, 0], [100, 100], 5)`

   d.   `pygame.draw.line(GREEN, screen, 0, 0, 100, 100, 5)`

   e.   `pygame.draw.line(5, GREEN, [0, 0], [100, 100], screen)`

14. What will this code draw?

```
offset = 0
while offset < 100:
    pygame.draw.line(screen, RED, [50+offset,20], [50+offset,60], 5)
    offset = offset + 10
```

   a. Ten vertical lines, 10 pixels apart, with a starting x coordinate of 50 and an ending coordinate of 140.

   b. Ten horizontal lines, 10 pixels part, with a starting y coordinate of 50 and an ending coordinate of 150.

   c. Ten vertical lines, 5 pixels apart, with a starting x coordinate of 50 and an ending coordinate of 100.

   d. Ten vertical lines, 10 pixels apart, with a starting x coordinate of 10 and an ending coordinate of 110.

   e. Ten vertical lines, 5 pixels apart, with a starting x coordinate of 10 and an ending coordinate of 150.

   f. Ten lines, all drawn on top of each other.

15. How wide will this ellipse be?

```
pygame.draw.ellipse(screen, BLACK, [0, 0, 100, 100], 2)
```

   a. 100 pixels

   b. 99 pixels

   c. 101 pixels

   d. 50 pixels

   e. 49 pixels

16. Where will the center of this ellipse be?

```
pygame.draw.ellipse(screen, BLACK, [1, 1, 3, 3], 1)
```

   a. (1, 1)

   b. (3, 3)

   c. (2, 2)

Short Answer Worksheet

1. Explain how the computer coordinate system differs from the standard Cartesian coordinate system. There are two main differences. List both.

2. Before a Python Pygame program can use any functions like `pygame.display.set_mode()`, what two lines of code must occur first?

3. Explain how `WHITE = (255, 255, 255)` represents a color.

4. When do we use variable names for colors in all uppercase, and when do we use variable names for colors in all lowercase? (This applies to all variables, not just colors.)

5. What does the `pygame.display.set_mode()` function do?

6. What does this `for event in pygame.event.get()` loop do?

7. What is `pygame.time.Clock` used for?

8. For this line of code:

   `pygame.draw.line(screen, GREEN, [0, 0], [100, 100], 5)`

   • What does `screen` do?

   • What does `[0, 0]` do?

   • What does `[100, 100]` do?

   • What does 5 do?

9. What is the best way to repeat something over and over in a drawing?

10. When drawing a rectangle, what happens if the specified line width is zero?

11. Describe the ellipse drawn in the code below.

    • What is the x, y of the origin coordinate?

    • What does the origin coordinate specify? The center of the circle?

    • What are the length and the width of the ellipse?

      `pygame.draw.ellipse(screen, BLACK, [20, 20, 250, 100], 2)`

12. When drawing an arc, what additional information is needed over drawing an ellipse?

13. Describe, in general, what are the three steps needed when printing text to the screen using graphics?

14. When drawing text, the first line of the three lines needed to draw text should actually be outside the main program loop. It should only run once at the start of the program. Why is this? You may need to ask.

15. What are the coordinates of the polygon that the code below draws?

    `pygame.draw.polygon(screen, BLACK, [[50,100],[0,200],[200,200],[100,50]], 5)`

16. What does `pygame.display.flip()` do?

17. What does `pygame.quit()` do?

18. Look up online how the `pygame.draw.circle` works. Get it working and paste a working sample here. I only need the one line of code that draws the circle, but make sure it is working by trying it out in a full working program.

Exercise

Check the appendix for the exercise "Create a Picture" that goes along with this chapter.

■ ■ ■

## CHAPTER 7

Back to Looping

Games involve a lot of complex loops. This is a challenge chapter to learn how to be an expert with loops. If you can understand the problems in this chapter, by the end of it you can certify yourself as a loop expert.

If becoming a loop expert isn't your goal, at least make sure you can write out the answers for the first eight problems. That will give you enough knowledge to continue this book. (Besides, being a loop expert never got anyone a date. Except for that guy in the *Groundhog Day* movie.)

There are video explanations for the answers online, and the answer code animates. Just hit the step button to see how the code operates.

Print Statement End Characters

By default, the print statement puts a *carriage return* at the end of what is printed out. As we explained back in the first chapter, the carriage return is a character that moves the next line of output to be printed to the next line. Most of the time this is what we want. Sometimes it isn't. If we want to continue printing on the same line, we can change the default character printed at the end. This is an example before we change the ending character:

```
print("Pink")
print("Octopus")
```

...which will print out:

```
Pink
Octopus
```

But if we wanted the code output to print on the same line, it can be done by using a new option to set the end character. For example:

```
print("Pink", end="")
print("Octopus")
```

This will print:

```
PinkOctopus
```

We can also use a space instead of setting it to an empty string:

```
print("Pink", end=" ")
print("Octopus")
```

This will print:

```
Pink Octopus
```

Here's another example, using a variable:

```
i = 0
print(i, end=" ")
i = 1
print(i, end=" ")
```

This will print:

```
0 1
```

Advanced Looping Problems

1. Write code that will print 10 asterisks (*) like the following:

    ```
    * * * * * * * * * *
    ```

    Have this code print using a for loop, and print each asterisk individually, rather than just printing 10 asterisks with 1 print statement. This can be done in 2 lines of code: a for loop and a print statement.

    When you have figured it out, or given up, here is the answer:
    ProgramArcadeGames.com/chapters/06_back_to_looping/problem_1.php

2. Write code that will print the following:

    ```
    * * * * * * * * * *
    * * * * *
    * * * * * * * * * * * * * * * * * * * *
    ```

    This is just like the prior problem but also printing 5 and 20 stars. Copy and paste from the prior problem, adjusting the for loop as needed.

    When you have figured it out, or given up, here is the answer:
    ProgramArcadeGames.com/chapters/06_back_to_looping/problem_2.php

3. Use two for loops, one of them nested inside the other, to print the following 10x10 rectangle:

```
* * * * * * * * * *
* * * * * * * * * *
* * * * * * * * * *
* * * * * * * * * *
* * * * * * * * * *
* * * * * * * * * *
* * * * * * * * * *
* * * * * * * * * *
```

To start, take a look at Problem 1. The code in Problem 1 generates 1 line of asterisks. It needs to be repeated 10 times. Work on this problem for at least 10 minutes before looking at the answer.

When you have figured it out, or given up, here it is: ProgramArcadeGames.com/chapters/06_back_to_looping/10x10box.php

4. Use two for loops, one of them nested, to print the following 5x10 rectangle:

```
* * * * *
* * * * *
* * * * *
* * * * *
* * * * *
* * * * *
* * * * *
* * * * *
* * * * *
* * * * *
```

This is a lot like the prior problem. Experiment with the ranges on the loops to find exactly what the numbers passed to the range function control.

When you have figured it out, or given up, here is the answer:
ProgramArcadeGames.com/chapters/06_back_to_looping/problem_4.php

5. Use two for loops, one of them nested, to print the following 20x5 rectangle:

```
* * * * * * * * * * * * * * * * * * * *
* * * * * * * * * * * * * * * * * * * *
* * * * * * * * * * * * * * * * * * * *
* * * * * * * * * * * * * * * * * * * *
* * * * * * * * * * * * * * * * * * * *
```

Again, like Problem 3 and Problem 4, but with different range values.

When you have figured it out, or given up, here is the answer:
ProgramArcadeGames.com/chapters/06_back_to_looping/problem_5.php

6. Write code that will print the following:

```
0 1 2 3 4 5 6 7 8 9
0 1 2 3 4 5 6 7 8 9
0 1 2 3 4 5 6 7 8 9
0 1 2 3 4 5 6 7 8 9
0 1 2 3 4 5 6 7 8 9
0 1 2 3 4 5 6 7 8 9
0 1 2 3 4 5 6 7 8 9
0 1 2 3 4 5 6 7 8 9
0 1 2 3 4 5 6 7 8 9
0 1 2 3 4 5 6 7 8 9
```

Use two nested loops. Print the first line with a loop, and not with:

```
print("0 1 2 3 4 5 6 7 8 9")
```

Tip: First, create a loop that prints the first line. Then enclose it in another loop that repeats the line 10 times. Use either i or j variables for what the program prints. This example and the next one help reinforce what those index variables are doing.

Work on this problem for at least 10 minutes before looking at the answer. The process of spending 10 minutes working on the answer is far more important than the answer itself. ProgramArcadeGames.com/chapters/06_back_to_looping/number_square_answer.php

7. Adjust the prior program to print:

```
0 0 0 0 0 0 0 0 0 0
1 1 1 1 1 1 1 1 1 1
2 2 2 2 2 2 2 2 2 2
3 3 3 3 3 3 3 3 3 3
4 4 4 4 4 4 4 4 4 4
5 5 5 5 5 5 5 5 5 5
6 6 6 6 6 6 6 6 6 6
7 7 7 7 7 7 7 7 7 7
8 8 8 8 8 8 8 8 8 8
9 9 9 9 9 9 9 9 9 9
```

Answer:
ProgramArcadeGames.com/chapters/06_back_to_looping/problem_7.php

8. Write code that will print the following:

```
0
0 1
0 1 2
0 1 2 3
0 1 2 3 4
0 1 2 3 4 5
0 1 2 3 4 5 6
0 1 2 3 4 5 6 7
0 1 2 3 4 5 6 7 8
0 1 2 3 4 5 6 7 8 9
```

Tip: This is just Problem 6, but the inside loop no longer loops a fixed number of times. Don't use `range(10)`, but adjust that range amount.

After working at least 10 minutes on the problem, here is the answer: ProgramArcadeGames.com/chapters/06_back_to_looping/top_right_triangle.php

Make sure you can write out the code for this and the prior problems. Yes, this practice is work, but it will pay off later and you'll save time in the long run.

9. Write code that will print the following:

```
0 1 2 3 4 5 6 7 8 9
  0 1 2 3 4 5 6 7 8
    0 1 2 3 4 5 6 7
      0 1 2 3 4 5 6
        0 1 2 3 4 5
          0 1 2 3 4
            0 1 2 3
              0 1 2
                0 1
                  0
```

This one is difficult. Tip: Two loops are needed inside the outer loop that controls each row. First, a loop prints spaces, then a loop prints the numbers. Loop both these for each row. To start with, try writing just one inside loop that prints:

```
0 1 2 3 4 5 6 7 8 9
0 1 2 3 4 5 6 7 8
0 1 2 3 4 5 6 7
0 1 2 3 4 5 6
0 1 2 3 4 5
0 1 2 3 4
0 1 2 3
0 1 2
0 1
0
```

Then once that is working, add a loop after the outside loop starts and before the already existing inside loop. Use this new loop to print enough spaces to right justify the other loops.

After working at least 10 minutes on the problem, here is the answer: ProgramArcadeGames.com/chapters/06_back_to_looping/bottom_left_ triangle.php

10. Write code that will print the following (Getting the alignment is hard, at least get the numbers):

```
1   2   3   4   5   6   7   8   9
2   4   6   8  10  12  14  16  18
3   6   9  12  15  18  21  24  27
4   8  12  16  20  24  28  32  36
5  10  15  20  25  30  35  40  45
6  12  18  24  30  36  42  48  54
7  14  21  28  35  42  49  56  63
8  16  24  32  40  48  56  64  72
9  18  27  36  45  54  63  72  81
```

Tip: Start by adjusting the code in Problem 1 to print:

```
0  0  0  0  0  0  0  0  0  0
0  1  2  3  4  5  6  7  8  9
0  2  4  6  8  10  12  14  16  18
0  3  6  9  12  15  18  21  24  27
0  4  8  12  16  20  24  28  32  36
0  5  10  15  20  25  30  35  40  45
0  6  12  18  24  30  36  42  48  54
0  7  14  21  28  35  42  49  56  63
0  8  16  24  32  40  48  56  64  72
0  9  18  27  36  45  54  63  72  81
```

Then adjust the code to print:

```
1  2  3  4  5  6  7  8  9
2  4  6  8  10  12  14  16  18
3  6  9  12  15  18  21  24  27
4  8  12  16  20  24  28  32  36
5  10  15  20  25  30  35  40  45
6  12  18  24  30  36  42  48  54
7  14  21  28  35  42  49  56  63
8  16  24  32  40  48  56  64  72
9  18  27  36  45  54  63  72  81
```

Finally, use an `if` to print spaces if the number being printed is less than 10.

After working at least 10 minutes on the problem, here is the answer: ProgramArcadeGames.com/chapters/06_back_to_looping/multiplication_ table.php

11. Write code that will print the following:

```
                    1
                  1 2 1
                1 2 3 2 1
              1 2 3 4 3 2 1
            1 2 3 4 5 4 3 2 1
          1 2 3 4 5 6 5 4 3 2 1
        1 2 3 4 5 6 7 6 5 4 3 2 1
      1 2 3 4 5 6 7 8 7 6 5 4 3 2 1
    1 2 3 4 5 6 7 8 9 8 7 6 5 4 3 2 1
```

Tip: first write code to print:

```
1
1 2
1 2 3
1 2 3 4
1 2 3 4 5
1 2 3 4 5 6
1 2 3 4 5 6 7
1 2 3 4 5 6 7 8
1 2 3 4 5 6 7 8 9
```

Then write code to print:

```
1
1 2 1
1 2 3 2 1
1 2 3 4 3 2 1
1 2 3 4 5 4 3 2 1
1 2 3 4 5 6 5 4 3 2 1
1 2 3 4 5 6 7 6 5 4 3 2 1
1 2 3 4 5 6 7 8 7 6 5 4 3 2 1
1 2 3 4 5 6 7 8 9 8 7 6 5 4 3 2 1
```

Then finish by adding spaces to print the final answer.

After working at least 10 minutes on the problem, here is the answer:
ProgramArcadeGames.com/chapters/06_back_to_looping/top_triangle.php

12.   Write code that will print the following:

```
                1
              1 2 1
            1 2 3 2 1
          1 2 3 4 3 2 1
        1 2 3 4 5 4 3 2 1
      1 2 3 4 5 6 5 4 3 2 1
    1 2 3 4 5 6 7 6 5 4 3 2 1
  1 2 3 4 5 6 7 8 7 6 5 4 3 2 1
1 2 3 4 5 6 7 8 9 8 7 6 5 4 3 2 1
  1 2 3 4 5 6 7 8
    1 2 3 4 5 6 7
      1 2 3 4 5 6
        1 2 3 4 5
          1 2 3 4
            1 2 3
              1 2
                1
```

This can be done by combining Problems 11 and 9.

After working at least 10 minutes on the problem, here is the answer:
ProgramArcadeGames.com/chapters/06_back_to_looping/three_quarters.php

13.   Write code that will print the following:

```
                1
              1 2 1
            1 2 3 2 1
          1 2 3 4 3 2 1
        1 2 3 4 5 4 3 2 1
      1 2 3 4 5 6 5 4 3 2 1
    1 2 3 4 5 6 7 6 5 4 3 2 1
  1 2 3 4 5 6 7 8 7 6 5 4 3 2 1
1 2 3 4 5 6 7 8 9 8 7 6 5 4 3 2 1
  1 2 3 4 5 6 7 8 7 6 5 4 3 2 1
    1 2 3 4 5 6 7 6 5 4 3 2 1
      1 2 3 4 5 6 5 4 3 2 1
        1 2 3 4 5 4 3 2 1
          1 2 3 4 3 2 1
            1 2 3 2 1
              1 2 1
                1
```

After working at least 10 minutes on the problem, here is the answer:
ProgramArcadeGames.com/chapters/06_back_to_looping/full_diamond.php

Review

Multiple Choice Quiz

1. What does this code display?

```
for i in range(3):
        print("*")
```

a. *
   *
   *

b. ***

c. 0
   1
   2

d. 012

2. What does this code display?

```
for i in range(3):
        print(i, end="")
```

a. *
   *
   *

b. ***

c. 0
   1
   2

d. 012

3. What does this code display?

```
for i in range(3):
        print("*", end="")
for j in range(3):
        print("*", end="")
```

a. ***
   ***

b. ***
   ***
   ***

c. ****** (6 asterisks)

d. ********* (9 asterisks)

012012

4. What does this code display?

```
for i in range(3):
        for j in range(3):
                print("*", end="")
```

a.   ***
     ***

b.   ***
     ***
     ***

c.   ****** (6 asterisks)

d.   ********* (9 asterisks)

     012012

5. What does this code display?

```
for i in range(3):
        for j in range(3):
                print("*", end="")
                print()
```

a.   (9 asterisks in a vertical line.)

b.   ***
     ***
     ***

c.   ********* (9 asterisks)

6. What does this code display?

```
for i in range(3):
        for j in range(3):
                print("*", end="")
        print()
```

a.   (9 asterisks in a vertical line.)

b.   ***

     ***

     ***

c.   ********* (9 asterisks)

116

7. What does this code display?

```
for i in range(3):
        for j in range(3):
                print("*", end="")
print()
```

   a.   (9 asterisks in a vertical line.)

   b.   ***
         ***
         ***

   c.   ********* (9 asterisks)

8. What does this code display?

```
for i in range(3):
    for j in range(3):
        print(i, end="")
    print()
```

   a.   000
         111
         222

   b.   012
         012
         012

   c.   012
         345
         678

Short Answer Worksheet

For each of the first two questions, write out your best guess as to what the code will print. Clearly label this as your guess. Then run the code and look at the output. Write if your guess was correct. If it was not, briefly describe what was different and why.

   Predicting what the code will do is important in writing programs and figuring out why programs don't run the way expected.

1. What does this program print out? (Remember: TWO answers. Your guess and the actual result.)

```
x = 0
while x < 10:
    print(x)
    x = x + 2
```

2. What does this program print out?

```
x = 1
while x < 64:
    print(x)
    x = x * 2
```

3. Why is the and x >= 0 not needed?

```
x = 0
while x < 10 and x >= 0:
    print(x)
    x = x + 2
```

4. What does this program print out? (0 pts) Explain.

```
x = 5
while x >= 0:
    print(x)
    if x == "1":
        print("Blast off!")
    x = x - 1
```

5. Fix the following code so it doesn't repeat forever, and keeps asking the user until he or she enters a number greater than zero:

```
x = float(input("Enter a number greater than zero: "))

while x <= 0:
    print("Too small. Enter a number greater than zero: ")
```

6. Fix the following code:

```
x = 10

while x < 0:
    print(x)
    x - 1

print("Blast-off")
```

7. What is wrong with this code? It runs but it has unnecessary code. Find all the unneeded code. Also, answer why it is not needed.

```
i = 0
for i in range(10):
    print(i)
    i += 1
```

8. Explain why the values printed for x are so different.

```
# Sample 1
x = 0
for i in range(10):
    x += 1
for j in range(10):
    x += 1
print(x)
```

```
# Sample 2
x = 0
for i in range(10):
    x += 1
    for j in range(10):
        x += 1
print(x)
```

Exercise

Check the appendix for the exercise "Loopy Lab" that goes along with this chapter.

CHAPTER 8

■ ■ ■

Introduction to Lists

So far this book has shown four types of data:

- String (a string is short for "string of characters," which normal people think of as text.)

- Integer

- Floating point

- Boolean

Python can display what type of data a value is with the type function.

This type function isn't useful for other programming in this book, but it is good to demonstrate the types of data introduced so far. Type the following into the interactive shell. (Don't create a new window and type this in as a program; it won't work.)

```
type(3)
type(3.145)
type("Hi there")
type(True)

>>> type(3)
<class 'int'>

>>> type(3.145)
<class 'float'>

>>> type("Hi there")
<class 'str'>

>>> type(True)
<class 'bool'>
```

It is also possible to use the type function on a variable to see what kind of data is in it.

```
x = 3
type(x)
```

More than one coin to collect? Use a list!

The two new types of data introduced in this chapter are *Lists* and *Tuples*. Lists are similar to another data structure called an *array*. A list can be resized, but an array cannot. A course in *data structures* will teach you the details, but it that is beyond the scope of this book. Try running the following commands in the interactive Python shell and see what is displayed:

```
type( (2, 3, 4, 5) )
type( [2, 3, 4, 5] )
```

Working with Lists

You've created grocery lists, to-do lists, bucket lists, but how do you create a list on the computer?

Even computers use lists

Try these examples using IDLE's command line. To create a list and print it out, try the following:

```
>>> x = [1,2]
>>> print(x)
[1, 2]
```

To print an individual element in a list:

```
>>> print(x[0])
1
```

This number with the item's location is called the *index*. Note that list locations start at zero. So a list or array with 10 elements does not have an element in spot [10]. Just spots [0] through [9]. It can be very confusing to create a list of 10 items and then not have an item 10, but most computer languages start counting at 0 rather than 1.

122

Think of a list as an ice cube tray that holds numbers, as shown in the figure below. The values are stored inside each tray spot, and written on the side of the tray are numbers starting at zero that identify the location of each spot.

Don't mix the index and the value!

Remember, there are two sets of numbers to consider when working with a list of numbers: the position and the value. The position, also known as index, refers to *where* a value is. The value is the actual number stored at that location. When working with a list or array, make sure to think if you need the *location* or the *value*.

It is easy to get the value given the location, but it is harder to get the location given the value. Chapter 16 is dedicated to answering how to find the location of a particular value.

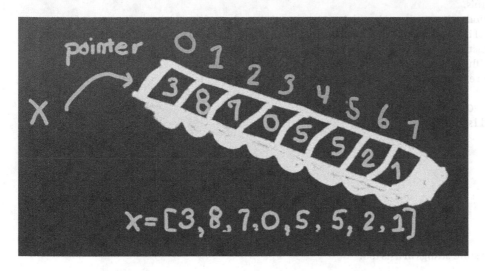

Lists are like ice cube trays

A program can assign new values to an individual element in a list. In the case below, the first spot at location zero (not one) is assigned the number 22.

```
>>> x[0] = 22
>>> print(x)
[22, 2]
```

Also, a program can create a tuple. This data type works just like a list but with two differences. First, it is created with parentheses rather than square brackets. Second, it is not possible to change the tuple once created. See below:

```
>>> x = (1, 2)
>>> print(x)
(1, 2)
>>> print(x[0])
1
>>> x[0] = 22
Traceback (most recent call last):
  File "<pyshell#18>", line 1, in <module>
    x[0] = 22
TypeError: 'tuple' object does not support item assignment
>>>
```

As can be seen from the output of the code above, we can't assign an item in the tuple a new value. Why would we want this limitation? First, the computer can run faster if it knows the value won't change. Second, some lists we don't want to change, such as a list of RGB colors for red. The color red doesn't change; therefore an immutable tuple is a better choice.

Iterating through a List

If a program needs to iterate through each item in a list, such as to print it out, there are two types of for loops that can do this.

The first method to iterate through each item in a loop is by using a for-each loop. This type of loop takes a collection of items and loops the code once per item. It will take a *copy* of the item and store it in a variable for processing.

The format of the command: for *item_variable* in *list_name*:

Here are some examples:

```
my_list = [101, 20, 10, 50, 60]
for item in my_list:
    print(item)
```

```
101
20
10
50
60
```

Programs can store strings in lists too:

```
my_list = ["Spoon", "Fork", "Knife"]
for item in my_list:
    print(item)
```

```
Spoon
Knife
Fork
```

Lists can even contain other lists. This iterates through each item in the main list but not in sublists.

```
my_list = [ [2,3], [4,3], [6,7] ]
for item in my_list:
    print(item)
```

```
[2,3]
[4,3]
[6,7]
```

The other way to iterate through a list is to use an *index variable* and directly access the list rather than through a copy of each item. To use an index variable, the program counts from 0 up to the length of the list. If there are 10 elements, the loop must go from 0 to 9 for a total of 10 elements.

The length of a list may be found by using the len function. Combining that with the range function allows the program to loop through the entire list.

```python
my_list = [101, 20, 10, 50, 60]
for i in range(len(my_list)):
    print(my_list[i])
```

```
101
20
10
50
60
```

This method is more complex, but is also more powerful. Because we are working directly with the list elements, rather than a copy, the list can be modified. The for-each loop does not allow modification of the original list.

Adding to a List

New items may be added to a list (but not a tuple) by using the append command. For example:

```python
my_list = [2, 4, 5, 6]
print(my_list)
my_list.append(9)
print(my_list)
```

```
[2, 4, 5, 6]
[2, 4, 5, 6, 9]
```

Side note: If performance while appending is a concern, it is very important to understand how a list is being implemented. For example, if a list is implemented as an *array data type*, then appending an item to the list is a lot like adding a new egg to a full egg carton. A new egg carton must be built with 13 spots. Then 12 eggs are moved over. Then the 13th egg is added. Finally the old egg carton is recycled. Because this can happen behind the scenes in a function, programmers may forget this and let the computer do all the work. It would be more efficient to simply tell the computer to make an egg carton with enough spots to begin with. Thankfully, Python does not implement a list as an array data type. But it is important to pay attention to your next semester data structures class and learn how all of this works.

To create a list from scratch, it is necessary to create a blank list and then use the append function. This example creates a list based upon user input:

```python
my_list = [] # Empty list
for i in range(5):
    userInput = input( "Enter an integer: " )
    userInput = int( userInput )
    my_list.append(userInput)
    print(my_list)
```

```
Enter an integer: 4
[4]
Enter an integer: 5
[4, 5]
```

```
Enter an integer: 3
[4, 5, 3]
Enter an integer: 1
[4, 5, 3, 1]
Enter an integer: 8
[4, 5, 3, 1, 8]
```

If a program needs to create an array of a specific length, all with the same value, a simple trick is to use the following code:

```
# Create an array with 100 zeros.
my_list = [0] * 100
```

Summing or Modifying a List

Creating a running total of an array is a common operation. Here's how it is done:

```
# Copy of the array to sum
my_list = [5,76,8,5,3,3,56,5,23]

# Initial sum should be zero
list_total = 0

# Loop from 0 up to the number of elements
# in the array:
for i in range(len(my_list)):
        # Add element 0, next 1, then 2, etc.
        list_total += my_list[i]

# Print the result
print(list_total)
```

The same thing can be done by using a for loop to iterate the array, rather than count through a range:

```
# Copy of the array to sum
my_list = [5, 76, 8, 5, 3, 3, 56, 5, 23]

# Initial sum should be zero
list_total = 0

# Loop through array, copying each item in the array into
# the variable named item.
for item in my_list:
        # Add each item
        list_total += item

# Print the result
print(list_total)
```

Numbers in an array can also be changed by using a for loop:

```
# Copy of the array to modify
my_list = [5, 76, 8, 5, 3, 3, 56, 5, 23]

# Loop from 0 up to the number of elements
# in the array:
for i in range(len(my_list)):
        # Modify the element by doubling it
        my_list[i] = my_list[i] * 2

# Print the result
print(my_list)
```

However version 2 *does not work* at doubling the values in an array. Why? Because an item is a *copy* of an element in the array. The code below doubles the copy, not the original array element.

```
# Copy of the array to modify
my_list = [5, 76, 8, 5, 3, 3, 56, 5, 23]

# Loop through each element in myArray
for item in my_list:
        # This doubles item, but does not change the array
        # because item is a copy of a single element.
        item = item * 2

# Print the result
print(my_list)
```

Slicing Strings

Strings are actually lists of characters. They can be treated like lists with each letter a separate item. Run the following code with both versions of x:

```
x = "This is a sample string"
#x = "0123456789"

print("x=", x)

# Accessing a single character
print("x[0]=", x[0])
print("x[1]=", x[1])

# Accessing from the right side
print("x[-1]=", x[-1])

# Access 0-5
print("x[:6]=", x[:6])
# Access 6
print("x[6:]=", x[6:])
# Access 6-8
print("x[6:9]=", x[6:9])
```

Strings in Python may be used with some of the mathematical operators. Try the following code and see what Python does:

```
a = "Hi"
b = "There"
c = "!"
print(a + b)
print(a + b + c)
print(3 * a)
print(a * 3)
print((a * 2) + (b * 2))
```

It is possible to get a length of a string. It is also possible to do this with any type of array.

```
a = "Hi There"
print(len(a))

b = [3, 4, 5, 6, 76, 4, 3, 3]
print(len(b))
```

Since a string is an array, a program can iterate through each character element just like an array:

```
for character in "This is a test.":
    print(character)
```

Exercise: Starting with the following code:

```
months = "JanFebMarAprMayJunJulAugSepOctNovDec"

n = int(input("Enter a month number: "))
```

Print the three-month abbreviation for the month number that the user enters. (Calculate the start position in the string, then use the info we just learned to print out the correct substring.)

Secret Codes

This code prints out every letter of a string individually:

```
plain_text = "This is a test. ABC abc"

for c in plain_text:
    print(c, end=" ")
```

Computers do not actually store letters of a string in memory; computers store a series of numbers. Each number represents a letter. The system that computers use to translate numbers to letters is called *Unicode*. The full name for the encoding is Universal Character Set Transformation Format 8-bit, usually abbreviated UTF-8.

The Unicode chart covers the Western alphabet using the numbers 0-127. Each Western letter is represented by one byte of memory. Other alphabets, like Cyrillic, can take multiple bytes to represent each letter. A partial copy of the Unicode chart is below:

Value	Character	Value	Character	Value	Character	Value	Character
40	(	61	=	82	R	103	g
41	)	62	>	83	S	104	h
42	*	63	?	84	T	105	i
43	+	64	@	85	U	106	j
44	,	65	A	86	V	107	k
45	-	66	B	87	W	108	l
46	.	67	C	88	X	109	m
47	/	68	D	89	Y	110	n
48	0	69	E	90	Z	111	o
49	1	70	F	91	[	112	p
50	2	71	G	92	\	113	q
51	3	72	H	93	]	114	r
52	4	73	I	94	^	115	s
53	5	74	J	95	_	116	t
54	6	75	K	96	`	117	u
55	7	76	L	97	a	118	v
56	8	77	M	98	b	119	w
57	9	78	N	99	c	120	x
58	:	79	O	100	d	121	y
59	;	80	P	101	e	122	z
60	<	81	Q	102	f		

For more information about ASCII (which has the same values as Unicode for the Western alphabet) see: http://en.wikipedia.org/wiki/ASCII

For a video that explains the beauty of Unicode, see here: http://hackaday.com/2013/09/27/utf-8-the-most-elegant-hack

This next set of code converts each of the letters in the prior example to its ordinal value using UTF-8:

```
plain_text = "This is a test. ABC abc"

for c in plain_text:
    print(ord(c), end=" ")
```

This next program takes each UTF-8 value and adds one to it. Then it prints the new UTF-8 value, then converts the value back to a letter.

```
plain_text = "This is a test. ABC abc"

for c in plain_text:
    x = ord(c)
    x = x + 1
    c2 = chr(x)
    print(c2, end="")
```

The next code listing takes each UTF-8 value and adds one to it, then converts the value back to a letter.

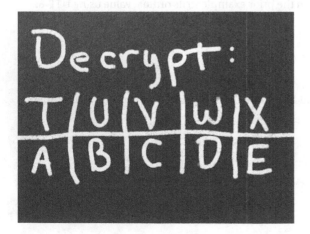

```
# Sample Python/Pygame Programs
# http://programarcadegames.com/

# Explanation video: http://youtu.be/sxFIxD8Gd3A

plain_text = "This is a test. ABC abc"

encrypted_text = ""
for c in plain_text:
    x = ord(c)
    x = x + 1
    c2 = chr(x)
    encrypted_text = encrypted_text + c2
print(encrypted_text)
```

Finally, the last code takes each UTF-8 value and subtracts one from it, then converts the value back to a letter. By feeding this program the output of the previous program, it serves as a decoder for text encoded by the prior example.

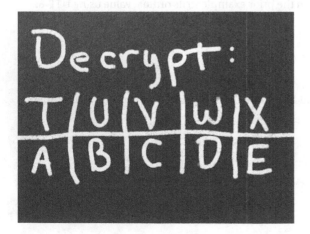

```
# Sample Python/Pygame Programs
# http://programarcadegames.com/

# Explanation video: http://youtu.be/sxFIxD8Gd3A

encrypted_text = "Uijt!jt!b!uftu/!BCD!bcd"

plain_text = ""
for c in encrypted_text:
    x = ord(c)
    x = x - 1
    c2 = chr(x)
    plain_text = plain_text + c2
print(plain_text)
```

Associative Arrays

Python is not limited to using numbers as an array index. It is also possible to use an *associative array*. An associative array works like this:

```
# Create an empty associative array
# (Note the curly braces.)
x = {}

# Add some stuff to it
x["fred"] = 2
x["scooby"] = 8
x["wilma"] = 1

# Fetch and print an item
print(x["fred"])
```

You won't really need associative arrays for this book, but I think it is important to point out that it is possible.

Review

Multiple Choice Quiz

1. What code will print out the first element?

   ```
   x = [1, 2, 3, 4, 5]
   ```

   a. `print(x[0])`

   b. `print(x[1])`

   c. `print(x(0))`

   d. `print(x(1))`

   e. `print(x)`

   f. `print([1])`

2. What code will change the first element?

   ```
   x = [1, 2, 3, 4, 5]
   ```

   a. `x[0] = 100`

   b. `x = 100`

   c. `x[1] = 100`

   d. `[1] = 100`

   e. `x(1) = 100`

3. What code will print each element of `my_list`?

   ```
   my_list = [101, 20, 10, 50, 60]
   ```

   a. ```
      for item in my_list:
          print(item)
      ```

   b. ```
      for item in my_list:
          print(my_list)
      ```

   c. ```
      for item in range(my_list):
          print(item)
      ```

   d. ```
      for my_list in item:
          print(item)
      ```

4. What code will add a new element to this list?

   ```
   my_list = [5, 6, 7]
   ```

   a. `my_list[8]`

   b. `my_list(8)`

   c. `my_list.add(8)`

   d. `my_list.append(8)`

   e. `my_list.add[8]`

5. What code will sum all the elements in this list?

```
my_array = [5, 76, 8, 5, 3, 3, 56, 5, 23]
```

a.
```
array_total = 0
for i in range(len(my_array)):
    array_total += my_array[i]
```

b.
```
array_total = 0
for i in range(my_array):
    array_total += my_array[i]
```

c.
```
array_total = 0
for i in range(len(my_array)):
    array_total += i
```

d.
```
i = 0
for i in range(len(my_array)):
    array_total += my_array
```

e.
```
i = 0
for i in my_array:
    array_total += my_array(i)
```

6. What does this code print?

```
my_array = [2, 4, 6]
for i in range(3):
    print(my_array)
```

a.
```
0
1
2
```

b.
```
1
2
3
```

c.
```
[2, 4, 6]
[2, 4, 6]
[2, 4, 6]
```

d. 246

e. [2, 4, 6]

f.
```
2
4
6
```

7. What does this code print?

```
my_array = [2, 4, 6]
for i in range(3):
        print(my_array[0])
```

```
0
1
2
```

```
2
2
2
```

```
[2, 4, 6]
[2, 4, 6]
[2, 4, 6]
```

```
246
```

```
[2, 4, 6]
```

```
2
4
6
```

8. What does this code print?

```
my_array = [2, 4, 6]
for i in range(3):
    print(i)
```

```
0
1
2
```

```
2
2
2
```

```
[2, 4, 6]
[2, 4, 6]
[2, 4, 6]
```

```
246
```

```
[2, 4, 6]
```

```
2
4
6
```

Short Answer Worksheet

In the following problems, if an error prevents an example from running, make certain to mention that as part of the results. Also, be precise. If program prints [1], doesn't say it prints 1.

1. List the four types of data we've covered, and give an example of each:

2. What does this code print out? For this and the following problems, make sure you understand WHY it prints what it does. You don't have to explain it, but if you don't understand why, make sure to ask. Otherwise you are wasting your time doing these.

    ```
    my_list = [5, 2, 6, 8, 101]
    print(my_list[1])
    print(my_list[4])
    print(my_list[5])
    ```

3. What does this code print out?

    ```
    my_list=[5, 2, 6, 8, 101]
    for my_item in my_list:
        print(my_item)
    ```

4. What does this code print out?

    ```
    my_list1 = [5, 2, 6, 8, 101]
    my_list2 = (5, 2, 6, 8, 101)
    my_list1[3] = 10
    print(my_list1)
    my_list2[2] = 10
    print(my_list2)
    ```

5. What does this code print out?

    ```
    my_list = [3 * 5]
    print(my_list)
    my_list = [3] * 5
    print(my_list)
    ```

6. What does this code print out?

    ```
    my_list = [5]
    for i in range(5):
            my_list.append(i)
    print(my_list)
    ```

7. What does this code print out?

    ```
    print(len("Hi"))
    print(len("Hi there."))
    print(len("Hi") + len("there."))
    print(len("2"))
    print(len(2))
    ```

8. What does this code print out?

```
print("Simpson" + "College")
print("Simpson" + "College"[1])
print( ("Simpson" + "College")[1] )
```

9. What does this code print out?

```
word = "Simpson"
for letter in word:
    print(letter)
```

10. What does this code print out?

```
word = "Simpson"
for i in range(3):
    word += "College"
print(word)
```

11. What does this code print out?

```
word = "Hi" * 3
print(word)
```

12. What does this code print out?

```
my_text = "The quick brown fox jumped over the lazy dogs."
print("The 3rd spot is: " + my_text[3])
print("The -1 spot is: " + my_text[-1])
```

13. What does this code print out?

```
s = "0123456789"
print(s[1])
print(s[:3])
print(s[3:])
```

14. Write a loop that will take in a list of five numbers from the user, adding each to an array. Then print the array. Try doing this without looking at the book.

15. Write a program that take an array like the following, and print the average. Use the len function, don't just use 15, because that won't work if the list size changes. (There is a sum function I haven't told you about. Don't use that. Sum the numbers individually as shown in the chapter.)

```
my_list = [3,12,3,5,3,4,6,8,5,3,5,6,3,2,4]
```

Exercise

Check the appendix for the exercise "Adventure" that goes along with this chapter.

■ ■ ■

## CHAPTER 9

Introduction to Animation

To begin our first animation, let's start with the base pygame program from Chapter 6 that opens up a blank screen. Source for pygame_base_template.py can be found here: ProgramArcadeGames.com/python_examples/f.php?file=pygame_base_template.py

We will put together a program to bounce a white rectangle around a screen with a black background. Feel free to pick your own colors; just make sure the background color is different than the rectangle color!

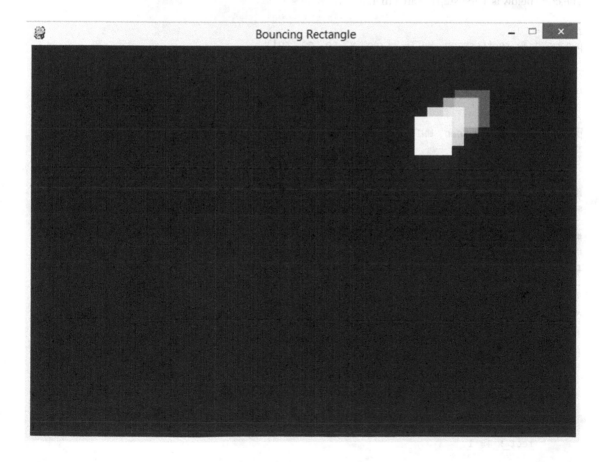

First step: start with the base template and flip the background color from white to black. This code should be around line 46.

```
screen.fill(BLACK)
```

Next up, draw the rectangle we plan to animate. A simple rectangle will suffice. This code should be placed after clearing the screen, and before flipping it.

```
pygame.draw.rect(screen, WHITE, [50, 50, 50, 50])
```

Each time through the loop the rectangle will be drawn at an (x,y) location of exactly (50,50). This is controlled by the first two 50s in the list. Until those numbers change, the square will not move.

The rectangle will be 50 pixels wide and 50 pixels tall. The dimensions are controlled by the last two numbers in the list. We could also call this rectangle a square, since it has the same width and height. I'll stick with calling it a rectangle because all squares are also rectangles, and depending on the monitor and resolution used, pixels aren't always square. Look up *Pixel Aspect Ratio* if you are really interested in this subject.

How do we keep changing the location rather than have it stuck at (50, 50)? Use a variable, of course! The code below is a first step towards that:

```
rect_x = 50
pygame.draw.rect(screen, WHITE, [rect_x, 50, 50, 50])
```

To move the rectangle to the right, x can be increased by one each frame. This code is close, but it does not quite do it:

```
rect_x = 50
pygame.draw.rect(screen, WHITE, [rect_x, 50, 50, 50])
rect_x += 1
```

The problem with the above code is that `rect_x` is reset back to 50 each time through the loop. To fix this problem, move the initialization of `rect_x` up outside of the loop. This next section of code will successfully slide the rectangle to the right.

```
# Starting x position of the rectangle
# Note how this is outside the main while loop.
rect_x = 50

# -------- Main Program Loop -----------
while not done:
        for event in pygame.event.get(): # User did something
                if event.type == pygame.QUIT: # If user clicked close
                        done = True # Flag that we are done so we exit this loop

        # Set the screen background
        screen.fill(BLACK)

        pygame.draw.rect(screen, WHITE, [rect_x, 50, 50, 50])
        rect_x += 1
```

To move the box faster, rather than increasing rect_x by 1, increase it by 5:

```
rect_x += 5
```

We can expand this code and increase both x and y, causing the square to move both down and right:

```
# Starting position of the rectangle
rect_x = 50
rect_y = 50

# -------- Main Program Loop -----------
while not done:
        for event in pygame.event.get():
                if event.type == pygame.QUIT:
                        done = True

        # Set the screen background
        screen.fill(BLACK)

        # Draw the rectangle
        pygame.draw.rect(screen, WHITE, [rect_x, rect_y, 50, 50])

        # Move the rectangle starting point
        rect_x += 5
        rect_y += 5
```

The direction and speed of the box's movement can be stored in a vector. This makes it easy for the direction and speed of a moving object to be changed. The next bit of code shows using variables to store the x and y change of (5, 5).

```
# Starting position of the rectangle
rect_x = 50
rect_y = 50

# Speed and direction of rectangle
rect_change_x = 5
rect_change_y = 5

# -------- Main Program Loop -----------
while done == False:
        for event in pygame.event.get(): # User did something
                if event.type == pygame.QUIT: # If user clicked close
                        done = True # Flag that we are done so we exit this loop

        # Set the screen background
        screen.fill(BLACK)

        # Draw the rectangle
        pygame.draw.rect(screen, WHITE, [rect_x, rect_y, 50, 50])

        # Move the rectangle starting point
        rect_x += rect_change_x
        rect_y += rect_change_y
```

Once the box hits the edge of the screen it will keep going. Nothing makes the rectangle bounce off the edge of the screen. To reverse the direction so the rectangle travels towards the right, rect_change_y needs to change from 5 to -5 once the rectangle gets to the bottom side of the screen. The rectangle is at the bottom when rect_y is greater than the height of the screen. The code below can do the check and reverse the direction:

```
# Bounce the rectangle if needed
if rect_y > 450:
        rect_change_y = rect_change_y * -1
```

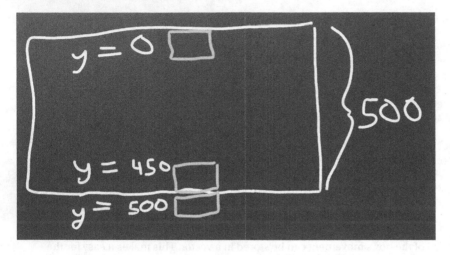

Rectangle location based on y coordinate

Why check rect_y against 450? If the screen is 500 pixels high, then checking against 500 would be a logical first guess. But remember the rectangle is drawn starting from the *top left* corner of the rectangle. If the rectangle was drawn starting at 500, it would draw from 500 to 550, totally off screen before it bounced.

Taking into account that the rectangle is 50 pixels high the correct bounce location is: $500-50=450$.

The code below will bounce the rectangle off all four sides of a 700x400 window:

```
# Bounce the rectangle if needed
if rect_y > 450 or rect_y < 0:
        rect_change_y = rect_change_y * -1
if rect_x > 650 or rect_x < 0:
        rect_change_x = rect_change_x * -1
```

Interested in a more complex shape than a rectangle? Several drawing commands can be used based off the rect_x and rect_y. The code below draws a red rectangle inside the white rectangle. The red rectangle is offset 10 pixels in the x,y directions from the upper left corner of the white rectangle. It also is 20 pixels smaller in both dimensions, resulting in 10 pixels of white surrounding the red rectangle. See the figure above.

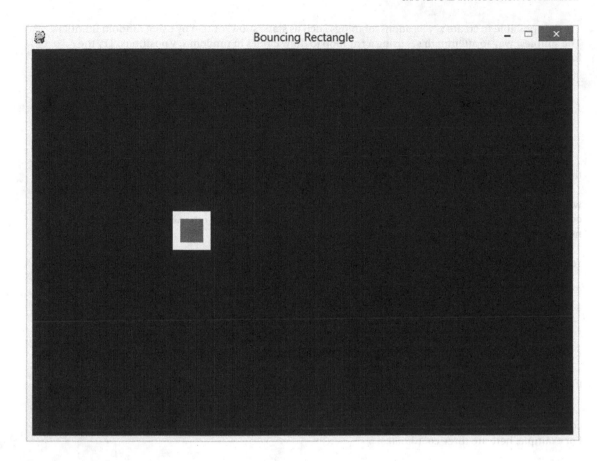

White rectangle with a red square in the middle

```
# Draw a red rectangle inside the white one
pygame.draw.rect(screen, WHITE, [rect_x, rect_y, 50, 50])
pygame.draw.rect(screen, RED, [rect_x + 10, rect_y + 10 ,30, 30])
```

Animating Snow

Animating only one item isn't enough? Need to animate more? How about being able to animate hundreds of objects at once? Let's expand on the code above and learn how to animate many objects.

Code Explanation

To start this program, begin with the base pygame template that opens up a blank screen. Again, source for pygame_base_template.py can be found here:

ProgramArcadeGames.com/python_examples/f.php?file=pygame_base_template.py

It is possible to create x, y locations for things such as stars, snow, or rain by using random numbers. The simplest way to attempt this is using a for loop to draw circles in random x, y positions. Try the following code inside of the main while loop.

```
for i in range(50):
    x = random.randrange(0, 400)
    y = random.randrange(0, 400)
        pygame.draw.circle(screen, WHITE, [x, y], 2)
```

Try it; this program has an odd problem! Twenty times per second, each time through the loop, it draws the snow in new random locations. Try adjusting the snowflake count and see how it changes the image.

Obviously, we need to randomly position the snowflakes and keep them in the same spot. We don't want to generate new positions 20 times per second. We need to keep a *list* of where they are. The program can use a python list to do this. This should be done *before* the main loop, otherwise the program will add 50 new snowflakes to the list every 1/20th of a second.

```
for i in range(50):
    x = random.randrange(0, 400)
    y = random.randrange(0, 400)
    snow_list.append([x, y])
```

Once the snowflake locations have been added, they can be accessed like a normal list. The following code would print both the x and y coordinates of the first location, stored in position zero:

```
print(snow_list[0])
```

What if we wanted just the x or y coordinate? We have lists inside lists. The main list has all the coordinates. Inside of that list, each coordinate is a list of an x (position 0), and a y coordinate (position 1). For example, here are three coordinates:

```
[[34, 10],
 [10, 50],
 [20, 18]]
```

To print the y coordinate at position 0, first select coordinate 0, and then the y value at position 1. The code will look like:

```
print(snow_list[0][1])
```

To print the x value of the 21st coordinate (position 20), first select coordinate 20, and then the x value at position 0:

```
print(snow_list[20][0])
```

Inside of the main while loop, a program may use a for loop to draw each of the items in the snow list. Remember, len(snow_list) will return the number of elements in the snowflake list.

```
# Process each snow flake in the list
for i in range(len(snow_list)):
        # Draw the snow flake
        pygame.draw.circle(screen, WHITE, snow_list[i], 2)
```

Remember, there are two types of for loops. The other type of loop can be used, and it would look like:

```
# Process A COPY of each snow flake's location in the list
for xy_coord in snow_list:
        # Draw the snow flake
        pygame.draw.circle(screen, WHITE, xy_coord, 2)
```

However, because we plan on modifying the snowflake's location we can't use this type of for loop because we'd be modifying the location of a copy of the snowflake's location rather than the actual snowflake's location.

If the program is to have all the objects in the array move down, like snow, then expanding the for loop created above will cause the y coordinate to increase:

```
# Process each snow flake in the list
for i in range(len(snow_list)):

        # Draw the snow flake
        pygame.draw.circle(screen, WHITE, snow_list[i], 2)

        # Move the snow flake down one pixel
        snow_list[i][1] += 1
```

This moves the snow downwards, but once off the screen nothing new appears. By adding the code below, the snow will reset to the top of the screen in a random location:

```
        # If the snow flake has moved off the bottom of the screen
        if snow_list[i][1] > 400:
                # Reset it just above the top
                y = random.randrange(-50, -10)
                snow_list[i][1] = y
                # Give it a new x position
                x = random.randrange(0, 400)
                snow_list[i][0] = x
```

It is also possible to add things to the list and have different sizes, shapes, colors, speeds, and directions for each item on the screen. This gets complex however because of the multiple types of data that need to be kept in the list. We will keep it simple for now, but once we learn about "classes" in Chapter 12, it will be easy to manage many different attributes for multiple objects.

Full Program Listing

```
"""

 Animating multiple objects using a list.
 Sample Python/Pygame Programs
 http://programarcadegames.com/

 Explanation video: http://youtu.be/Gkhz3FuhGoI
"""
```

```python
# Import a library of functions called 'pygame'
import pygame
import random

# Initialize the game engine
pygame.init()

BLACK = [0, 0, 0]
WHITE = [255, 255, 255]

# Set the height and width of the screen
SIZE = [400, 400]

screen = pygame.display.set_mode(SIZE)
pygame.display.set_caption("Snow Animation")

# Create an empty array
snow_list = []

# Loop 50 times and add a snow flake in a random x,y position
for i in range(50):
    x = random.randrange(0, 400)
    y = random.randrange(0, 400)
    snow_list.append([x, y])

clock = pygame.time.Clock()

# Loop until the user clicks the close button.
done = False
while not done:

    for event in pygame.event.get():    # User did something
        if event.type == pygame.QUIT:   # If user clicked close
            done = True    # Flag that we are done so we exit this loop

    # Set the screen background
    screen.fill(BLACK)

    # Process each snow flake in the list
    for i in range(len(snow_list)):

        # Draw the snow flake
        pygame.draw.circle(screen, WHITE, snow_list[i], 2)

        # Move the snow flake down one pixel
        snow_list[i][1] += 1
```

```
    # If the snow flake has moved off the bottom of the screen
    if snow_list[i][1] > 400:
        # Reset it just above the top
        y = random.randrange(-50, -10)
        snow_list[i][1] = y
        # Give it a new x position
        x = random.randrange(0, 400)
        snow_list[i][0] = x

# Go ahead and update the screen with what we've drawn.
pygame.display.flip()
clock.tick(20)

pygame.quit()
```

This example shows each snowflake moving the same direction. What if each item needs to be animated separately, with its own direction? If you need this for your game, see Chapter 13 on how to use classes. The "Classes and Graphics" Exercise in the appendix steps you through how to have hundreds of different items animated, each with their own direction.

3D Animation

Extending from a 2D environment into a 3D environment complete with game physics isn't as hard as it would seem. While it is beyond the scope of this book, it is worthwhile to see how it is done.

There is a freely available 3D program called *Blender* that has a "game engine" that allows programmers to create 3D games. The 3D objects in the game can have Python code attached to them that controls their actions in the game.

Blender-based Game

Look at the figure above. This shows a green tray with several objects in it. The blue object is controlled by a Python script that moves it around the tray bumping into the other objects. The script, shown below, has many of the same features that the 2D programs have. There is a main loop, there is a list for x,y locations, and there are variables controlling the vector.

The main program loop is controlled by Blender. The python code shown in the listing is called by Blender for each "frame" the game renders. This is why the Python code does not show a main program loop. It does exist, however.

The blue object has a location held in x, y, z format. It can be accessed and changed by using the blue_object.position variable. Array position 0 holds x, position 1 holds y, and position 2 holds the z location.

Rather than the change_x and change_y variables used in the 2D examples in this changer, this Blender example uses the associative array locations:

```
blue_object["x_change"]
blue_object["y_change"]
```

The if statements check to see if the blue object has reached the borders of the screen and the direction needs to reverse. Unlike pixels used in the 2D games, locations of objects may be a floating point number type. To position an item between 5 and 6, setting its location to 5.5 is permissible.

```
# Import Blender Game Engine
import bge

# Get a reference to the blue object
cont = bge.logic.getCurrentController()
blue_object = cont.owner

# Print the x,y coordinates where the blue object is
print(blue_object.position[0], blue_object.position[1] )

# Change x,y coordinates according to x_change and
# y_change. x_change and y_change are game properties
# associated with the blue object.
blue_object.position[0] += blue_object["x_change"]
blue_object.position[1] += blue_object["y_change"]

# Check to see of the object has gone to the edge.
# If so reverse direction. Do so with all 4 edges.
if blue_object.position[0] > 6 and blue_object["x_change"] > 0:
    blue_object["x_change"] *= -1

if blue_object.position[0] < -6 and blue_object["x_change"] < 0:
    blue_object["x_change"] *= -1

if blue_object.position[1] > 6 and blue_object["y_change"] > 0:
    blue_object["y_change"] *= -1

if blue_object.position[1] < -6 and blue_object["y_change"] < 0:
    blue_object["y_change"] *= -1
```

Blender may be downloaded from: http://www.blender.org/

A full blender example file is available at: ProgramArcadeGames.com/chapters/ 08_intro_to_animation/simple_block_move.blend.

Review

Multiple Choice Quiz

1. In the bouncing rectangle program, if rect_change_x is positive and rect_change_y is negative, which way will the rectangle travel?

    a. Up

    b. Up and right

    c. Right

    d. Down and right

    e. Down

    f. Down and left

    g. Left

    h. Up and left

2. In the bouncing rectangle program, if rect_change_x is zero and rect_change_y is positive, which way will the rectangle travel?

    a. Up

    b. Up and right

    c. Right

    d. Down and right

    e. Down

    f. Down and left

    g. Left

    h. Up and left

3. This code is supposed to draw a white rectangle. But when the program is run, no rectangle shows up. Why?

```
import pygame

# Define some colors
BLACK    = (   0,   0,   0)
WHITE    = ( 255, 255, 255)

pygame.init()

# Set the height and width of the screen
size = [700, 500]
screen = pygame.display.set_mode(size)
```

```
    # Loop until the user clicks the close button.
    done = False

    # Used to manage how fast the screen updates
    clock = pygame.time.Clock()

    # -------- Main Program Loop -----------
    while not done:
        for event in pygame.event.get():
            if event.type == pygame.QUIT:
                done = True

        # Set the screen background
        screen.fill(BLACK)

        # Draw the rectangle
        pygame.draw.rect(screen, WHITE, [50, 50, 50, 50])

        # Limit to 20 frames per second
        clock.tick(20)

    # Be IDLE friendly. If you forget this line, the program will 'hang'
    # on exit.
    pygame.quit()
```

a.   The rectangle dimensions are offscreen.

b.   There is no flip command.

c.   The rectangle is the same color as the background.

d.   The rectangle is drawn outside the main program loop.

e.   The rectangle is too small to see.

f.   The rectangle should be drawn earlier in the code.

4.   This code is supposed to draw a white rectangle. But when the program is run, no rectangle shows up. Curiously, when the user hits the close button, the rectangle briefly appears before the program closes. Why?

```
import pygame

# Define some colors
BLACK    = (   0,   0,   0)
WHITE    = ( 255, 255, 255)

pygame.init()

# Set the height and width of the screen
size = [700, 500]
screen = pygame.display.set_mode(size)

# Loop until the user clicks the close button.
done = False
```

```
# Used to manage how fast the screen updates
clock = pygame.time.Clock()

# -------- Main Program Loop -----------
while not done:
    for event in pygame.event.get():
        if event.type == pygame.QUIT:
            done = True

    # Set the screen background
    screen.fill(BLACK)

    # Draw the rectangle
    pygame.draw.rect(screen, WHITE, [50, 50, 50, 50])

    # Limit to 20 frames per second
    clock.tick(20)

# Go ahead and update the screen with what we've drawn.
pygame.display.flip()

# Be IDLE friendly. If you forget this line, the program will 'hang'
# on exit.
pygame.quit()
```

a. The rectangle dimensions are offscreen.

b. The flip is unindented and doesn't show until after the program ends.

c. The rectangle is the same color as the background.

d. The rectangle is drawn outside the main program loop.

e. The rectangle is too small to see.

f. The flip should be done before the rectangle is drawn.

5. This version of "The Bouncing Rectangle" doesn't work. The rectangle won't move. Why?

```
import pygame

# Define some colors
BLACK    = (   0,   0,   0)
WHITE    = ( 255, 255, 255)

pygame.init()

# Set the height and width of the screen
size = [700, 500]
screen = pygame.display.set_mode(size)

#Loop until the user clicks the close button.
done = False
```

```
    # Used to manage how fast the screen updates
    clock = pygame.time.Clock()

    # Speed and direction of rectangle
    rect_change_x = 5
    rect_change_y = 5

    # -------- Main Program Loop -----------
    while not done:
        for event in pygame.event.get():
            if event.type == pygame.QUIT:
                done=True

        # Starting position of the rectangle
        rect_x = 50
        rect_y = 50

        # Move the rectangle starting point
        rect_x += rect_change_x
        rect_y += rect_change_y

        # Bounce the ball if needed
        if rect_y > 450 or rect_y < 0:
            rect_change_y = rect_change_y * -1
        if rect_x > 650 or rect_x < 0:
            rect_change_x = rect_change_x * -1

        # Set the screen background
        screen.fill(BLACK)

        # Draw the rectangle
        pygame.draw.rect(screen, WHITE, [rect_x, rect_y, 50, 50])

        # Limit to 20 frames per second
        clock.tick(20)

        # Go ahead and update the screen with what we've drawn.
        pygame.display.flip()

# Be IDLE friendly. If you forget this line, the program will 'hang'
# on exit.
pygame.quit ()
```

a.   pygame.draw.rect doesn't change where the rectangle is drawn based on the variables.

b.   rect_x and rect_y are reset to 50 each time through the loop.

c.   The 50,50 in the draw command also needs to be changed to rect_x,rect_y

d.   The lines to adjust rect_x and rect_y need to be outside the while loop.

6. What is the correct code to make the rectangle bounce of the left and right sides of the screen?

   a. ```
      if rect_x > 450 or rect_x < 0:
          rect_x = rect_x * -1
      ```

   b. ```
      if rect_x > 450 or rect_x < 0:
          rect_change_x = rect_change_x * -1
      ```

   c. ```
      if rect_y > 450 or rect_y < 0:
          rect_y = rect_y * -1
      ```

   d. ```
      if rect_y > 450 or rect_y < 0:
          rect_change_y = rect_change_y * -1
      ```

7. Why does this code not work for drawing stars?

   ```
   for i in range(50):
       x = random.randrange(0,400)
       y = random.randrange(0,400)
       pygame.draw.circle(screen, WHITE, [x, y], 2)
   ```

   a. The stars are drawn offscreen.

   b. The variable i should be used when drawing stars.

   c. The stars get brand-new locations each time a frame is drawn.

   d. The stars are drawn too small to be seen.

   e. The x and y coordinates are reversed.

Short Answer Worksheet

1. Why does using this code in the main loop not work to move the rectangle?

   ```
   rect_x = 50
   pygame.draw.rect(screen, WHITE, [rect_x, 50, 50, 50])
   rect_x += 1
   ```

2. The example code to bounce a rectangle used a total of four variables. What did each variable represent?

3. If the screen is 400 pixels tall, and the shape is 20 pixels high, at what point should the code check to see if the shape is in contact with the bottom of the screen.

4. Explain what is wrong with the following code (explain it, don't just correct the code):

   ```
   if rect_y > 450 or rect_y < 0:
       rect_y = rect_y * -1
   ```

5. A student is animating a stick figure. He creates separate variables for tracking the position of the head, torso, legs, and arms. When the figure moves to the right he adds one to each of the variables. Explain an easier way to do this that only requires one pair of x, y variables.

6. When drawing a starry background, explain why it doesn't work to put code like this in the main program loop:

```
for i in range(50):
    x = random.randrange(0, 400)
    y = random.randrange(0, 400)
    pygame.draw.circle(screen, WHITE, [x, y], 2)
```

7. Explain how to animate dozens of items at the same time.

8. If you have a list of coordinates like the following, what code would be required to print out the array location that holds the number 33?

```
stars = [[ 3,  4],
         [33, 94],
         [ 0,  0]]
```

9. This code example causes snow to fall:

```
# Process each snow flake in the list
for i in range(len(snow_list)):

    # Get the x and y from the lies
    x = snow_list[i][0]
    y = snow_list[i][1]

    # Draw the snow flake
    pygame.draw.circle(screen, WHITE, [x, y], 2)

    # Move the snow flake down one pixel
    snow_list[i][1] += 1
```

So does the example below. Explain why this example works as well.

```
# Process each snow flake in the list
for i in range(len(snow_list)):

    # Draw the snow flake
    pygame.draw.circle(screen, WHITE, snow_list[i], 2)

    # Move the snow flake down one pixel
    snow_list[i][1] += 1
```

10. Take a look at the radar_sweep.py program. You can find this example under the "graphics examples" subsection on the examples page. The radar_sweep.py is near the end of that list. Explain how this program animates the sweep to go in a circle.

Exercise

Check the appendix for the exercise "Animation" that goes along with this chapter.

CHAPTER 10

Functions

Functions are used for two reasons. First, they make code easier to read and understand. Second, they allow code to be used more than once.

Imagine a set of code that draws a tree as shown below. To do this, the programmer executes the following commands:

```
pygame.draw.rect(screen, BROWN, [60, 400, 30, 45])
pygame.draw.polygon(screen, GREEN, [[150, 400], [75, 250], [0, 400]])
pygame.draw.polygon(screen, GREEN, [[140, 350], [75, 230], [10, 350]])
```

Simple Tree

Those three lines of code don't really pop out as obviously drawing a tree! If we have multiple trees or complex objects, it starts getting hard to understand what is being drawn.

By defining a function we can make the program easier to read. To define a function, start by using the def command. After the def command goes the function name. In this case we are calling it draw_tree. We use the same rules for function names that we use for variable names.

Following the function name will be a set of parentheses and a colon. All the commands for the function will be indented inside. See the example below:

```
def draw_tree():
    pygame.draw.rect(screen, BROWN, [60, 400, 30, 45])
    pygame.draw.polygon(screen, GREEN, [[150, 400], [75, 250], [0, 400]])
    pygame.draw.polygon(screen, GREEN, [[140, 350], [75, 230], [10, 350]])
```

By itself, this code will not cause a tree to draw. It will tell the computer *how* to do draw_tree. You have to *call* the function to actually run the code in the function and get the tree to draw:

```
draw_tree()
```

With a whole library of functions defining different things to be drawn, a final program might look like:

```
draw_tree()
draw_house()
draw_car()
draw_killer_bunny()
```

Remember that draw_tree has three lines of code. Each one of these other commands, like draw_house, has multiple lines of code. By using functions, we can repeat the commands without repeating all the code contained within, making for a much smaller program.

Function names are very important. If the function names are descriptive, even a nonprogrammer should be able to read a set of code and get an idea what is happening. Function names follow the same rules as variable names and should start with a lowercase letter.

Function Parameters

Functions can take *parameters*. Chances are, you've already used parameters in math class. In the equation for the volume of a sphere below, the function v takes one parameter: r which represents the radius. This function can be used to determine the volume of any sphere, no matter what the radius is. These parameters are used to increase the flexibility of a function by altering the result based on parameters passed to it.

$$v(r) = \frac{4}{3}pr^3$$

For example, our function called draw_tree() draws the tree in one specific place. But the function could be changed to take a parameter that specifies *where* to draw the tree. For example draw_tree(screen, 0, 230) would draw the tree at an (x, y) location of (0, 230).

Adjusting the function for the tree might look like:

```
def draw_tree(screen, x, y):
    pygame.draw.rect(screen, BROWN, [60+x, 170+y, 30, 45])
    pygame.draw.polygon(screen, GREEN, [[150+x,170+y],[75+x,20+y], [x,170+y]])
    pygame.draw.polygon(screen, GREEN, [[140+x,120+y], [75+x,y], [10+x,120+y]])
```

This would allow us to draw multiple trees wherever we like:

```
draw_tree(screen, 0, 230)
draw_tree(screen, 200, 230)
draw_tree(screen, 400, 230)
```

Here is a different function that can be run without using graphics. This function will calculate and print out the volume of a sphere:

```
def volume_sphere(radius):
    pi = 3.141592653589
    volume = (4 / 3) * pi * radius ** 3
    print("The volume is", volume)
```

Parameters are assigned values when a function is called, not when it is defined.

The name of the function is volume_sphere. The data going into the functions will be stored in a new variable called radius. The resulting volume is printed to the screen. The radius variable does not get a value here. Frequently new programmers get confused because parameter variables aren't given a value when the function is defined, so it doesn't look legal. Parameters are given a value when the function is called.

To call this function, use:

```
volume_sphere(22)
```

The radius variable in the function is created and initialized with a value of 22. The function's code is run once the execution reaches the call to the function.

What if we need to pass in more than one value? Multiple parameters can be passed to a function, each parameter separated by a comma:

```
def volume_cylinder(radius, height):
    pi = 3.141592653589
    volume = pi * radius ** 2 * height
    print("The volume is", volume)
```

That function may be called by:

```
volume_cylinder(12, 3)
```

Parameters are done in order, so radius will get the 12, and height will get the 3 value.

Returning and Capturing Values

Unfortunately, these example functions are limited. Why? If a person wanted to use the volume_cylinder function to calculate the volume in a six-pack, it wouldn't work. It only prints out the volume of one cylinder. It is not possible to use the function's result for one cylinder's volume in an equation and multiply it by six to get a six-pack volume.

Returning Values

This can be solved by using a return statement. For example:

```
# Add two numbers and return the results
def sum_two_numbers(a, b):
    result = a + b
    return result
```

Return is not a function and does not use parentheses. Don't do return(result).

This only gets us halfway there. Because if we call the function now, not much happens. The numbers get added. They get returned to us. But we do nothing with the result.

```
# This doesn't do much, because we don't capture the result
sum_two_numbers(22, 15)
```

Capturing Returned Values

We need to capture the result. We do that by setting a variable equal to the value the function returned:

```
# Store the function's result into a variable
my_result = sum_two_numbers(22, 15)
print(my_result)
```

Now the result isn't lost. It is stored in my_result, which we can print or use some other way.

Improving the volume_cylinder Example

```
def volume_cylinder(radius, height):
    pi = 3.141592653589
    volume = pi * radius ** 2 * height
    return volume
```

Because of the return, this function could be used later on as part of an equation to calculate the volume of a six-pack like this:

```
six_pack_volume = volume_cylinder(2.5, 5) * 6
```

The value returned from volume_cylinder goes into the equation and is multiplied by six.

There is a big difference between a function that *prints* a value and a function that *returns* a value. Look at the code below and try it out.

```
# Function that prints the result
def sum_print(a, b):
    result = a + b
    print(result)

# Function that returns the results
def sum_return(a, b):
    result = a + b
    return result

# This prints the sum of 4+4
sum_print(4, 4)

# This does not
sum_return(4, 4)

# This will not set x1 to the sum
# It actually gets a value of 'None'
x1 = sum_print(4, 4)

# This will
x2 = sum_return(4, 4)
```

When first working with functions it is not unusual to get stuck looking at code like this:

```
def calculate_average(a, b):
    """ Calculate an average of two numbers """
    result = (a * b) / 2
    return result

# Pretend you have some code here
x = 45
y = 56

# Wait, how do I print the result of this?
calculate_average(x, y)
```

How do we print the result of `calculate_average`? The program can't print the `result` because that variable only exists inside the function. Instead, use a variable to capture the result:

```
def calculate_average(a, b):
    """ Calculate an average of two numbers """
    result = (a * b) / 2
    return result

# Pretend you have some code here
x = 45
y = 56

average = calculate_average(x, y)
print(average)
```

157

Documenting Functions

Functions in Python typically have a comment as the first statement of the function. This comment is delimited using three double quotes and is called a *docstring*. A function may look like:

```python
def volume_cylinder(radius, height):
    """Returns volume of a cylinder given radius, height."""
    pi = 3.141592653589
    volume = pi * radius ** 2 * height
    return volume
```

The great thing about using docstrings in functions is that the comment can be pulled out and put into a web site documenting your code using a tool like http://sphinx-doc.org/. Most languages have similar tools that can help make documenting your code a breeze. This can save a lot of time as you start working on larger programs.

Variable Scope

The use of functions introduces the concept of *scope*. Scope is where in the code a variable is alive and can be accessed. For example, look at the code below:

```python
# Define a simple function that sets
# x equal to 22
def f():
    x = 22


# Call the function
f()
# This fails, x only exists in f()
print(x)
```

The last line will generate an error because x only exists inside of the f() function. The variable is created when f() is called and the memory it uses is freed as soon as f() finishes.

Here's where it gets complicated.

A more confusing rule is accessing variables created outside of the f() function. In the following code, x is created before the f() function, and thus can be read from inside the f() function.

```python
# Create the x variable and set to 44
x = 44


# Define a simple function that prints x
def f():
    print(x)


# Call the function
f()
```

Variables created ahead of a function may be read inside of the function *only if the function does not change the value*. This code, very similar to the code above, will fail. The computer will claim it doesn't know what x is.

```
# Create the x variable and set to 44
x = 44

# Define a simple function that prints x
def f():
    x += 1
    print(x)

# Call the function
f()
```

Other languages have more complex rules around the creation of variables and scope than Python does. Because Python is straightforward, it is a good introductory language.

Pass-by-copy

Functions pass their values by creating a copy of the original. For example:

```
# Define a simple function that prints x
def f(x):
    x += 1
    print(x)

# Set y
y = 10
# Call the function
f(y)
# Print y to see if it changed
print(y)
```

The value of y does not change, even though the f() function increases the value passed to it. Each of the variables listed as a parameter in a function is a brand new variable. The value of that variable is copied from where it is called.

This is reasonably straightforward in the prior example. Where it gets confusing is if both the code that calls the function and the function itself have variables named the same. The code below is identical to the prior listing, but rather than use y it uses x.

```
# Define a simple function that prints x
def f(x):
    x += 1
    print(x)

# Set x
x = 10
# Call the function
f(x)
# Print x to see if it changed
print(x)
```

The output is the same as the program that uses y. Even though both the function and the surrounding code use x for a variable name, there are actually *two* different variables. There is the variable x that exists inside of the function and a different variable x that exists outside the function.

Functions Calling Functions

It is entirely possible for a function to call another function. For example, say the functions like the following were defined:

```
def arm_out(which_arm, palm_up_or_down):
    # code would go here

def hand_grab(hand, arm):
    # code goes here
```

Then another function could be created that calls the other functions:

```
def macarena():
    arm_out("right", "down")
    arm_out("left", "down")
    arm_out("right", "up")
    arm_out("left", "up")
    hand_grab("right", "left arm")
    hand_grab("left", "right arm")
    # etc
```

Main Functions and Globals

Global variables are pure evil.

As programs get large it is important to keep the code organized and put into functions. Python allows us to write code at "indent level 0." This describes most of the code we've written so far. Our code is lined up on the left and not contained in functions.

This philosophy is like heaping your clothes on the middle of your floor or keeping all your tools in a pile on the workbench. It only works well when you don't have much stuff. Even when you don't have much stuff it is still messy.

All your code and all your variables should be placed in functions. This will keep your code organized. It will also help when you need to track down a bug in the program. Variables created at "indent level 0" are called *global variables*. Global variables are a *very bad thing*. Why? Because any piece of code anywhere can change their value. If you have a 50,000-line program, each line of code can change that global variable. If instead you keep the variable in a function, then only that code in the function can change the variable. Thus, if you have an unexpected value in a variable, you only need to look through the maybe 50 lines of code in your function. Otherwise you have to check every line of code in your entire program!

A better way to write a program in Python would be to follow this pattern:

```
def main():
    print("Hello world.")

main()
```

160

In this case all the code that I normally would have run at indent level 0 is placed in the main function. The last line of the file calls main.

But wait! There's another problem we need to fix. In Chapter 15, we will talk about how to break our program into multiple files. We can use the import command to bring in functions from other modules we created. If we used the import command on this module, it would automatically start running the main function. We don't want that. We want the program that imports it to control when the function is called.

To fix this problem we can have our program check a global variable defined automatically by Python. (I know, I just said global variables were bad, right?) That variable is called __name__, with two underscores before and after it. We can check it to see if this code is being *imported* or *run*. If the code is being run, Python will automatically set the value of that variable to __main__. By using an if statement we will only call the main function if the code is being run. Otherwise the code will just *define* the main function. The code that imported it can call the function when desired.

This is how all your Python code *should* be run:

```python
def main():
    print("Hello world.")

if __name__ == "__main__":
    main()
```

One of the reasons I love Python as a first language is that you aren't required to use this complexity until you need it. Other languages, like Java, require it no matter how small your program.

To make things easier in this book we do *not* show our examples using this pattern. But after this book your programs will likely be complex enough that it will make life easier if you don't "throw all your clothes in a pile," so to speak.

If you are super enthused about programming, try writing your programs starting this way now. While it may be a bit more challenging to begin with, it will make writing programs easier later on. It is also a good way to learn about how to properly manage your data and its scope.

Here is an example that shows how to do the base pygame template using this pattern:
programarcadegames.com/python_examples/f.php?file=pygame_base_template_proper.py

Using this template is not required. I'm OK for a short time if you pile your clothes in the middle of the floor. I'm just happy you are wearing clothes. (For the neat freaks, we can clean this program up even more when we get to the chapter on Python classes.)

Short Examples

For each of the examples below, think about what would print. Check to see if you are right. If you didn't guess correctly, spend to the time to understand why.

```python
# Example 1
def a():
    print("A")

def b():
    print("B")

def c():
    print("C")

a()
```

```
# Example 2
def a():
    b()
    print("A")

def b():
    c()
    print("B")

def c():
    print("C")

a()

# Example 3
def a():
    print("A")
    b()

def b():
    print("B")
    c()

def c():
    print("C")

a()

# Example 4
def a():
    print("A start")
    b()
    print("A end")

def b():
    print("B start")
    c()
    print("B end")

def c():
    print("C start and end")
a()

# Example 5
def a(x):
    print("A start, x =",x)
    b(x + 1)
    print("A end, x =",x)
```

```
def b(x):
    print("B start, x =",x)
    c(x + 1)
    print("B end, x =",x)

def c(x):
    print("C start and end, x =",x)

a(5)

# Example 6
def a(x):
    x = x + 1

x = 3
a(x)

print(x)

# Example 7
def a(x):
    x = x + 1
    return x

x = 3
a(x)

print(x)

# Example 8
def a(x):
    x = x + 1
    return x

x = 3
x = a(x)

print(x)

# Example 9
def a(x, y):
    x = x + 1
    y = y + 1
    print(x, y)

x = 10
y = 20
a(y, x)
```

```
# Example 10
def a(x, y):
    x = x + 1
    y = y + 1
    return x
    return y

x = 10
y = 20
z = a(x, y)

print(z)

# Example 11
def a(x, y):
    x = x + 1
    y = y + 1
    return x, y

x = 10
y = 20
z = a(x, y)

print(z)

# Example 12
def a(x, y):
    x = x + 1
    y = y + 1
    return x, y

x = 10
y = 20
x2, y2 = a(x, y) # Most computer languages don't support this

print(x2)
print(y2)

# Example 13
def a(my_data):
    print("function a, my_data =  ", my_data)
    my_data = 20
    print("function a, my_data =  ", my_data)

my_data = 10

print("global scope, my_data =", my_data)
a(my_data)
print("global scope, my_data =", my_data)
```

```
# Example 14
def a(my_list):
    print("function a, list =  ", my_list)
    my_list = [10, 20, 30]
    print("function a, list =  ", my_list)

my_list = [5, 2, 4]

print("global scope, list =", my_list)
a(my_list)
print("global scope, list =", my_list)

# Example 15
# New concept!
# Covered in more detail in Chapter 13
def a(my_list):
    print("function a, list =  ", my_list)
    my_list[0] = 1000
    print("function a, list =  ", my_list)

my_list = [5, 2, 4]

print("global scope, list =", my_list)
a(my_list)
print("global scope, list =", my_list)
```

Mudball Game Example

```
"""
This is a sample text-only game that demonstrates the use of functions.
The game is called "Mudball" and the players take turns lobbing mudballs
at each other until someone gets hit.
"""

import math
import random

def print_instructions():
    """ This function prints the instructions. """

    # You can use the triple-quote string in a print statement to
    # print multiple lines.
    print("""
Welcome to Mudball! The idea is to hit the other player with a mudball.
Enter your angle (in degrees) and the amount of PSI to charge your gun
with.
    """)
```

```python
def calculate_distance(psi, angle_in_degrees):
    """ Calculate the distance the mudball flies. """
    angle_in_radians = math.radians(angle_in_degrees)
    distance = .5 * psi ** 2 * math.sin(angle_in_radians) * math.cos(angle_in_radians)
    return distance

def get_user_input(name):
    """ Get the user input for psi and angle. Return as a list of two
    numbers. """
    # Later on in the 'exceptions' chapter, we will learn how to modify
    # this code to not crash the game if the user types in something that
    # isn't a valid number.
    psi = float(input(name + " charge the gun with how many psi? "))
    angle = float(input(name + " move the gun at what angle? "))
    return psi, angle

def get_player_names():
    """ Get a list of names from the players. """
    print("Enter player names. Enter as many players as you like.")
    done = False
    players = []
    while not done:
        player = input("Enter player (hit enter to quit): ")
        if len(player) > 0:
            players.append(player)
        else:
            done = True

    print()
    return players

def process_player_turn(player_name, distance_apart):
    """ The code runs the turn for each player.
    If it returns False, keep going with the game.
    If it returns True, someone has won, so stop. """
    psi, angle = get_user_input(player_name)

    distance_mudball = calculate_distance(psi, angle)
    difference = distance_mudball - distance_apart

    # By looking ahead to the chapter on print formatting, these
    # lines could be made to print the numbers is a nice formatted
    # manner.
    if difference > 1:
        print("You went", difference, "yards too far!")
    elif difference < -1:
        print("You were", difference * -1, "yards too short!")
    else:
        print("Hit!", player_name, "wins!")
        return True
```

```
    print()
    return False

def main():
    """ Main program. """

    # Get the game started.
    print_instructions()
    player_names = get_player_names()
    distance_apart = random.randrange(50, 150)

    # Keep looking until someone wins
    done = False
    while not done:
        # Loop for each player
        for player_name in player_names:
            # Process their turn
            done = process_player_turn(player_name, distance_apart)
            # If someone won, 'break' out of this loop and end the game.
            if done:
                break

if __name__ == "__main__":
    main()
```

Review

Multiple Choice Quiz

1. What does this code print?

```
def f():
    print("f")

def g():
    print("g")

print("a")
```

a. f

b. a

c. g

d. f
   g
   a

e. a
   f
   g

2. What does this code print?

```
def f():
    print("f")

def g():
    print("g")

g()
print("a")
f()
```

    a. f

    b. a

    c. g

    d. g
        a
        f

    e. f
        g
        a

    f. a
        f
        g

3. What does this code print?

```
def f(a):
    print(a)

a = 5
f(a + 1)
```

    a. 0

    b. 5

    c. Nothing

    d. 6

    e. a+1

    f. a

4. What does this code print?

```
def f(a, b):
    print(a)
    print(b)

a = 1
b = 2
f(b, a)
```

   a. 1
       2

   b. 2
       1

   c. a
       b

   d. b
       a

5. What does this code print?

```
def f(a):
    return a + 1

b = f(5)
print(b)
```

   a. 5

   b. 6

   c. a+1

   d. b

   e. a

6. What is wrong with this code?

```python
def sum_list(list):
    sum = 0
    for item in list:
        sum + = item
        return sum

list=[45, 2, 10, -5, 100]
print(sum_list(list))
```

   a. The return statement should print the sum instead.

   b. The return statement should be unindented one tab stop.

   c. The return statement should be unindented two tab stops.

   d. The variable i should be used instead of item.

   e. The sum_list function may not be placed inside the print statement.

7. What will this print?

```python
a = 3

def f():
    print(a)

f()
```

   a. f

   b. 3

   c. Nothing

   d. An error, a is undefined.

8. What will this print?

```python
a = 3

def f():
        a = a + 1
    print(a)

f()
```

   a. f

   b. 4

   c. Nothing

   d. An error, a is undefined.

9. What will this print?

```
def f(a):
    return a + 1

print( f( f(5) ) )
```

a. 5

b. 6

c. 7

d. An error.

10. What will this print?

```
def foo():
    x = 3
    print("foo has been called")

x = 10
print("x=", x)
foo()
print("x=", x)
```

a. x= 10
    foo has been called
    x= 10

b. x= 3
    foo has been called
    x= 10

c. x= 10
    foo has been called
    x= 3

d. An error.

Short Answer Worksheet

For the code below, write a prediction on what it will output. Then run the code and state if your prediction was accurate or not. If your prediction is incorrect, make sure you understand why.

1. Block 1 (Remember, guess AND actual.)

```
for i in range(5):
    print(i + 1)
```

2. Block 2

```
for i in range(5):
    print(i)
    i = i + 1
```

171

3. Block 3

```
x = 0
for i in range(5):
    x += 1
print(x)
```

4. Block 4

```
x = 0
for i in range(5):
    for j in range(5):
        x += 1
print(x)
```

5. Block 5

```
for i in range(5):
    for j in range(5):
        print(i, j)
```

6. Block 6

```
for i in range(5):
    for j in range(5):
        print("*", end="")
        print()
```

7. Block 7

```
for i in range(5):
    for j in range(5):
        print("*", end="")
    print()
```

8. Block 8

```
for i in range(5):
    for j in range(5):
        print("*", end="")
print()
```

9. Block 9

```
# This is supposed to sum a list of numbers
# What is the mistake here?
my_list = [5, 8, 10, 4, 5]
i = 0
```

```
    for i in my_list:
        i = i + my_list[i]
    print(i)
```

10.   Block 10

```
    for i in range(5):
        x = 0
        for j in range(5):
            x += 1
    print(x)
```

11.   Block 11

```
    import random
    play_again = "y"
    while play_again == "y":
        for i in range(5):
            print(random.randrange(2), end="")
        print()
        play_again = input("Play again? ")
    print("Bye!")
```

12.   Block 12

```
    def f1(x):
        print(x)
    y = 3
    f1(y)
```

13.   Block 13

```
    def f2(x):
        x = x + 1
        print(x)
    y = 3
    f2(y)
    print(y)
```

14.   Block 14

```
    def f3(x):
        x = x + 1
        print(x)
    x = 3
    f3(x)
    print(x)
```

15. Block 15

```
def f4(x):
    z = x + 1
    print(z)
x = 3
f4(x)
print(z)
```

16. Block 16

```
def foo(x):
    x = x + 1
    print("x=", x)

x = 10
print("x=", x)
foo(x)
print("x=", x)
```

17. Block 17

```
def f():
    print("f start")
    g()
    h()
    print("f end")

def g():
    print("g start")
    h()
    print("g end")

def h():
    print("h")

f()
```

18. Block 18

```
def foo():
    x = 3
    print("foo has been called")

x = 10
print("x=", x)
foo()
print("x=", x)
```

19. Block 19 (This demonstrates a new concept that won't be fully explained until Chapter 13.)

```
def a(x):
    print("a", x)
    x = x + 1
    print("a", x)

x = 1
print("main", x)
a(x)
print("main", x)

def b(y):
    print("b", y[1])
    y[1] = y[1] + 1
    print("b", y[1])

y=[123, 5]
print("main", y[1])
b(y)
print("main", y[1])

def c(y):
    print("c", y[1])
    y = [101, 102]
    print("c", y[1])

y = [123, 5]
print("main", y[1])
c(y)
print("main", y[1])
```

Correcting Code

This next section involves finding the mistakes in the code. If you can't find the mistake, check out the video on-line for the answer and an explanation on what is wrong.

1. Correct the following code: (Don't let it print out the word "None.")

```
def sum(a, b, c):
    print(a + b + c)

print(sum(10, 11, 12))
```

2. Correct the following code: (x should increase by one, but it doesn't.)

```
def increase(x):
    return x + 1

x = 10
print("X is", x, " I will now increase x." )
increase(x)
print("X is now", x)
```

3. Correct the following code:

```
def print_hello:
    print("Hello")

print_hello()
```

4. Correct the following code:

```
def count_to_ten():
    for i in range[10]:
        print(i)

count_to_ten()
```

5. Correct the following code:

```
def sum_list(list):
    for i in list:
        sum = i
        return sum

list = [45, 2, 10, -5, 100]
print(sum_list(list))
```

6. Correct the following code: (This almost reverses the string. What is wrong?)

```
def reverse(text):
    result = ""
    text_length = len(text)
    for i in range(text_length):
        result = result + text[i * -1]
    return result

text = "Programming is the coolest thing ever."
print(reverse(text))
```

7. Correct the following code:

```
def get_user_choice():
    while True:
        command = input("Command: ")
        if command = f or command = m or command = s or command = d or command = q:
            return command

        print("Hey, that's not a command. Here are your options:" )
        print("f - Full speed ahead")
        print("m - Moderate speed")
        print("s - Status")
        print("d - Drink")
        print("q - Quit")

user_command = get_user_choice()
print("You entered:", user_command)
```

For this section, write code that satisfies the following items:

1. Write a function that prints out "Hello World."

2. Write code that will call the function in the prior problem.

3. Write a function that prints out "Hello Bob" and will take a parameter to let the caller specify the name. Do not put an input statement inside the function! Use a parameter.

4. Write code that will call the function in the prior problem.

5. Write a function that will take two numbers as parameters (not as input from the user) and print their product (i.e., multiply them).

6. Write code that will call the prior function.

7. Write a function that takes in two parameters. The first parameter will be a string named phrase. The second parameter will be a number named count. Print phrase to the screen count times. (e.g., the function takes in "Hello" and 5 then prints "Hello" five times.)

8. Write code to call the previous function.

9. Write code for a function that takes in a number and returns the square of that number. (I'm not asking for the square root but the number squared.) Note, this function should RETURN the answer, not print it out.

10. Write code to call the function above and print the output.

11. Write a function that takes three numbers as parameters and returns the centrifugal force. The formula for centrifugal force is: $F = m\dfrac{v^2}{r}$ F is force, m is mass, r is radius, and v is angular velocity.

12. Write code to call the function above and display the result.

13. Write a function that takes a list of numbers as a parameter and prints out each number individually using a `for` loop.

Exercise

Check the appendix for the exercise "Functions" that goes along with this chapter.

CHAPTER 11

■ ■ ■

Controllers and Graphics

How do we get objects to move using the keyboard, mouse, or a game controller?

So far, we've shown how to animate items on the screen, but not how to *interact* with them. How do we use a mouse, keyboard, or game controller to control the action onscreen? Thankfully this is pretty easy.

To begin with, it is necessary to have an object that can be moved around the screen. The best way to do this is to have a *function* that takes in an x and y coordinate, then draws an object at that location. So back to Chapter 10! Let's take a look at how to write a function to draw an object.

All the pygame draw functions require a screen parameter to let Pygame know which window to draw on. We will need to pass this in to any function we create to draw an object on the screen.

The function also needs to know where to draw the object on the screen. The function needs an x and y. We pass the location to the function as a parameter. Here is example code that defines a function that will draw a snowman when called:

```
def draw_snowman(screen, x, y):
    # Draw a circle for the head
    pygame.draw.ellipse(screen, WHITE, [35+x, 0+y, 25, 25])
    # Draw the middle snowman circle
    pygame.draw.ellipse(screen, WHITE, [23+x, 20+y, 50, 50])
    # Draw the bottom snowman circle
    pygame.draw.ellipse(screen, WHITE, [0+x, 65+y, 100, 100])
```

Then, in the main program loop, multiple snowmen can be drawn, as seen in the figure below.

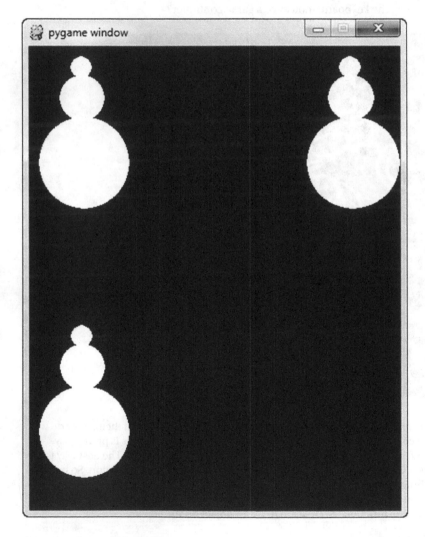

Snowmen drawn by a function

```
# Snowman in upper left
draw_snowman(screen, 10, 10)

# Snowman in upper right
draw_snowman(screen, 300, 10)

# Snowman in lower left
draw_snowman(screen, 10, 300)
```

A full working example is available online at:

ProgramArcadeGames.com/python_examples/f.php?file=functions_and_graphics.py

Chances are, from a prior lab you already have a code that draws something cool. But how do you get that into a function? Let's take an example of code that draws a stick figure:

```
# Head
pygame.draw.ellipse(screen, BLACK, [96,83,10,10], 0)

# Legs
pygame.draw.line(screen, BLACK, [100,100], [105,110], 2)
pygame.draw.line(screen, BLACK, [100,100], [95,110], 2)

# Body
pygame.draw.line(screen, RED, [100,100], [100,90], 2)

# Arms
pygame.draw.line(screen, RED, [100,90], [104,100], 2)
pygame.draw.line(screen, RED, [100,90], [96,100], 2)
```

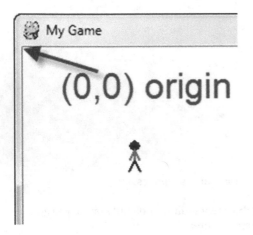

Stick Figure

This code can easily be put in a function by adding a function def and indenting the code under it. We'll need to bring in all the data that the function needs to draw the stick figure. We need the screen variable to tell the function what window to draw on, and an x and y coordinate for where to draw the stick figure.

But we can't define the function in the middle of our program loop! The code should be removed from the main part of the program. Function declarations should go at the start of the program. We need to move that code to the top. See the figure to help visualize.

```
def draw_stick_figure(screen,x,y):
    # Head
    pygame.draw.ellipse(screen, BLACK, [96,83,10,10], 0)

    # Legs
    pygame.draw.line(screen, BLACK, [100,100], [105,110], 2)
    pygame.draw.line(screen, BLACK, [100,100], [95,110], 2)

    # Body
    pygame.draw.line(screen, RED, [100,100], [100,90], 2)

    # Arms
    pygame.draw.line(screen, RED, [100,90], [104,100], 2)
    pygame.draw.line(screen, RED, [100,90], [96,100], 2)
```

```
10   green     = (  0, 255,   0)
11   red       = ( 255,  0,   0)
12
13   def draw_stick_figure(screen,x,y):
14       # Head
15       pygame.draw.ellipse(screen,black,[96+x,83+y,10,10
16
17       # Legs
18       pygame.draw.line(screen,black,[100+x,100+y],[105+x,110+y]
19       pygame.draw.line(screen,black,[100+x,100+y],[95+x,110+y],2
20
21       # Body
22       pygame.draw.line(screen,red,[100+x,100+y],[100+x,90+y],2)
23
24       # Arms
25       pygame.draw.line(screen,red,[100+x,90+y],[104+x,100+y],2)
26       pygame.draw.line(screen,red,[100+x,90+y],[96+x,100+y],2)
27
28   pygame.init()
29
30   # Set the width and height of the screen [width,height]
31   size=[700,500]
32   screen=pygame.display.set_mode(size)
33
34   pygame.display.set_caption("My Game")
35
36   #Loop until the user clicks the close button.
37   done=False
38
39   # Used to manage how fast the screen updates
40   clock=pygame.time.Clock()
41
42   # -------- Main Program Loop -----------
43   while done==False:
44       # ALL EVENT PROCESSING SHOULD GO BELOW THIS COMMENT
45       for event in pygame.event.get(): # User did something
46           if event.type == pygame.QUIT: # If user clicked close
47               done=True # Flag that we are done so we exit this loop
48       # ALL EVENT PROCESSING SHOULD GO ABOVE THIS COMMENT
49
50       # ALL CODE TO DRAW SHOULD GO BELOW THIS COMMENT
51
52       # First, clear the screen to white. Don't put other drawing comman
53       # above this, or they will be erased with this command.
54       screen.fill(white)
55
56       # Head
57       pygame.draw.ellipse(screen,black,[96+x,       ,10],0
58
59       # Le
60       pygame.draw.line(screen,black,[100+x,        x,  0+y],2)
61       pygame.draw.line(screen,black,[100+x,100+y],[9  x,1 0+y],2)
62
63       # Body
64       pygame.draw.line(screen,red,[100+x,100+y],[100+x,90+y],2)
65
66       # Arms
67       pygame.draw.line(screen,red,[100+x,90+y],[10  x,100+y],2)
68       pygame.draw.line(screen,red,[100+x,90    ,[96+x,100+],2)
69
70       # Call draw stick figure function
71       draw_stick_figure(screen, 50, 50)
72
```

New Function

New function call

Making a Function and Putting it in the Right Place

Right now, this code takes in an x and y coordinate. Unfortunately it doesn't actually do anything with them. You can specify any coordinate you want; the stick figure always draws in *in the same exact spot*. Not very useful. The next code example literally adds in the x and y coordinate to the code we had before.

```
def draw_stick_figure(screen, x, y):
    # Head
    pygame.draw.ellipse(screen, BLACK,[96+x,83+y,10,10],0)

    # Legs
    pygame.draw.line(screen, BLACK, [100+x,100+y], [105+x,110+y], 2)
    pygame.draw.line(screen, BLACK, [100+x,100+y], [95+x,110+y], 2)

    # Body
    pygame.draw.line(screen, RED, [100+x,100+y], [100+x,90+y], 2)

    # Arms
    pygame.draw.line(screen, RED, [100+x,90+y], [104+x,100+y], 2)
    pygame.draw.line(screen, RED, [100+x,90+y], [96+x,100+y], 2)
```

But the problem is that the figure is already drawn a certain distance from the origin. It assumes an origin of (0, 0) and draws the stick figure down and over about 100 pixels. See the next figure and how the stick figure is not drawn at the (0, 0) coordinate passed in.

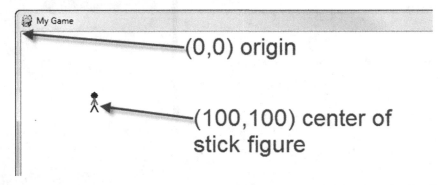

Stick Figure

By adding x and y in the function, we shift the origin of the stick figure by that amount. For example, if we call:

```
draw_stick_figure(screen, 50, 50)
```

The code does not put a stick figure at (50, 50). It shifts the origin down and over 50 pixels. Since our stick figure was already being drawn at about (100, 100), with the origin shift, the figure is about (150, 150). How do we fix this so that the figure is actually drawn where the function call requests?

```
def draw_stick_figure(screen,x,y):
    # Head
    pygame.draw.ellipse(screen,black,[96+x,83+y,10,10],0)    ──── Smallest x value

    # Legs
    pygame.draw.line(screen,black,[100+x,100+y],[105+x,110+y],2)
    pygame.draw.line(screen,black,[100+x,100+y],[95+x,110+y],2)    ──── Smallest y value

    # Body
    pygame.draw.line(screen,red,[100+x,100+y],[100+x,90+y],2)

    # Arms
    pygame.draw.line(screen,red,[100+x,90+y],[104+x,100+y],2)
    pygame.draw.line(screen,red,[100+x,90+y],[96+x,100+y],2)
```

Finding the Smallest X and Y Values

Find the smallest x value and the smallest y value as shown in the figure above. Then subtract that value from each x and y in the function. Don't mess with the height and width values. Here's an example where we subtracted the smallest x and y values:

```
def draw_stick_figure(screen, x, y):
    # Head
    pygame.draw.ellipse(screen, BLACK,[96-95+x,83-83+y,10,10],0)

    # Legs
    pygame.draw.line(screen, BLACK, [100-95+x,100-83+y], [105-95+x,110-83+y], 2)
    pygame.draw.line(screen, BLACK, [100-95+x,100-83+y], [95-95+x,110-83+y], 2)

    # Body
    pygame.draw.line(screen, RED, [100-95+x,100-83+y], [100-95+x,90-83+y], 2)

    # Arms
    pygame.draw.line(screen, RED, [100-95+x,90-83+y], [104-95+x,100-83+y], 2)
    pygame.draw.line(screen, RED, [100-95+x,90-83+y], [96-95+x,100-83+y], 2)
```

Or, to make a program simpler, do the subtraction yourself:

```
def draw_stick_figure(screen, x, y):
    # Head
    pygame.draw.ellipse(screen, BLACK, [1+x,y,10,10], 0)

    # Legs
    pygame.draw.line(screen, BLACK ,[5+x,17+y], [10+x,27+y], 2)
    pygame.draw.line(screen, BLACK, [5+x,17+y], [x,27+y], 2)

    # Body
    pygame.draw.line(screen, RED, [5+x,17+y], [5+x,7+y], 2)

    # Arms
    pygame.draw.line(screen, RED, [5+x,7+y], [9+x,17+y], 2)
    pygame.draw.line(screen, RED, [5+x,7+y], [1+x,17+y], 2)
```

Mouse

Great, now we know how to write a function to draw an object at specific coordinates. How do we get those coordinates? The easiest to work with is the mouse. It takes one line of code to get the coordinates:

```
pos = pygame.mouse.get_pos()
```

The trick is that coordinates are returned as a list, or more specifically a non-modifiable tuple. Both the x and y values are stored in the same variable. So if we do a print(pos) we get what is shown in the following figure.

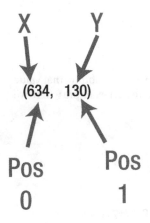

Coordinates

The variable pos is a tuple of two numbers. The x coordinate is in position 0 of array and the y coordinate is in the position 1. These can easily be fetched out and passed to the function that draws the item:

```
# Game logic
pos = pygame.mouse.get_pos()
x = pos[0]
y = pos[1]

# Drawing section
draw_stick_figure(screen, x, y)
```

Getting the mouse should go in the game logic part of the main program loop. The function call should go in the drawing part of the main program loop.

The only problem with this is that the mouse pointer draws right on top of the stick figure, making it hard to see, as shown in the next figure.

Stick Figure with Mouse Cursor on Top

The mouse can be hidden by using the following code right before the main program loop:

```
# Hide the mouse cursor
pygame.mouse.set_visible(False)
```

A full working example can be found here:

ProgramArcadeGames.com/python_examples/f.php?file=move_mouse.py

Keyboard

Controlling with the keyboard is a bit more complex. We can't just grab the x and y from the mouse. The keyboard doesn't give us an x and y. We need to:

- Create an initial x and y for our start position.
- Set a velocity in pixels per frame when an arrow key is pressed down. (keydown)
- Reset the velocity to zero when an arrow key is released. (keyup)
- Adjust the x and y each frame depending on the velocity.

It seems complex, but this is just like the bouncing rectangle we did before, with the exception that the speed is controlled by the keyboard.

To start with, set the location and speed *before* the main loop starts:

```
# Speed in pixels per frame
x_speed = 0
y_speed = 0

# Current position
x_coord = 10
y_coord = 10
```

Inside the main while loop of the program, we need to add some items to our event processing loop. In addition to looking for a pygame.QUIT event, the program needs to look for keyboard events. An event is generated each time the user presses a key.

A pygame.KEYDOWN event is generated when a key is pressed down. A pygame.KEYUP event is generated when the user lets up on a key. When the user presses a key, the speed vector is set to 3 or -3 pixels per frame. When the user lets up on a key the speed vector is reset back to zero. Finally, the coordinates of the object are adjusted by the vector, and then the object is drawn. See the code example below:

```python
for event in pygame.event.get():
    if event.type == pygame.QUIT:
        done = True

    # User pressed down on a key
    elif event.type == pygame.KEYDOWN:
        # Figure out if it was an arrow key. If so
        # adjust speed.
        if event.key == pygame.K_LEFT:
            x_speed = -3
        elif event.key == pygame.K_RIGHT:
            x_speed = 3
        elif event.key == pygame.K_UP:
            y_speed = -3
        elif event.key == pygame.K_DOWN:
            y_speed = 3

    # User let up on a key
    elif event.type == pygame.KEYUP:
        # If it is an arrow key, reset vector back to zero
        if event.key == pygame.K_LEFT or event.key == pygame.K_RIGHT:
            x_speed = 0
        elif event.key == pygame.K_UP or event.key == pygame.K_DOWN:
            y_speed = 0

# Move the object according to the speed vector.
x_coord += x_speed
y_coord += y_speed

# Draw the stick figure
draw_stick_figure(screen, x_coord, y_coord)
```

For a full example see:

ProgramArcadeGames.com/python_examples/f.php?file=move_keyboard.py

Note that this example does not prevent the character from moving off the edge of the screen. To do this, in the game logic section, a set of if statements would be needed to check the x_coord and y_coord values. If they are outside the boundaries of the screen, then reset the coordinates to the edge. The exact code for this is left as an exercise for the reader.

The table below shows a full list of key-codes that can be used in Pygame:

Pygame Code	ASCII	Common Name
K_BACKSPACE	\b	backspace
K_RETURN	\r	return
K_TAB	\t	tab
K_ESCAPE	^[	escape
K_SPACE		space
K_COMMA	,	comma sign
K_MINUS	-	minus
K_PERIOD	.	period slash
K_SLASH	/	forward
K_0	0	0
K_1	1	1
K_2	2	2
K_3	3	3
K_4	4	4
K_5	5	5
K_6	6	6
K_7	7	7
K_8	8	8
K_9	9	9
K_SEMICOLON	;	semicolon sign
K_EQUALS	=	equals sign
K_LEFTBRACKET	[	left
K_RIGHTBRACKET	]	right
K_BACKSLASH	\	backslash bracket
K_BACKQUOTE	`	grave
K_a	a	a
K_b	b	b
K_c	c	c
K_d	d	d
K_e	e	e
K_f	f	f
K_g	g	g
K_h	h	h
K_i	i	i

(*continued*)

Pygame Code	ASCII	Common Name
K_j	j	j
K_k	k	k
K_l	l	l
K_m	m	m
K_n	n	n
K_o	o	o
K_p	p	p
K_q	q	q
K_r	r	r
K_s	s	s
K_t	t	t
K_u	u	u
K_v	v	v
K_w	w	w
K_x	x	x
K_y	y	y
K_z	z	z
K_DELETE	delete	
K_KP0	keypad	0
K_KP1	keypad	1
K_KP2	keypad	2
K_KP3	keypad	3
K_KP4	keypad	4
K_KP5	keypad	5
K_KP6	keypad	6
K_KP7	keypad	7
K_KP8	keypad	8
K_KP9	keypad	9 period
K_KP_PERIOD	.	keypad divide
K_KP_DIVIDE	/	keypad multiply
K_KP_MULTIPLY	*	keypad minus
K_KP_MINUS	-	keypad plus
K_KP_PLUS	+	keypad enter
K_KP_ENTER	\r	keypad equals
K_KP_EQUALS	=	keypad

(*continued*)

Pygame Code	ASCII	Common Name
K_UP	up	arrow
K_DOWN	down	arrow
K_RIGHT	right	arrow
K_LEFT	left	arrow
K_INSERT	insert	
K_HOME	home	
K_END	end	
K_PAGEUP	page	up
K_PAGEDOWN	page	down
K_F1	F1	
K_F2	F2	
K_F3	F3	
K_F4	F4	
K_F5	F5	
K_F6	F6	
K_F7	F7	
K_F8	F8	
K_F9	F9	
K_F10	F10	
K_F11	F11	
K_F12	F12	
K_NUMLOCK	numlock	
K_CAPSLOCK	capslock	
K_RSHIFT	right	shift
K_LSHIFT	left	shift
K_RCTRL	right	ctrl
K_LCTRL	left	ctrl
K_RALT	right	alt
K_LALT	left	alt

Game Controller

Game controllers require a different set of code, but the idea is still simple.

To begin, check to see if the computer has a joystick, and initialize it before use. This should only be done once. Do it ahead of the main program loop:

```
# Current position
x_coord = 10
y_coord = 10

# Count the joysticks the computer has
joystick_count = pygame.joystick.get_count()
if joystick_count == 0:
    # No joysticks!
    print("Error, I didn't find any joysticks.")
else:
    # Use joystick #0 and initialize it
    my_joystick = pygame.joystick.Joystick(0)
    my_joystick.init()
```

A joystick will return two floating-point values. If the joystick is perfectly centered it will return (0, 0). If the joystick is fully up and to the left it will return (-1, -1). If the joystick is down and to the right it will return (1, 1). If the joystick is somewhere in between, values are scaled accordingly. See the controller images starting at the following figures to get an idea how it works.

Center (0,0)

Up Left (-1,-1)

Up (0,-1)

Up Right (1,-1)

193

Right (1,0)

Down Right (1,1)

Down (0,1)

Down Left (-1,1)

Left (-1,0)

Inside the main program loop, the values of the joystick returns may be multiplied according to how far an object should move. In the case of the code below, moving the joystick fully in a direction will move it 10 pixels per frame because the joystick values are multiplied by 10.

```
# This goes in the main program loop!

# As long as there is a joystick
if joystick_count != 0:

    # This gets the position of the axis on the game controller
    # It returns a number between -1.0 and +1.0
    horiz_axis_pos = my_joystick.get_axis(0)
    vert_axis_pos = my_joystick.get_axis(1)

    # Move x according to the axis. We multiply by 10 to speed up the movement.
    # Convert to an integer because we can't draw at pixel 3.5, just 3 or 4.
    x_coord = x_coord + int(horiz_axis_pos * 10)
    y_coord = y_coord + int(vert_axis_pos * 10)
```

```
# Clear the screen
screen.fill(WHITE)

# Draw the item at the proper coordinates
draw_stick_figure(screen, x_coord, y_coord)
```

For a full example, see

ProgramArcadeGames.com/python_examples/f.php?file=move_game_controller.py.

Controllers have a lot of joysticks, buttons, and even hat switches. Below is an example program and screenshot that prints everything to the screen showing what each game controller is doing. Take heed that game controllers must be plugged in before this program starts, or the program can't detect them.

Joystick Calls Program

```
"""
Sample Python/Pygame Programs
http://programarcadegames.com/

Show everything we can pull off the joystick
```

```python
"""
import pygame

# Define some colors
BLACK = (0, 0, 0)
WHITE = (255, 255, 255)


class TextPrint(object):
    """
    This is a simple class that will help us print to the screen
    It has nothing to do with the joysticks, just outputting the
    information.
    """
    def __init__(self):
        """ Constructor """
        self.reset()
        self.x_pos = 10
        self.y_pos = 10
        self.font = pygame.font.Font(None, 20)

    def print(self, my_screen, text_string):
        """ Draw text onto the screen. """
        text_bitmap = self.font.render(text_string, True, BLACK)
        my_screen.blit(text_bitmap, [self.x_pos, self.y_pos])
        self.y_pos += self.line_height

    def reset(self):
        """ Reset text to the top of the screen. """
        self.x_pos = 10
        self.y_pos = 10
        self.line_height = 15

    def indent(self):
        """ Indent the next line of text """
        self.x_pos += 10

    def unindent(self):
        """ Unindent the next line of text """
        self.x_pos -= 10

pygame.init()

# Set the width and height of the screen [width,height]
size = [500, 700]
screen = pygame.display.set_mode(size)
```

```python
pygame.display.set_caption("My Game")

# Loop until the user clicks the close button.
done = False

# Used to manage how fast the screen updates
clock = pygame.time.Clock()

# Initialize the joysticks
pygame.joystick.init()

# Get ready to print
textPrint = TextPrint()

# -------- Main Program Loop -----------
while not done:
    # EVENT PROCESSING STEP
    for event in pygame.event.get():
        if event.type == pygame.QUIT:
            done = True

        # Possible joystick actions: JOYAXISMOTION JOYBALLMOTION JOYBUTTONDOWN
        # JOYBUTTONUP JOYHATMOTION
        if event.type == pygame.JOYBUTTONDOWN:
            print("Joystick button pressed.")
        if event.type == pygame.JOYBUTTONUP:
            print("Joystick button released.")

    # DRAWING STEP
    # First, clear the screen to white. Don't put other drawing commands
    # above this, or they will be erased with this command.
    screen.fill(WHITE)
    textPrint.reset()

    # Get count of joysticks
    joystick_count = pygame.joystick.get_count()

    textPrint.print(screen, "Number of joysticks: {}".format(joystick_count))
    textPrint.indent()

    # For each joystick:
    for i in range(joystick_count):
        joystick = pygame.joystick.Joystick(i)
        joystick.init()
```

```python
            textPrint.print(screen, "Joystick {}".format(i))
            textPrint.indent()

            # Get the name from the OS for the controller/joystick
            name = joystick.get_name()
            textPrint.print(screen, "Joystick name: {}".format(name))

            # Usually axis run in pairs, up/down for one, and left/right for
            # the other.
            axes = joystick.get_numaxes()
            textPrint.print(screen, "Number of axes: {}".format(axes))
            textPrint.indent()

            for i in range(axes):
                axis = joystick.get_axis(i)
                textPrint.print(screen, "Axis {} value: {:>6.3f}".format(i, axis))
            textPrint.unindent()

            buttons = joystick.get_numbuttons()
            textPrint.print(screen, "Number of buttons: {}".format(buttons))
            textPrint.indent()

            for i in range(buttons):
                button = joystick.get_button(i)
                textPrint.print(screen, "Button {:>2} value: {}".format(i, button))
            textPrint.unindent()

            # Hat switch. All or nothing for direction, not like joysticks.
            # Value comes back in an array.
            hats = joystick.get_numhats()
            textPrint.print(screen, "Number of hats: {}".format(hats))
            textPrint.indent()

            for i in range(hats):
                hat = joystick.get_hat(i)
                textPrint.print(screen, "Hat {} value: {}".format(i, str(hat)))
            textPrint.unindent()

            textPrint.unindent()

    # ALL CODE TO DRAW SHOULD GO ABOVE THIS COMMENT

    # Go ahead and update the screen with what we've drawn.
    pygame.display.flip()

    # Limit to 60 frames per second
    clock.tick(60)

pygame.quit()
```

Review

Multiple Choice Quiz

1. What code will draw a circle at the specified x and y locations?

   a. ```
      def draw_circle(screen, x, y):
          pygame.draw.ellipse(screen, WHITE, [x, y, 25, 25])
      ```

   b. ```
      def draw_circle(screen,x,y):
          pygame.draw.ellipse(screen, WHITE, [x, y, 25 + x, 25 + y])
      ```

   c. ```
      def draw_circle(screen, x, y):
          pygame.draw.ellipse(screen, WHITE, [0, 0, 25 + x, 25 + y])
      ```

2. The following code draws an "X." What would the code look like if it was moved from the main program loop to a function, with the ability to specify how the coordinates of X appear?

   ```
   pygame.draw.line(screen, RED, [80, 80], [100, 100], 2)
   pygame.draw.line(screen, RED, [80, 100], [100, 80], 2)
   ```

   a. ```
      def draw_x(screen, x, y):
          pygame.draw.line(screen, RED, [80, 80], [100, 100], 2)
          pygame.draw.line(screen, RED, [80, 100], [100, 80], 2)
      ```

   b. ```
      def draw_x(screen, x, y):
          pygame.draw.line(screen, RED, [80+x, 80+y], [100, 100], 2)
          pygame.draw.line(screen, RED, [80+x, 100+y], [100, 80], 2)
      ```

   c. ```
      def draw_x(screen, x, y):
          pygame.draw.line(screen, RED, [x, y], [20+x, 20+y], 2)
          pygame.draw.line(screen, RED, [x, 20+y], [20+x, y], 2)
      ```

   d. ```
      def draw_x(screen, x, y):
          pygame.draw.line(screen, RED, [x, y], [20, 20], 2)
          pygame.draw.line(screen, RED, [x, 20+y], [20, 0], 2)
      ```

   e. ```
      def draw_x(screen, x, y):
          pygame.draw.line(screen, RED, [80+x, 80+y], [100+x, 100+y], 2)
          pygame.draw.line(screen, RED, [80+x, 100+y], [100+x, 80+y], 2)
      ```

3. code will get the x and y position of the mouse?

   a. ```
      pos = pygame.mouse.get_pos()
      x = pos[0]
      y = pos[1]
      ```

   b. ```
      pos = pygame.mouse.get_pos()
      x = pos[x]
      y = pos[y]
      ```

   c. ```
      pos = pygame.mouse.get_pos()
      x = pos(x)
      y = pos(y)
      ```
      ```

      d.   `x = pygame.mouse.get_pos(x)`
              `y = pygame.mouse.get_pos(y)`

      e.   `x = pygame.mouse.get_pos(0)`
              `y = pygame.mouse.get_pos(1)`

4.   In the keyboard example, if x_speed and y_speed were both set to 3, then:

    a.   The object would be set to location (3, 3).

    b.   The object would move down and to the right at 3 pixels per frame.

    c.   The object would move down and to the right at 3 pixels per second.

    d.   The object would move up and to the right at 3 pixels per second.

    e.   The object would move up and to the left 3 pixels per frame.

5.   The call axes = joystick.get_numaxes() will return how many axes for a game controller?

    a.   2

    b.   4

    c.   One for each analog joystick on the game controller.

    d.   Two for each analog joystick on the game controller.

    e.   One for each button on the game controller.

6.   Depending on the button state, what value will the variable button be assigned using this code?
    `button = joystick.get_button( 0 )`

    a.   0 or 1

    b.   On or Off

    c.   Up or Down

    d.   True or False

7.   What is the difference between a hat on a game controller and a joystick?

    a.   Nothing, they are just different names for the same thing.

    b.   A hat can be moved in small amounts; an analog joystick is all or nothing.

    c.   An analog joystick can be moved in small amounts; a hat is all or nothing.

8.   What axis values will be returned when the joystick is moved up and to the left?

    a.   (-1, -1)

    b.   (1, 1)

    c.   (0, 0)

9. What axis values will be returned when the joystick is centered?

    a. (-1, -1)

    b. (1, 1)

    c. (0, 0)

10. What code would move an object based on the position of the joystick on the game controller?

    a. ```
        horiz_axis_pos = my_joystick.get_axis(0)
        vert_axis_pos = my_joystick.get_axis(1)
        ```

    b.  ```
        x_coord = int(x_coord + horiz_axis_pos * 10)
        y_coord = int(y_coord + vert_axis_pos * 10)
        ```

    c. ```
        x_coord = my_joystick.get_axis(0)
        y_coord = my_joystick.get_axis(1)
        ```

    d.  ```
        x_coord = my_joystick.get_axis(0)*10
        y_coord = my_joystick.get_axis(1)*10
        ```

Short Answer Worksheet

1. What's wrong with this code that uses a function to draw a stick figure? Assume the colors are already defined and the rest of the program is OK. What is wrong with the code in the function?

    ```
    def draw_stick_figure(screen, x, y):
        # Head
        pygame.draw.ellipse(screen, BLACK, [96,83,10,10], 0)

        # Legs
        pygame.draw.line(screen, BLACK, [100,100], [105,110], 2)
        pygame.draw.line(screen, BLACK, [100,100], [95,110], 2)

        # Body
        pygame.draw.line(screen, RED, [100,100], [100,90], 2)

        # Arms
        pygame.draw.line(screen, RED, [100,90], [104,100], 2)
        pygame.draw.line(screen, RED, [100,90], [96,100], 2)
    ```

2. Show how to only grab the x coordinate of where the mouse is.

3. Why is it important to keep the event processing loop together and only have one of them? It is more than organization; there will be subtle hard-to-detect errors. What are they and why will they happen without the event processing loop together? (Review "The Event Processing Loop" in Chapter 5 if needed.)

4. When we created a bouncing rectangle, we multiplied the speed times -1 when the rectangle hit the edge of the screen. Explain why that technique won't work for moving an object with the keyboard.

5. Why does movement with the keyboard or game controller need to have a starting x, y location, but the mouse doesn't?

6. What values will a game controller return if it is held all the way down and to the right?

Exercise

Check the appendix for the exercise "Functions and User Control" that goes along with this chapter.

CHAPTER 12

■ ■ ■

Bitmapped Graphics and Sound

To move beyond the simplistic shapes offered by drawing circles and rectangles, our programs need the ability to work with *bitmapped graphics*. Bitmapped graphics can be photos or images created and saved from a drawing program.

But graphics aren't enough. Games need sound too! This chapter shows how to put graphics and sound in your game.

Storing the Program in a Folder

The programs we've made so far only involve one file. Now that we are including images and sounds, there are more files that are part of our program. It is easy to get these files mixed up with other programs we are making. The way to keep everything neat and separated out is to put each of these programs into its own folder. Before beginning any project like this, click the "new folder" button, and use that new folder as a spot to put all the new files as shown in the following figure.

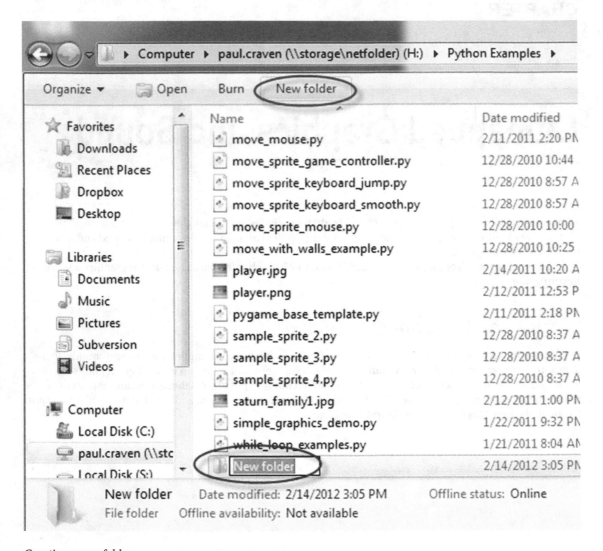

Creating a new folder

Setting a Background Image

Need to set a background image for your game? Find an image like what is seen in the figure below. If you are looking online in a web browser, you can usually right-click on an image and save it onto the computer. Save the image to the folder that we just created for our game.

Make sure you don't use copyrighted images! Using a reverse-image search will make it easy to double check that you did not copy it.

Background Image

Any bitmap images used in a game should already be sized for how it should appear on the screen. Don't take a 5000x5000 pixel image from a high-resolution camera and then try to load it into a window only 800x600. Use a graphics program (even MS Paint will work) and resize/crop the image before using it in your Python program.

Loading an image is a simple process and involves only one line of code. There is a lot going on in that one line of code, so the explanation of the line will be broken into three parts. The first version of the our load command will load a file called saturn_family1.jpg. This file must be located in the same directory that the Python program is in, or the computer will not find it:

```
pygame.image.load("saturn_family1.jpg")
```

That code may load the image, but we have no way to reference that image and display it! We need a variable set equal to what the load() command returns. In the next version of our load command, we create a new variable named background_image. See below for version two:

```
background_image = pygame.image.load("saturn_family1.jpg")
```

Finally, the image needs to be converted to a format that pygame can more easily work with. To do that, we append .convert() to the command to call the convert function. The function .convert() is a method in the Image class. We'll talk more about classes, objects, and methods in Chapter 13.

All images should be loaded using code similar to the line below. Just change the variable name and file name as needed.

```
background_image = pygame.image.load("saturn_family1.jpg").convert()
```

Loading the image should be done *before* the main program loop. While it would be possible to load it in the main program loop, this would cause the program to fetch the image from the disk 20 or so times per second. This is completely unnecessary. It is only necessary to do it once at program startup.

To display the image use the blit command. This blits the image bits to the screen. We've already used this command once before when displaying text onto a game window back in Chapter 6.

The blit command is a method in the screen variable, so we need to start our command by screen. blit. Next, we need to pass the image to blit and where to blit it. This command should be done *inside* the loop so the image gets drawn each frame. See below:

```
screen.blit(background_image, [0, 0])
```

This code blits the image held in background_image to the screen starting at (0, 0).

Moving an Image

Now we want to load an image and move it around the screen. We will start off with a simple orange space ship. You can get this and many other great assets from http://kenney.nl/. See the figure below. The image for the ship can be downloaded from the book's web site, or you can find a .gif or .png that you like with a white or black background. Don't use a .jpg.

Player image

To load the image we need the same type of command that we used with the background image. In this case, I'm assuming the file is saved as player.png.

```
player_image = pygame.image.load("player.png").convert()
```

Inside the main program loop, the mouse coordinates are retrieved, and passed to another blit function as the coordinates to draw the image:

```
# Get the current mouse position. This returns the position
# as a list of two numbers.
player_position = pygame.mouse.get_pos()
x = player_position[0]
y = player_position[1]

# Copy image to screen:
screen.blit(player_image, [x, y])
```

This demonstrates a problem. The image is a spaceship with a solid black background. So when the image is drawn the program shows the figure below.

The image's solid black bakground is obvious

We only want the spaceship, not a rectangular background! But all images we can load are rectangles, so how do we show only the part of the image we want? The way to get around this is to tell the program to make one color transparent and not display. This can be done immediately after loading. The following makes the color black (assuming BLACK is already defined as a variable) transparent:

```
player_image.set_colorkey(BLACK)
```

This will work for most files ending in .gif and .png. This does not work well for most .jpg files. The jpeg image format is great for holding photographs, but it does subtly change the image as part of the algorithm that makes the image smaller. Images in .gif and .png are also compressed, but the algorithms used in those formats do not change the image. The format .bmp isn't compressed at all, and it results in huge files. Because the .jpg format changes the format, this means that not all of the background color will be the exactly the same. In the next figure the spaceship has been saved as a jpeg with a white background. The white around the ship is not exactly (255, 255, 255), but just really close.

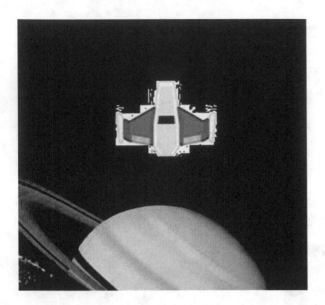

JPEG compression artifacts

If you are picking out an image that will be transparent, choose a .gif or .png. These are the best formats for graphic art type of images. Photos should be .jpg. Keep in mind it is not possible to change a .jpg to another format just by renaming the file extension to .png. It is still a .jpg even if you call it something different. It requires conversion in a graphics program to change it to a different format. But once in a .jpg format, it has been altered and converting it to a .png won't fix those alterations.

Here are three great places to find free images to use in your program:

```
http://kenney.nl; http://opengameart.org; and http://hasgraphics.com/
```

Sounds

In this section we'll play a laser sound when the mouse button is clicked. This sound originally came from Kenney.nl. You can download and save the sound here: ProgramArcadeGames.com/python_examples/en/laser5.ogg

Like images, sounds must be loaded before they are used. This should be done once sometime before the main program loop. The following command loads a sound file and creates a variable named click_sound to reference it:

```
click_sound = pygame.mixer.Sound("laser5.ogg")
```

We can play the sound by using the following command:

```
click_sound.play()
```

But where do we put this command? If we put it in the main program loop it will play it 20 times or so per second. Really annoying. We need a trigger. Some action occurs, then we play the sound. For example, this sound can be played when the user hits the mouse button with the following code:

```
for event in pygame.event.get():
    if event.type == pygame.QUIT:
        done = True
    elif event.type == pygame.MOUSEBUTTONDOWN:
        click_sound.play()
```

Uncompressed sound files usually end in .wav. These files are larger than other formats because no algorithm has been run on them to make them smaller. There is also the ever popular .mp3 format, although that format has patents that can make it undesirable for certain applications. Another format that is free to use is the OGG Vorbis format that ends in .ogg.

Pygame does not play all .wav files that can be found on the Internet. If you have a file that isn't working, you can try using the program http://sourceforge.net/projects/audacity to convert it to an ogg-vorbis type of sound file that ends in .ogg. This file format is small and reliable for use with pygame.

If you want background music to play in your program, then check out the online example section for:

ProgramArcadeGames.com/en/python_examples/f.php?file=background_music.py

Please note that you can't redistribute copyrighted music with your program. Even if you make a video of your program with copyrighted music in the background, YouTube and similar video sights will flag you for copyright violation.

Great places to find free sounds to use in your program:

OpenGameArt.org and www.freesound.org

Full Listing

```
"""
 Sample Python/Pygame Programs
 http://programarcadegames.com/

 Explanation video: http://youtu.be/4YqIKncMJNs
 Explanation video: http://youtu.be/ONAK8VZIcI4
 Explanation video: http://youtu.be/_6c4o41BIms
"""

import pygame

# Define some colors
WHITE = (255, 255, 255)
BLACK = (0, 0, 0)

# Call this function so the Pygame library can initialize itself
pygame.init()

# Create an 800x600 sized screen
screen = pygame.display.set_mode([800, 600])
```

```
# This sets the name of the window
pygame.display.set_caption('CMSC 150 is cool')

clock = pygame.time.Clock()

# Before the loop, load the sounds:
click_sound = pygame.mixer.Sound("laser5.ogg")

# Set positions of graphics
background_position = [0, 0]

# Load and set up graphics.
background_image = pygame.image.load("saturn_family1.jpg").convert()
player_image = pygame.image.load("playerShip1_orange.png").convert()
player_image.set_colorkey(BLACK)

done = False

while not done:
    for event in pygame.event.get():
        if event.type == pygame.QUIT:
            done = True
        elif event.type == pygame.MOUSEBUTTONDOWN:
            click_sound.play()

    # Copy image to screen:
    screen.blit(background_image, background_position)

    # Get the current mouse position. This returns the position
    # as a list of two numbers.
    player_position = pygame.mouse.get_pos()
    x = player_position[0]
    y = player_position[1]

    # Copy image to screen:
    screen.blit(player_image, [x, y])

    pygame.display.flip()

    clock.tick(60)

pygame.quit()
```

Review

Multiple Choice Quiz

1. Should the following line go inside, or outside of the main program loop?

    ```
    background_image = pygame.image.load("saturn_family1.jpg").convert()
    ```

    a. Outside the loop, because it isn't a good idea to load the image from the disk 20 times per second.

    b. Inside the loop, because the background image needs to be redrawn every frame.

2. In the following code, what does the [0, 0] do?

    ```
    screen.blit(background_image, [0, 0])
    ```

    a. Default dimensions of the bitmap.

    b. Specifies the x and y of the top left coordinate of where to start drawing the bitmap on the screen.

    c. Draw the bitmap in the center of the screen.

3. Should the following line go inside or outside of the main program loop?

    ```
    screen.blit(background_image, [0, 0])
    ```

    a. Outside the loop, because it isn't a good idea to load the image from the disk 20 times per second.

    b. Inside the loop, because the background image needs to be redrawn every frame.

4. Given this line of code, what code will get the x value of the current mouse position?

    ```
    player_position = pygame.mouse.get_pos()
    ```

    a. `x = player_position[x]`

    b. `x = player_position[0]`

    c. `x = player_position.x`

    d. `x[0] = player_position`

5. What types of image file formats are loss-less (i.e., they do not change the image)? Choose the best answer.

    a. `png, jpg, gif`

    b. `png, gif`

    c. `png`

    d. `jpg`

213

    e.   `gif`

    f.   `jpg, gif`

6. What does this code do?

```
player_image.set_colorkey(WHITE)
```

    a.   Makes the bitmap background white.

    b.   Sets all the white pixels to be transparent instead.

    c.   Sets the next color to be drawn to white.

    d.   Clears the screen to a white color.

    e.   Draws the player image in white.

7. What is wrong with section of code?

```
for event in pygame.event.get():
    if event.type == pygame.QUIT:
        done=True
    if event.type == pygame.MOUSEBUTTONDOWN:
        click_sound = pygame.mixer.Sound("click.wav")
        click_sound.play()
```

    a.   Pygame doesn't support .wav files.

    b.   The colorkey hasn't been set for click_sound yet.

    c.   Sounds should be loaded at the start of the program, not in the main program loop.

    d.   Sounds should not be played in a main program loop.

Short Answer Worksheet

1. This is about the time that many people learning to program run into problems with Windows hiding file extensions. Briefly explain how to make Windows show file extensions. If you don't remember, go back to Chapter 1 to see the details.

2. For the following file extensions:

- .jpg
- .wav
- .gif
- .png
- .ogg
- .bmp
- .mp3

...match the extension to the category it best fits:

- Photos

- Graphic art

- Uncompressed images

- Songs and sound effects

- Uncompressed sounds

3. Should an image be loaded inside the main program loop or before it? Should the program blit the image in the main program loop or before it?

4. How can a person change an image from one format to another? For example, how do you change a .jpg to a .gif? Why does changing the file extension not really work? (Ask if you can't figure it out.)

5. Explain why an image that was originally saved as a .jpg doesn't work with setting a background color even after it is converted to a .png.

6. Briefly explain how to play background music in a game and how to automatically start playing a new song when the current song ends.

Exercise

Check the appendix for the exercise "Bitmapped Graphics and User Control" that goes along with this chapter.

■ ■ ■

Introduction to Classes

Classes and objects are very powerful programming tools. They make programming easier. In fact, you are already familiar with the concept of classes and objects. A class is a classification of an object. Like person or image. An object is a particular instance of a class. Like Mary is an instance of Person.

Objects have attributes, such as a person's name, height, and age. Objects also have methods. Methods define what an object can do: like run, jump, or sit.

Why Learn About Classes?

Each character in an adventure game needs data: a name, location, strength; are they raising their arm; what direction they are headed; etc. Plus those characters *do* things. They run, jump, hit, and talk.

Without classes, our Python code to store this data might look like:

```
name = "Link"
sex = "Male"
max_hit_points = 50
current_hit_points = 50
```

In order to do anything with this character, we'll need to pass that data to a function:

```
def display_character(name, sex, max_hit_points, current_hit_points):
    print(name, sex, max_hit_points, current_hit_points)
```

Now imagine creating a program that has a set of variables like that for each character, monster, and item in our game. Then we need to create functions that work with those items. We've now waded into a quagmire of data. All of a sudden this doesn't sound like fun at all.

But wait, it gets worse! As our game expands, we may need to add new fields to describe our character. In this case we've added max_speed:

```
name = "Link"
sex = "Male"
max_hit_points = 50
current_hit_points = 50
max_speed = 10
```

```
def display_character(name, sex, max_hit_points, current_hit_points, max_speed):
    print(name, sex, max_hit_points, current_hit_points)
```

In example above, there is only one function. But in a large video game, we might have hundreds of functions that deal with the main character. Adding a new field to help describe what a character has and can do would require us to go through each one of those functions and add it to the parameter list. That would be a *lot* of work. And perhaps we need to add max_speed to different types of characters such as monsters. There needs to be a better way. Somehow our program needs to package up those data fields so they can be managed easily.

Defining and Creating Simple Classes

A better way to manage multiple data attributes is to *define* a structure that has all of the information. Then we can give that grouping of information a name, like *Character* or *Address*. This can be easily done in Python and any other modern language by using a *class*.

For example, we can *define* a class representing a character in a game:

```
class Character():
    """ This is a class that represents the main character in a game. """
    def __init__(self):
        """ This is a method that sets up the variables in the object. """
        self.name = "Link"
        self.sex = "Male"
        self.max_hit_points = 50
        self.current_hit_points = 50
        self.max_speed = 10
        self.armor_amount = 8
```

Here's another example; we *define* a class to hold all the fields for an address:

```
class Address():
    """ Hold all the fields for a mailing address. """
    def __init__(self):
        """ Set up the address fields. """
        self.name = ""
        self.line1 = ""
        self.line2 = ""
        self.city = ""
        self.state = ""
        self.zip = ""
```

In the code above, Address is the *class name*. The variables in the class, such as name and city, are called *attributes* or *fields*. (Note the similarities and differences between declaring a class and declaring a function.)

Unlike functions and variables, class names should begin with an uppercase letter. While it is possible to begin a class with a lowercase letter, it is not considered good practice.

The def __init__(self): in a special function called a *constructor* that is run automatically when the class is created. We'll discuss the constructor more in a bit.

The self. is kind of like the pronoun *my*. When inside the class Address we are talking about *my* name, *my* city, etc. We don't want to use self. outside of the class definition for Address, to refer to an Address field. Why? Because just like the pronoun "my," it means someone totally different when said by a different person!

To better visualize classes and how they relate, programmers often make diagrams. A diagram for the Address class would look like the next figure. See how the class name is on top with the name of each attribute listed below. To the right of each attribute is the data type, such as string or integer.

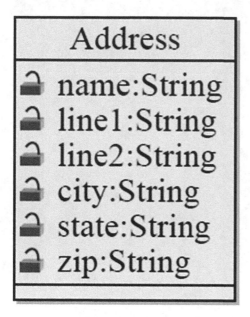

Class Diagram

The class code *defines* a class but it does not actually create an *instance* of one. The code told the computer what fields an address has and what the initial default values will be. We don't actually have an address yet though. We can define a class without creating one just like we can define a function without calling it. To create a class and set the fields, look at the example below:

```
# Create an address
home_address = Address()

# Set the fields in the address
home_address.name = "John Smith"
home_address.line1 = "701 N. C Street"
home_address.line2 = "Carver Science Building"
home_address.city = "Indianola"
home_address.state = "IA"
home_address.zip = "50125"
```

An instance of the address class is created in line 2 with Address(). Note how the class Address name is used, followed by parentheses. The variable name can be anything that follows normal naming rules.

To set the fields in the class, a program must use the *dot operator*. This operator is the period that is between the home_address and the field name. See how the last 6 lines use the dot operator to set each field value.

A very common mistake when working with classes is to forget to specify which instance of the class you want to work with. If only one address is created, it is natural to assume the computer will know to use that address you are talking about. This is not the case, however. See the example below:

```
class Address():
    def __init__(self):
        self.name = ""
        self.line1 = ""
        self.line2 = ""
        self.city = ""
        self.state = ""
        self.zip = ""

# Create an address
my_address = Address()

# Alert! This does not set the address's name!
name = "Dr. Craven"

# This doesn't set the name for the address either
Address.name = "Dr. Craven"

# This does work:
my_address.name = "Dr. Craven"
```

A second address can be created and fields from both instances may be used. See the example below (line numbers added for readability):

```
001 class Address():
002     def __init__(self):
003         self.name = ""
004         self.line1 = ""
005         self.line2 = ""
006         self.city = ""
007         self.state = ""
008         self.zip = ""
009
010 # Create an address
011 home_address = Address()
012
013 # Set the fields in the address
014 home_address.name = "John Smith"
```

```
015 home_address.line1 = "701 N. C Street"
016 home_address.line2 = "Carver Science Building"
017 home_address.city = "Indianola"
018 home_address.state = "IA"
019 home_address.zip = "50125"
020
021 # Create another address
022 vacation_home_address = Address()
023
024 # Set the fields in the address
025 vacation_home_address.name = "John Smith"
026 vacation_home_address.line1 = "1122 Main Street"
027 vacation_home_address.line2 = ""
028 vacation_home_address.city = "Panama City Beach"
029 vacation_home_address.state = "FL"
030 vacation_home_address.zip = "32407"
031
032 print("The client's main home is in " + home_address.city)
033 print("His vacation home is in " + vacation_home_address.city)
```

Line 11 creates the first instance of Address; line 22 creates the second instance. The variable home_address points to the first instance and vacation_home_address points to the second.

Lines 25–30 set the fields in this new class instance. Line 32 prints the city for the home address, because home_address appears before the dot operator. Line 33 prints the vacation address because vacation_home_address appears before the dot operator.

In the example Address is called the *class* because it defines a new classification for a data object. The variables home_address and vacation_home_address refer to *objects* because they refer to actual instances of the class Address. A simple definition of an object is that it is an instance of a class. Like Bob and Nancy are instances of a Human class.

By using www.pythontutor.com we can visualize the execution of the code (see below). There are three variables in play. One points to the class definition of Address. The other two variables point to the different address objects and their data.

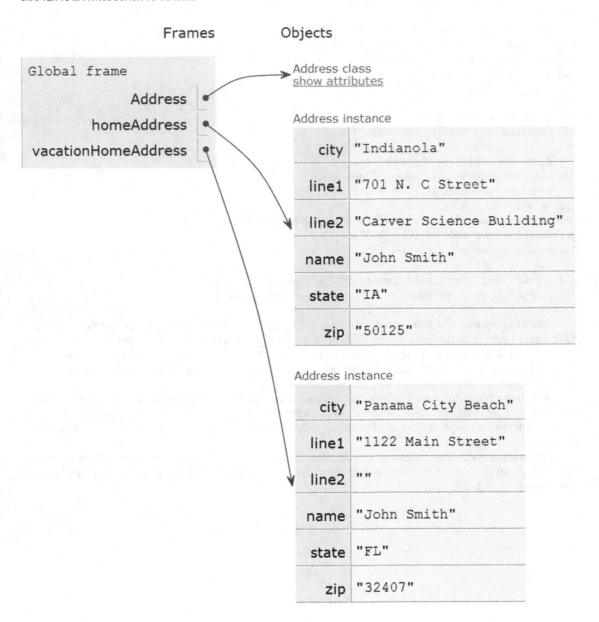

Two Addresses

Putting lots of data fields into a class makes it easy to pass data in and out of a function. In the code below, the function takes in an address as a parameter and prints it out on the screen. It is not necessary to pass parameters for each field of the address.

```
# Print an address to the screen
def print_address(address):
    print(address.name)
    # If there is a line1 in the address, print it
    if len(address.line1) > 0:
        print(address.line1)
    # If there is a line2 in the address, print it
    if len(address.line2) > 0:
        print( address.line2 )
    print(address.city + ", " + address.state + " " + address.zip)

print_address(home_address)
print()
print_address(vacation_home_address)
```

Adding Methods to Classes

In addition to attributes, classes may have *methods*. A method is a function that exists inside of a class. Expanding the earlier example of a Dog class from the review problem 1 above, the code below adds a method for a dog barking.

```
class Dog():
    def __init__(self):
        self.age = 0
        self.name = ""
        self.weight = 0

    def bark(self):
        print("Woof")
```

The method definition is contained in lines 7–8 above. Method definitions in a class look almost exactly like function definitions. The big difference is the addition of a parameter self on line 7. The first parameter of any method in a class must be self. This parameter is required even if the function does not use it.

Here are the important items to keep in mind when creating methods for classes:

- Attributes should be listed first, methods after.

- The first parameter of any method must be self.

- Method definitions are indented exactly one tab stop.

Methods may be called in a manner similar to referencing attributes from an object. See the example code below.

```
001 my_dog = Dog()
002
003 my_dog.name = "Spot"
004 my_dog.weight = 20
005 my_dog.age = 3
006
007 my_dog.bark()
```

Line 1 creates the dog. Lines 3–5 set the attributes of the object. Line 7 calls the bark function. Note that even through the bark function has one parameter, self, the call does not pass in anything. This is because the first parameter is assumed to be a reference to the dog object itself. Behind the scenes, Python makes a call that looks like:

```
# Example, not actually legal
Dog.bark(my_dog)
```

If the bark function needs to make reference to any of the attributes, then it does so using the self reference variable. For example, we can change the Dog class so that when the dog barks, it also prints out the dog's name. In the code below, the name attribute is accessed using a dot operator and the self reference.

```
def bark(self):
    print("Woof says", self.name)
```

Attributes are adjectives, and methods are verbs. The drawing for the class would look like the next figure.

Dog Class

Example: Ball Class

This example code could be used in Python/pygame to draw a ball. Having all the parameters contained in a class makes data management easier. The diagram for the Ball class is shown in the next figure.

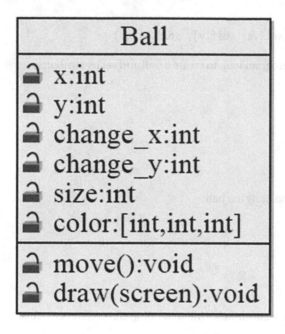

Ball Class

```
class Ball():
    def __init__(self):
        # --- Class Attributes ---
        # Ball position
        self.x = 0
        self.y = 0

        # Ball's vector
        self.change_x = 0
        self.change_y = 0

        # Ball size
        self.size = 10

        # Ball color
        self.color = [255,255,255]
```

```
        # --- Class Methods ---
    def move(self):
        self.x += self.change_x
        self.y += self.change_y

    def draw(self, screen):
        pygame.draw.circle(screen, self.color, [self.x, self.y], self.size )
```

Below is the code that would go ahead of the main program loop to create a ball and set its attributes:

```
theBall = Ball()
theBall.x = 100
theBall.y = 100
theBall.change_x = 2
theBall.change_y = 1
theBall.color = [255,0,0]
```

This code would go inside the main loop to move and draw the ball:

```
theBall.move()
theBall.draw(screen)
```

References

Here's where we separate the true programmers from the want-to-be's. Understanding class references. Take a look at the following code:

```
class Person():
    def __init__(self):
        self.name = ""
        self.money = 0

bob = Person()
bob.name = "Bob"
bob.money = 100

nancy = Person()
nancy.name = "Nancy"

print(bob.name, "has", bob.money, "dollars.")
print(nancy.name, "has", nancy.money, "dollars.")
```

The code above creates two instances of the Person() class, and using www.pythontutor.com we can visualize the two classes in the next figure.

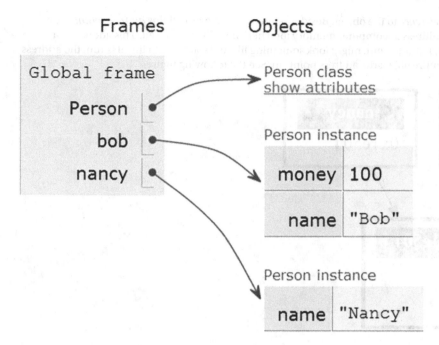

Two Persons

The code above has nothing new. But the code below does:

```python
class Person():
    def __init__(self):
        self.name = ""
        self.money = 0

bob = Person()
bob.name = "Bob"
bob.money = 100

nancy = bob
nancy.name = "Nancy"

print(bob.name, "has", bob.money, "dollars.")
print(nancy.name, "has", nancy.money, "dollars.")
```

See the difference on line 10 with nancy = bob?

A common misconception when working with objects is to assume that the variable bob *is* the Person object. This is not the case. The variable bob is a *reference* to the Person object. That is, it stores the memory address of where the object is and not the object itself.

If bob actually was the object, then line 9 could create a *copy* of the object and there would be two objects in existence. The output of the program would show both Bob and Nancy having 100 dollars. But when run, the program outputs the following instead:

```
Nancy has 100 dollars.
Nancy has 100 dollars.
```

What bob stores is a *reference* to the object. Besides reference, one may call this *address*, *pointer*, or *handle*. A reference is an address in computer memory for where the object is stored. This address is a hexadecimal number that, if printed out, might look something like 0x1e504. When line 9 is run, the address is copied rather than the entire object the address points to. See the following figure.

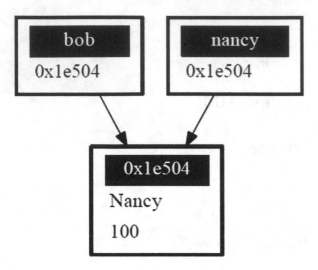

Class References

We can also run this in www.pythontutor.com to see how both of the variables are pointing to the same object.

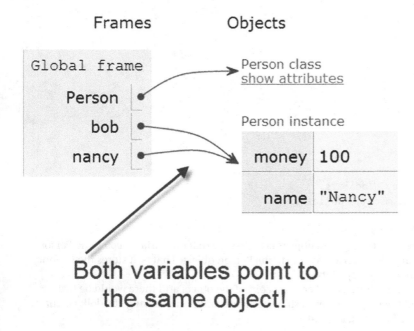

One Person, Two Pointers

Functions and References

Look at the code example below. Line 1 creates a function that takes in a number as a parameter. The variable money is a variable that contains a copy of the data that was passed in. Adding 100 to that number does not change the number that was stored in bob.money on line 11. Thus, the print statement on line 14 prints out 100 and not 200.

```python
def give_money1(money):
    money += 100

class Person():
    def __init__(self):
        self.name = ""
        self.money = 0

bob = Person()
bob.name = "Bob"
bob.money = 100

give_money1(bob.money)
print(bob.money)
```

Running on http://www.pythontutor.com/visualize.html#mode=display, we see that there are two instances of the money variable. One is a copy and local to the give_money1 function.

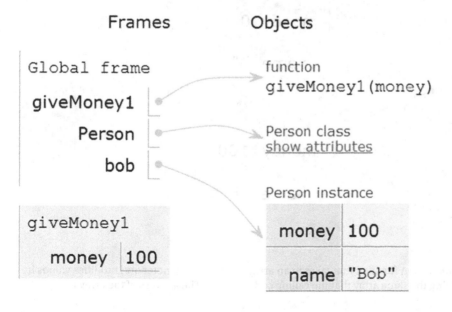

Function References

Look at the additional code below. This code does cause bob.money to increase and the print statement to print 200.

```
def give_money2(person):
    person.money += 100

give_money2(bob)
print(bob.money)
```

Why is this? Because person contains a copy of the memory address of the object, not the actual object itself. One can think of it as a bank account number. The function has a copy of the bank account number, not a copy of the whole bank account. So using the copy of the bank account number to deposit 100 dollars causes Bob's bank account balance to go up.

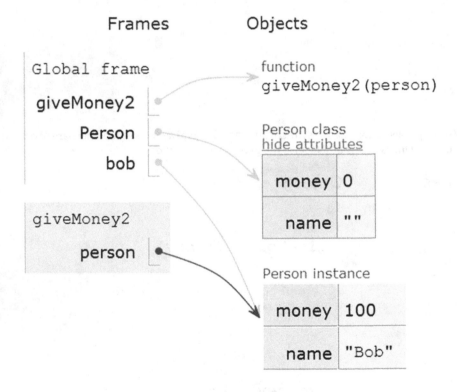

Function References

Arrays work the same way. A function that takes in an array (list) as a parameter and modifies values in that array will be modifying the same array that the calling code created. The address of the array is copied, not the entire array.

Review Questions

1. Create a class called `Cat`. Give it attributes for name, color, and weight. Give it a method called `meow`.

2. Create an instance of the cat class, set the attributes, and call the meow method.

3. Create a class called `Monster`. Give it an attribute for name and an integer attribute for health. Create a method called `decrease_health` that takes in a parameter `amount` and decreases the health by that much. Inside that method, print that the animal died if its health goes below zero.

Constructors

There's a terrible problem with our class for Dog listed below. When we create a dog, by default the dog has no name. Dogs should have names! We should not allow dogs to be born and then never be given a name. Yet the code below allows this to happen, and that dog will never have a name.

```
class Dog()
    def __init__(self):
        self.name = ""

my_dog = Dog()
```

Python doesn't want this to happen. That's why Python classes have a special function that is called any time an instance of that class is created. By adding a function called a *constructor*, a programmer can add code that is automatically run each time an instance of the class is created. See the example constructor code below:

```
class Dog():
    def __init__(self):
        """ Constructor. Called when creating an object of this type. """
        self.name = ""
        print("A new dog is born!")

# This creates the dog
my_dog = Dog()
```

The constructor starts on line 2. It must be named `__init__`. There are two underscores before the `init` and two underscores after. A common mistake is to only use one.

The constructor must take in `self` as the first parameter just like other methods in a class. When the program is run, it will print:

```
A new dog is born!
```

When a Dog object is created on line 8, the `__init__` function is automatically called and the message is printed to the screen.

Avoid This Mistake

Put everything for a method into just one definition. Don't define it twice. For example:

```
# Wrong:
class Dog():
    def __init__(self):
        self.age = 0
        self.name = ""
        self.weight = 0

    def __init__(self):
        print("New dog!")
```

The computer will just ignore the first __init__ and go with the last definition. Instead do this:

```
# Correct:
class Dog():
    def __init__(self):
        self.age = 0
        self.name = ""
        self.weight = 0
        print("New dog!")
```

A constructor can be used for initializing and setting data for the object. The example Dog class above still allows the name attribute to be left blank after the creation of the dog object. How do we keep this from happening? Many objects need to have values right when they are created. The constructor function can be used to make this happen. See the code below:

```
001 class Dog():
002
003     def __init__(self, new_name):
004         """ Constructor. """
005         self.name = new_name
006
007 # This creates the dog
008 my_dog = Dog("Spot")
009
010 # Print the name to verify it was set
011 print(my_dog.name)
012
013 # This line will give an error because
014 # a name is not passed in.
015 herDog = Dog()
```

On line 3 the constructor function now has an additional parameter named new_name. The value of this parameter is used to set the name attribute in the Dog class on line 8. It is no longer possible to create a Dog class without a name. The code on line 15 tries this. It will cause a Python error and it will not run. A common mistake is to name the parameter of the __init__ function the same as the attribute and assume that the values will automatically synchronize. This does not happen.

Review Questions

1. Should class names begin with an upper or lowercase letter?

2. Should method names begin with an upper or lowercase letter?

3. Should attribute names begin with an upper or lowercase letter?

4. Which should be listed first in a class, attributes or methods?

5. What are other names for a reference?

6. What is another name for an instance variable?

7. What is the name for an instance of a class?

8. Create a class called Star that will print out "A star is born!" every time it is created.

9. Create a class called Monster with attributes for health and a name. Add a constructor to the class that sets the health and name of the object with data passed in as parameters.

Inheritance

Another powerful feature of using classes and objects is the ability to make use of *inheritance*. It is possible to create a class and inherit all of the attributes and methods of a *parent class*.

For example, a program may create a class called Boat that has all the attributes needed to represent a boat in a game:

```
class Boat():
    def __init__(self):
        self.tonnage = 0
        self.name = ""
        self.isDocked = True

    def dock(self):
        if self.isDocked:
            print("You are already docked.")
        else:
            self.isDocked = True
            print("Docking")

    def undock(self):
        if not self.isDocked:
            print("You aren't docked.")
        else:
            self.isDocked = False
            print("Undocking")
```

To test out our code:

```
b = Boat()

b.dock()
b.undock()
b.undock()
b.dock()
b.dock()
```

The outputs:

```
You are already docked.
Undocking
You aren't docked.
Docking
You are already docked.
```

Our program also needs a submarine. Our submarine can do everything a boat can, plus we need a command for submerge. Without inheritance we have two options.

- One, add the submerge() command to our boat. This isn't a great idea because we don't want to give the impression that our boats normally submerge.

- Two, we could create a copy of the Boat class and call it Submarine. In this class we'd add the submerge() command. This is easy at first, but things become harder if we change the Boat class. A programmer would need to remember that we'd need to change not only the Boat class but also make the same changes to the Submarine class. Keeping this code synchronized is time consuming and error prone.

Luckily, there is a better way. Our program can create *child classes* that will inherit all the attributes and methods of the *parent class*. The child classes may then add fields and methods that correspond to their needs. For example:

```
class Submarine(Boat):
    def submerge(self):
        print("Submerge!")
```

Line 1 is the important part. Just by putting Boat in between the parentheses during the class declaration, we have automatically picked up every attribute and method that is in the Boat class. If we update Boat, then the child class Submarine will automatically get these updates. Inheritance is that easy!

The next code example is diagrammed out in the figure below.

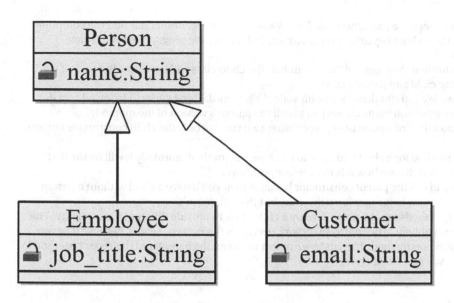

Class Diagram

```
001 class Person():
002     def __init__(self):
003         self.name = ""
004
005 class Employee(Person):
006     def __init__(self):
007         # Call the parent/super class constructor first
008         super().__init__()
009
010         # Now set up our variables
011         self.job_title = ""
012
013 class Customer(Person):
014     def __init__(self):
015         super().__init__()
016         self.email = ""
017
018 john_smith = Person()
019 john_smith.name = "John Smith"
020
021 jane_employee = Employee()
022 jane_employee.name = "Jane Employee"
023 jane_employee.job_title = "Web Developer"
024
025 bob_customer = Customer()
026 bob_customer.name = "Bob Customer"
027 bob_customer.email = "send_me@spam.com"
```

By placing Person between the parentheses on lines 5 and 13, the programmer has told the computer that Person is a parent class to both Employee and Customer. This allows the program to set the name attribute on lines 19 and 22.

Methods are also inherited. Any method the parent has, the child class will have, too. But what if we have a method in both the child and parent class?

We have two options. We can run them both with super() keyword. Using super() followed by a dot operator, and then finally a method name allows you to call the parent's version of the method.

The code above shows the first option using super where we run not only the child constructor but also the parent constructor.

If you are writing a method for a child and want to call a parent method, normally it will be the first statement in the child method. Notice how it is in the example above.

All constructors should call the parent constructor because then you'd have a child without a parent and that is just sad. In fact, some languages force this rule, but Python doesn't.

The second option? Methods may be *overridden* by a child class to provide different functionality. The example below shows both options. The Employee.report overrides the Person.report because it never calls and runs the parent report method. The Customer report does call the parent and the report method in Customer adds to the Person functionality.

```python
class Person():
    def __init__(self):
        self.name = ""

    def report(self):
        # Basic report
        print("Report for", self.name)

class Employee(Person):
    def __init__(self):
        # Call the parent/super class constructor first
        super().__init__()

        # Now set up our variables
        self.job_title = ""

    def report(self):
        # Here we override report and just do this:
        print("Employee report for", self.name)

class Customer(Person):
    def __init__(self):
        super().__init__()
        self.email = ""

    def report(self):
        # Run the parent report:
        super().report()
        # Now add our own stuff to the end so we do both
        print("Customer e-mail:", self.email)
```

```
john_smith = Person()
john_smith.name = "John Smith"

jane_employee = Employee()
jane_employee.name = "Jane Employee"
jane_employee.job_title = "Web Developer"

bob_customer = Customer()
bob_customer.name = "Bob Customer"
bob_customer.email = "send_me@spam.com"

john_smith.report()
jane_employee.report()
bob_customer.report()
```

Is-A and Has-A Relationships

Classes have two main types of relationships. They are "is a" and "has a" relationships.

A parent class should always be a more general, abstract version of the child class. This type of child to parent relationship is called an *is a* relationship. For example, a parent class Animal could have a child class Dog. The Dog class could have a child class Poodle. Another example, a dolphin *is a* mammal. It does not work the other way: a mammal is not necessarily a dolphin. So the class Dolphin should never be a parent to a class Mammal. Likewise a class Table should not be a parent to a class Chair because a chair is not a table.

The other type of relationship is the *has a* relationship. These relationships are implemented in code by class attributes. A dog has a name, and so the Dog class has an attribute for name. Likewise a person could have a dog, and that would be implemented by having the Person class have an attribute for Dog. The Person class would not derive from Dog because that would be some kind of insult.

Looking at the prior code example we can see:

- Employee is a person.

- Customer is a person.

- Person has a name.

- Employee has a job title.

- Customer has an e-mail.

Static Variables vs. Instance Variables

The difference between static and instance variables is confusing. Thankfully it isn't necessary to completely understand the difference right now. But if you stick with programming, it will be. Therefore we will briefly introduce it here.

There are also some oddities with Python that kept *me* confused the first several years I've made this book available. So you might see older videos and examples where I get it wrong.

An *instance variable* is the type of class variable we've used so far. Each instance of the class gets its own value. For example, in a room full of people each person will have their own age. Some of the ages may be the same, but we still need to track each age individually.

With instance variables, we can't just say "age" with a room full of people. We need to specify *whose* age we are talking about. Also, if there are no people in the room, then referring to an age when there are no people to have an age makes no sense.

With *static variables* the value is the same for every single instance of the class. Even if there are no instances, there still is a value for a static variable. For example, we might have a count static variable for the number of Human classes in existence. No humans? The value is zero, but it still exists.

In the example below, ClassA creates an instance variable. ClassB creates a static variable.

```
001 # Example of an instance variable
002 class ClassA():
003     def __init__(self):
004         self.y = 3
005
006 # Example of a static variable
007 class ClassB():
008     x = 7
009
010 # Create class instances
011 a = ClassA()
012 b = ClassB()
013
014 # Two ways to print the static variable.
015 # The second way is the proper way to do it.
016 print(b.x)
017 print(ClassB.x)
018
019 # One way to print an instance variable.
020 # The second generates an error, because we don't know what instance
021 # to reference.
022 print(a.y)
023 print(ClassA.y)
```

In the example above, lines 16 and 17 print out the static variable. Line 17 is the proper way to do so. Unlike before, we can refer to the class name when using static variables, rather than a variable that points to a particular instance. Because we are working with the class name, by looking at line 17 we instantly can tell we are working with a static variable. Line 16 could be either an instance or static variable. That confusion makes line 17 the better choice.

Line 22 prints out the instance variable, just like we've done in prior examples. Line 23 will generate an error because each instance of y is different (it is an instance variable after all), and we aren't telling the computer what instance of ClassA we are talking about.

Instance Variables Hiding Static Variables

This is one feature of Python I dislike. It is possible to have a static variable and an instance variable *with the same name*. Look at the example below:

```
# Class with a static variable
class ClassB():
    x = 7

# Create a class instance
b = ClassB()

# This prints 7
print(b.x)

# This also prints 7
print(ClassB.x)

# Set x to a new value using the class name
ClassB.x = 8

# This also prints 8
print(b.x)

# This prints 8
print(ClassB.x)

# Set x to a new value using the instance.
# Wait! Actually, it doesn't set x to a new value!
# It creates a brand new variable, x. This x
# is an instance variable. The static variable is
# also called x. But they are two different
# variables. This is super-confusing and is bad
# practice.
b.x = 9

# This prints 9
print(b.x)

# This prints 8. NOT 9!!!
print(ClassB.x)
```

Allowing instance variables to hide static variables caused confusion for me for many years!

Review

Multiple Choice Quiz

1. Select the best class definition for an alien:

   a. ```
      class Alien():
          def __init__(self):
              self.name = ""
              self.height = 7.2
              self.weight = 156
      ```

   b. ```
      class alien():
          def __init__(self):
              self.name = ""
              self.height = 7.2
              self.weight = 156
      ```

   c. ```
      class alien.name = ""
      class alien.height = 7.2
      class alien.weight = 156
      ```

   d. ```
      class alien(
          def __init__(self):
              self.name = ""
              self.height = 7.2
              self.weight = 156
      )
      ```

2. What does this code do?

   ```
   d1 = Dog()
   d2 = Dog()
   ```

   a. Creates two objects, of type `Dog`.

   b. Creates two classes, of type `Dog`.

   c. Creates one object, of type `Dog`.

3. What does this code do?

   ```
   d1 = Dog()
   d2 = d1
   ```

   a. Creates two objects, of type `Dog`.

   b. Creates two classes, of type `Dog`.

   c. Creates one object, of type `Dog`.

4. What is wrong with the following code:

```
class Book():
    def open(self):
        print("You opened the book")

    def __init__(self):
        self.pages = 347
```

a. There should be a self. in front of pages.

b. Book should not be capitalized.

c. The __init__ with attributes should be listed first.

d. open should be capitalized.

5. What is wrong with the following code:

```
class Ball():
    def __init__(self):
        self.x = 0
        self.y = 0
        self.change_x = 0
        self.change_y = 0

    x += change_x
    y += change_y
```

a. The ball should not be at location 0, 0

b. The variables should be set equal to "".

c. The code to add to x and y must be in a method.

d. The code to set the variables to zero should be inside a method.

e. All classes must have at least one method

f. self should be in between the parentheses.

6. What is wrong with the following code:

```
class Ball():
    def __init__(self):
        self.x = 0
        self.y = 0

Ball.x = 50
Ball.y = 100
```

a. Lines 3 and 4 should not have self. in front.

b. Ball. does not refer to an instance of the class.

c. Lines 3 and 5 should be used to set x and y to 50 and 100.

d. Ball. on lines 6 and 7 should be lowercase.

241

7. What is wrong with the following code:

```
class Ball():
    def __init__(self):
        self.x = 0
        self.y = 0

        b = Ball()
        b.x = 50
        b.y = 100
```

a. Lines 6–8 should be in a method.

b. Lines 6–8 should not be indented.

c. Lines 7 and 8 should have self. instead of b.

d. Line 6 should have self in between the parentheses.

8. What will this print?

```
class Ball():
    def __init__(self):
        self.x = 0
        self.y = 0

b1 = Ball()
b2 = b1

b1.x = 40
b2.x = 50
b1.x += 5
b2.x += 5
print(b1.x, b2.x)
```

a. 40 40

b. 60 60

c. 45 55

d. 55 55

e. 40 50

9. What will this print?

```
class Account():
    def __init__(self):
        self.money = 0

    def deposit(self, amount):
        self.money += amount

account = Account()
money = 100
account.deposit(50)
print(money, account.money)
```

   a. 150 150

   b. 100 50

   c. 100 100

   d. 50 100

   e. 50 50

   f. 100 150

10. What is wrong with the following:

```
class Dog():
    def __init__(self, new_name):
        """ Constructor.
        Called when creating an object of this type """

        name = new_name
        print("A new dog is born!")

# This creates the dog
my_dog = Dog("Rover")
```

   a. On line 6, there should be a self. in front of new_name

   b. On line 6, there should be a self. in front of name

   c. Line 10 has 1 parameter, yet in line 2 we can see __init__ takes two parameters.

   d. Lines 9 and 10 should be indented.

   e. Lines 6 to 7 should not be indented.

Short Answer Worksheet

Section 1:

1. What is the difference between a class and an object?

2. What is the difference between a function and a method?

3. Write code to create an instance of this class and set its attributes:

```
class Dog():
    def __init__(self):
        self.age = 0
        self.name = ""
        self.weight = 0
```

4. Write code to create *two different* instances of this class and set attributes for both objects:

```
class Person():
    def __init__(self):
        self.name = ""
        self.cell_phone = ""
        self.email = ""
```

5. For the code below, write a class that has the appropriate class name and attributes that will allow the code to work.

```
my_bird = Bird()
my_bird.color = "green"
my_bird.name = "Sunny"
my_bird.breed = "Sun Conure"
```

6. Define a class that would represent a character in a simple 2D game. Include attributes for the position, name, and strength.

7. The following code runs, but it is not correct. What did the programmer do wrong?

```
class Person():
    def __init__(self):
        self.name = ""
        self.money = 0

nancy = Person()
name = "Nancy"
money = 100
```

8. Take a look at the code. It does not run. What is the error that prevents it from running?

```
class Person():
    def __init__(self):
        self.name = ""
        self.money = 0

bob = Person()
print(bob.name, "has", money, "dollars.")
```

9. Even with that error fixed, the program will not print out:

   Bob has 0 dollars.

   Instead it just prints out:

   has 0 dollars.

   Why is this the case?

10. Take pairs of the following items, and list some of the "has-a" relationships, and the "is-a" relationships between them.

   - Checking account
   - Person
   - Mortgage account
   - Customer
   - Withdraw
   - Bank Account
   - SSN
   - Transaction
   - Address
   - Deposit

11. In Python, how is an "is-a" relationship implemented? Give an example.

12. In Python, how is a "has-a" relationship implemented? Give an example.

13. How does this change if an object is allowed more than one item of a given type? (Ask if you aren't sure.)

Section 2:

To answer the next four questions, create one program. In that program will be the answers for all four questions. Make sure the program runs, and then copy/paste from the program to answer each of the questions below.

You should have a program that starts with three class definitions, one each for the first three questions. Then you should have code that will create instances of each class, and that will be the answer to the last problem.

1. Write code that defines a class named `Animal`:

   - Add an attribute for the animal name.

   - Add an `eat()` method for `Animal` that prints "Munch munch."

   - A `make_noise()` method for `Animal` that prints "Grrr says [animal name]."

   - Add a constructor for the `Animal` class that prints "An animal has been born."

2. A class named `Cat`:

   - Make `Animal` the parent.

   - A `make_noise()` method for `Cat` that prints "Meow says [animal name]."

   - A constructor for `Cat` that prints "A cat has been born."

   - Modify the constructor so it calls the parent constructor as well.

3. A class named `Dog`:

   - Make `Animal` the parent.

   - A `make_noise()` method for `Dog` that prints "Bark says [animal name]."

   - A constructor for `Dog` that prints "A dog has been born."

   - Modify the constructor so it calls the parent constructor as well.

4. A main program with:

   - Code that creates a cat, two dogs, and an animal.

   - Sets the name for each animal.

   - Code that calls `eat()` and `make_noise()` for each animal. (Don't forget this!)

Exercise

Check the appendix for the exercise "Classes and Graphics" that goes along with this chapter.

CHAPTER 14

■ ■ ■

Introduction to Sprites

Our games need support for handling objects that collide. Balls bouncing off paddles, laser beams hitting aliens, or our favorite character collecting a coin. All these examples require collision detection.

The pygame library has support for *sprites*. A sprite is a two-dimensional image that is part of the larger graphical scene. Typically a sprite will be some kind of object in the scene that will be interacted with like a car, frog, or little plumber guy.

Originally, video game consoles had built-in hardware support for sprites. Now this specialized hardware support is no longer needed, but we still use the term sprite.

Basic Sprites and Collisions

Let's step through an example program that uses sprites. This example shows how to create a screen of black blocks and collect them using a red block controlled by the mouse as shown in the figure below. The program keeps score on how many blocks have been collected. The code for this example may be found at:

ProgramArcadeGames.com/python_examples/f.php?file=sprite_collect_blocks.py

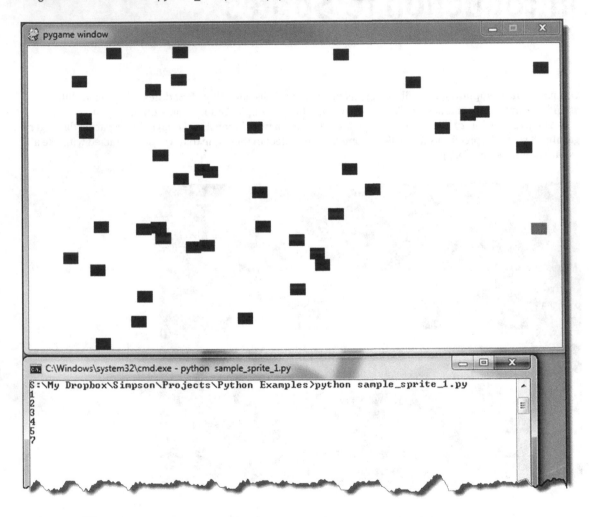

Example Sprite Game

The first few lines of our program start off like other games we've done (line numbers added for clarity):

```
001 import pygame
002 import random
003
004 # Define some colors
```

```
005 BLACK = (  0,   0,   0)
006 WHITE = (255, 255, 255)
007 RED   = (255,   0,   0)
```

The pygame library is imported for sprite support on line 1. The random library is imported for the random placement of blocks on line 2. The definition of colors is standard in lines 5–7; there is nothing new in this example yet.

```
009 class Block(pygame.sprite.Sprite):
010     """
011     This class represents the ball.
012     It derives from the "Sprite" class in pygame.
013     """
```

Line 9 starts the definition of the Block class. Note that on line 9 this class is a child class of the Sprite class. The pygame.sprite. specifies the library and package, which will be discussed later in Chapter 15. All the default functionality of the Sprite class will now be a part of the Block class.

```
015     def __init__(self, color, width, height):
016         """ Constructor. Pass in the color of the block,
017         and its x and y position. """
018
019         # Call the parent class (Sprite) constructor
020         super().__init__()
```

The constructor for the Block class on line 15 takes in a parameter for self just like any other constructor. It also takes in parameters that define the object's color, height, and width.

It is important to call the parent class constructor in Sprite to allow sprites to initialize. This is done on line 20.

```
022         # Create an image of the block, and fill it with a color.
023         # This could also be an image loaded from the disk.
024         self.image = pygame.Surface([width, height])
025         self.image.fill(color)
```

Lines 24 and 25 create the image that will eventually appear on the screen. Line 24 creates a blank image. Line 25 fills it with black. If the program needs something other than a black square, these are the lines of code to modify.

For example, look at the code below:

```
def __init__(self, color, width, height):
    """
    Ellipse Constructor. Pass in the color of the ellipse,
    and its size
    """
    # Call the parent class (Sprite) constructor
    super().__init__()
```

```
# Set the background color and set it to be transparent
self.image = pygame.Surface([width, height])
self.image.fill(WHITE)
self.image.set_colorkey(WHITE)

# Draw the ellipse
pygame.draw.ellipse(self.image, color, [0, 0, width, height])
```

If the code above was substituted, then everything would be in the form of ellipses. Line 29 draws the ellipse and line 26 makes white a transparent color so the background shows up. This is the same concept used in Chapter 12 for making the white background of an image transparent.

```
def __init__(self):
    """ Graphic Sprite Constructor. """

    # Call the parent class (Sprite) constructor
    super().__init__()

    # Load the image
    self.image = pygame.image.load("player.png").convert()

    # Set our transparent color
    self.image.set_colorkey(WHITE)
```

If instead a bitmapped graphic is desired, substituting the lines of code above will load a graphic (line 22) and set white to the transparent background color (line 25). In this case, the dimensions of the sprite will automatically be set to the graphic dimensions, and it would no longer be necessary to pass them in. See how line 15 no longer has those parameters.

There is one more important line that we need in our constructor, no matter what kind of sprite we have:

```
027         # Fetch the rectangle object that has the dimensions of the image
028         # image.
029         # Update the position of this object by setting the values
030         # of rect.x and rect.y
031         self.rect = self.image.get_rect()
```

The attribute rect is a variable that is an instance of the Rect class that pygame provides. The rectangle represents the dimensions of the sprite. This rectangle class has attributes for x and y that may be set. Pygame will draw the sprite where the x and y attributes are. So to move this sprite, a programmer needs to set mySpriteRef.rect.x and mySpriteRef.rect.y where mySpriteRef is the variable that points to the sprite.

We are done with the Block class. Time to move on to the initialization code.

```
033 # Initialize pygame
034 pygame.init()
035
036 # Set the height and width of the screen
037 screen_width = 700
038 screen_height = 400
039 screen = pygame.display.set_mode([screen_width, screen_height])
```

The code above initializes pygame and creates a window for the game. There is nothing new here from other pygame programs.

```
041 # This is a list of 'sprites.' Each block in the program is
042 # added to this list. The list is managed by a class called 'Group.'
043 block_list = pygame.sprite.Group()
044
045 # This is a list of every sprite.
046 # All blocks and the player block as well.
047 all_sprites_list = pygame.sprite.Group()
```

A major advantage of working with sprites is the ability to work with them in groups. We can draw and move all the sprites with one command if they are in a group. We can also check for sprite collisions against an entire group.

The above code creates two lists. The variable all_sprites_list will contain every sprite in the game. This list will be used to draw all the sprites. The variable block_list holds each object that the player can collide with. In this example it will include every object in the game but the player. We don't want the player in this list because when we check for the player colliding with objects in the block_list, pygame will go ahead and always return the player as colliding if it is part of that list.

```
049 for i in range(50):
050     # This represents a block
051     block = Block(BLACK, 20, 15)
052
053     # Set a random location for the block
054     block.rect.x = random.randrange(screen_width)
055     block.rect.y = random.randrange(screen_height)
056
057     # Add the block to the list of objects
058     block_list.add(block)
059     all_sprites_list.add(block)
```

The loop starting on line 49 adds 50 black sprite blocks to the screen. Line 51 creates a new block, sets the color, the width, and the height. Lines 54 and 55 set the coordinates for where this object will appear. Line 58 adds the block to the list of blocks the player can collide with. Line 59 adds it to the list of all blocks. This should be very similar to the code you wrote back in Exercise 13.

```
061 # Create a RED player block
062 player = Block(RED, 20, 15)
063 all_sprites_list.add(player)
```

Lines 61–63 set up the player for our game. Line 62 creates a red block that will eventually function as the player. This block is added to the all_sprites_list in line 63 so it can be drawn, but not the block_list.

```
065 # Loop until the user clicks the close button.
066 done = False
067
068 # Used to manage how fast the screen updates
069 clock = pygame.time.Clock()
070
```

```
071 score = 0
072
073 # -------- Main Program Loop -----------
074 while not done:
075     for event in pygame.event.get():
076         if event.type == pygame.QUIT:
077             done = True
078
079     # Clear the screen
080     screen.fill(WHITE)
```

The code above is a standard program loop first introduced back in Chapter 6. Line 71 initializes our score variable to 0.

```
082     # Get the current mouse position. This returns the position
083     # as a list of two numbers.
084     pos = pygame.mouse.get_pos()
085
086     # Fetch the x and y out of the list,
087         # just like we'd fetch letters out of a string.
088     # Set the player object to the mouse location
089     player.rect.x = pos[0]
090     player.rect.y = pos[1]
```

Line 84 fetches the mouse position similar to other pygame programs discussed before. The important new part is contained in lines 89–90 where the rectangle containing the sprite is moved to a new location. Remember this rect was created back on line 31 and this code won't work without that line.

```
092     # See if the player block has collided with anything.
093     blocks_hit_list = pygame.sprite.spritecollide(player, block_list, True)
```

This line of code takes the sprite referenced by player and checks it against all sprites in block_list. The code returns a list of sprites that overlap. If there are no overlapping sprites, it returns an empty list. The Boolean True will remove the colliding sprites from the list. If it is set to False the sprites will not be removed.

```
095     # Check the list of collisions.
096     for block in blocks_hit_list:
097         score += 1
098         print(score)
```

This loops for each sprite in the collision list created back in line 93. If there are sprites in that list, increase the score for each collision. Then print the score to the screen. Note that the print on line 98 will not print the score to the main window with the sprites, but the console window instead. Figuring out how to make the score display on the main window is part of Exercise "Sprite Collecting."

```
100     # Draw all the spites
101     all_sprites_list.draw(screen)
```

The Group class that `all_sprites_list` is a member of has a method called `draw`. This method loops through each sprite in the list and calls that sprite's `draw` method. This means that with only one line of code, a program can cause every sprite in the `all_sprites_list` to draw.

```
103     # Go ahead and update the screen with what we've drawn.
104     pygame.display.flip()
105
106     # Limit to 60 frames per second
107     clock.tick(60)
108
109 pygame.quit()
```

Lines 103–109 flip the screen and call the quit method when the main loop is done.

Moving Sprites

In the example so far, only the player sprite moves. How could a program cause all the sprites to move? This can be done easily; just two steps are required.

The first step is to add a new method to the Block class. This new method is called `update`. The update function will be called automatically when `update` is called for the entire list.

Put this in the sprite:

```
def update(self):
    """ Called each frame. """

    # Move block down one pixel
    self.rect.y += 1
```

Put this in the main program loop:

```
# Call the update() method for all blocks in the block_list
block_list.update()
```

The code isn't perfect because the blocks fall off the screen and do not reappear. This code will improve the update function so that the blocks will reappear up top.

```
def update(self):
    # Move the block down one pixel
    self.rect.y += 1
    if self.rect.y > screen_height:
                self.rect.y = random.randrange(-100, -10)
                self.rect.x = random.randrange(0, screen_width)
```

If the program should reset blocks that are collected to the top of the screen, the sprite can be changed with the following code:

```
def reset_pos(self):
    """ Reset position to the top of the screen, at a random x location.
    Called by update() or the main program loop if there is a collision.
    """
```

```
        self.rect.y = random.randrange(-300, -20)
        self.rect.x = random.randrange(0, screen_width)

def update(self):
    """ Called each frame. """

    # Move block down one pixel
    self.rect.y += 1

    # If block is too far down, reset to top of screen.
    if self.rect.y > 410:
        self.reset_pos()
```

Rather than destroying the blocks when the collision occurs, the program may instead call the reset_pos function, and the block will move to the top of the screen ready to be collected.

```
# See if the player block has collided with anything.
blocks_hit_list = pygame.sprite.spritecollide(player, block_list, False)

# Check the list of collisions.
for block in blocks_hit_list:
    score += 1
    print(score)

    # Reset block to the top of the screen to fall again.
    block.reset_pos()
```

The full code for this example is here:

ProgramArcadeGames.com/python_examples/f.php?file=moving_sprites.py

If you'd rather see code for sprites that bounce, look here:

ProgramArcadeGames.com/python_examples/f.php?file=moving_sprites_bounce.py

If you want them to move in circles:

ProgramArcadeGames.com/python_examples/f.php?file=sprite_circle_movement.py

The Game Class

Back in Chapter 10 we introduced functions. At the end of the chapter we talked about an option to use a main function. As programs get large this technique helps us avoid problems that can come from having a lot of code to sort through. Our programs aren't quite that large yet. However I know some people like to organize things properly from the start.

For those people in that camp, here's another optional technique to organize your code. (If you aren't in that camp, you can skip this section and circle back later when your programs get too large.) Watch the video to get an idea of how the program works.

ProgramArcadeGames.com/python_examples/f.php?file=game_class_example.py

Other Examples

Here are several other examples of what you can do with sprites. A few of these also include a linked video that explains how the code works.

Shooting things

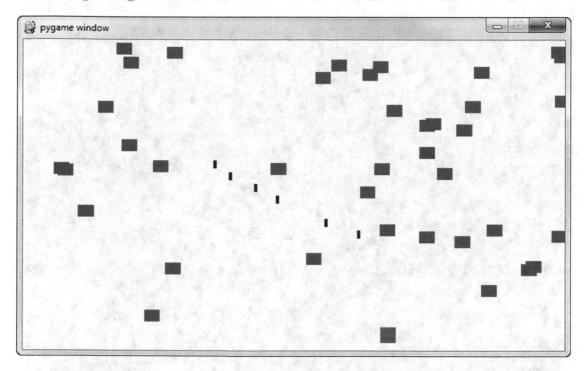

Shooting things

Interested in a shoot-em-up game? Something like the classic Space Invaders? This example shows how to create sprites to represent bullets:

ProgramArcadeGames.com/python_examples/f.php?file=bullets.py

Walls

Are you looking for more of an adventure games? You don't want your player to wander all over the place? This shows how to add walls that prevent player movement:

ProgramArcadeGames.com/python_examples/f.php?file=move_with_walls_example.py

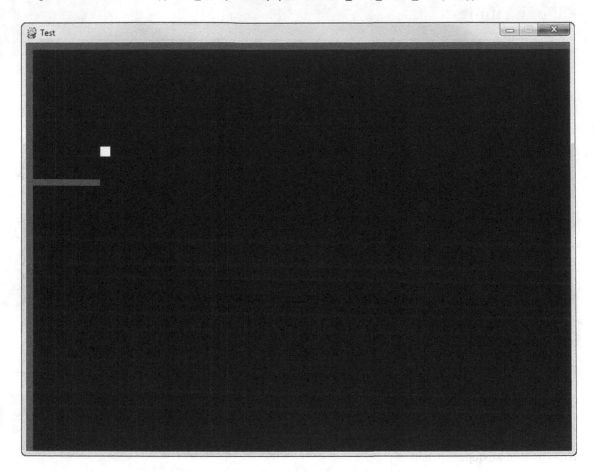

Move with walls we can run into

Wait? One room isn't enough of an adventure? You want your player to move from screen to screen? We can do that! Look through this example where the player may run through a multi-room maze:

ProgramArcadeGames.com/python_examples/f.php?file=maze_runner.py

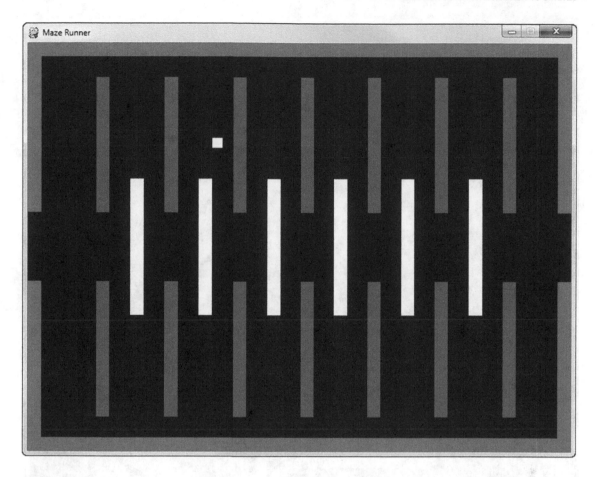

Multi-room maze

Platforms

Interested in creating a platformer, like Donkey Kong? We need to use the same idea as our example with walls, but add some gravity:

ProgramArcadeGames.com/python_examples/f.php?file=platform_jumper.py

Jump around platforms

Good platformers can move side to side. This is a side scrolling platformer:

ProgramArcadeGames.com/python_examples/f.php?file=platform_scroller.py

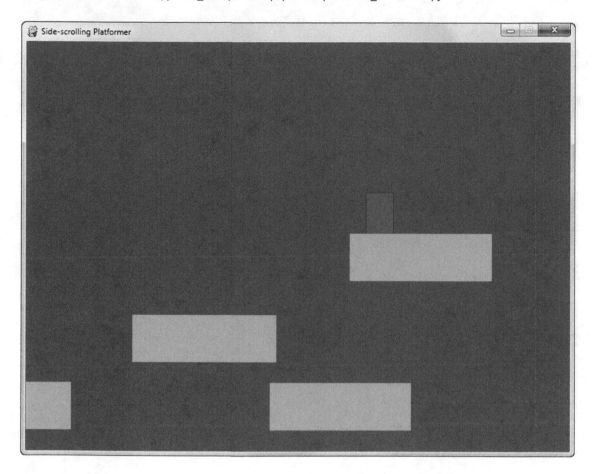

Side scrolling platformer

Even cooler platform games have platforms that move! See how that is done with this example:

ProgramArcadeGames.com/python_examples/f.php?file=platform_moving.py

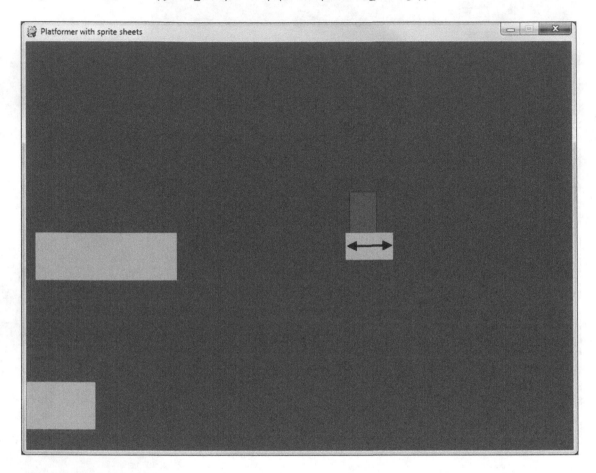

Moving platforms

Snake/Centipede

I occasionally come across readers that want to make a snake or centipede type of game. You have a multi-segment snake that you can control. This requires each segment to be held in a list. While it requires learning two new commands, the concept behind how to do this game isn't difficult.

Control a snake or centipede going around the screen:

ProgramArcadeGames.com/python_examples/f.php?file=snake.py

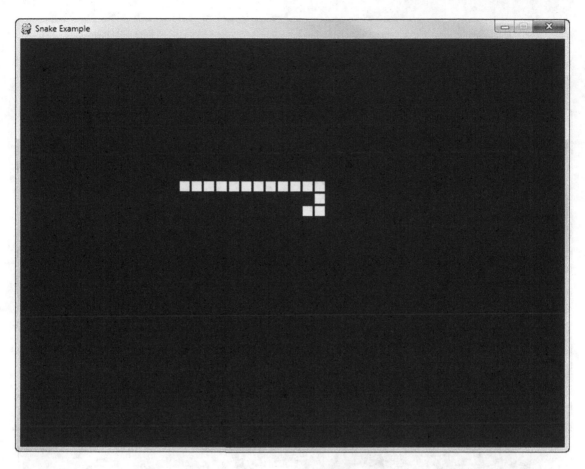

Snake

Using Sprite Sheets

This is an extensive example that uses sprite sheets to provide the graphics behind a platformer game. It supports multiple levels and moving platforms as well. The game is broken into multiple files. ProgramArcadeGames.com/python_examples/en/sprite_sheets

Sprite sheet platformer

Review
Multiple Choice Quiz

1. What is a Sprite?

   a. A graphic image that he computer can easily track, draw on the screen, and detect collisions with.

   b. A very bright color that seems to glow.

   c. A function that draws images to the screen.

   d. A sprite is to Tinkerbell as a human is to Bob.

2. Which option best describes how a programmer use sprites in his or her program?

    a. Derive a new class from `pygame.sprite.Sprite`, and then create instances of those sprites and add them to sprite groups.

    b. Create instances of `pygame.sprite.Sprite` and add them to sprite groups.

    c. Use functions to draw images directly to the screen

    d. Use bitmaps and blit images to the screen.

3. What is the standard way to draw sprites in a program?

    a. Add a sprite to a group. Then call `.draw(screen)` on the group.

    b. Call the sprite's `.draw(screen)` method.

    c. Call the sprite's `.update(screen)` method.

    d. Call the sprite's `.blit(screen)` method.

4. How does a program move a sprite pointed to by `mysprite`?

    a. Set new `mysprite.rect.x` and `mysprite.rect.y` values.

    b. Set new `mysprite.x` and `mysprite.y` values.

    c. Call `mysprite.draw(x,y)` with the desired x and y values.

    d. Call `mysprite.move(x,y)` with the desired x and y values.

5. How does a sprite move itself?

    a. Create an `update()` method. Change `self.rect.x` and `self.rect.y` values.

    b. Create an `update()` method. Change `rect.x` and `rect.y` values.

    c. Create a `move()` method. Change `self.x` and `self.y` values.

6. If a programmer creates his/her own constructor for a sprite, what must be the first line of that constructor?

    a. `super().__init__()`

    b. `self.image = pygame.Surface([width, height])`

    c. `self.image.set_colorkey(white)`

7. If a programmer wants to create a transparent background for a sprite, what type of image should be avoided?

    a. jpg

    b. png

    c. gif

8. What does the True do in this line of code?

    ```
    sprites_hit_list = pygame.sprite.spritecollide(sprite, sprite_list, True)
    ```

    a. Removes `sprite` if any sprite in `sprite_list` is overlapping.

    b. Creates an explosion effect when the sprites collide.

    c. Creates a sound effect when the sprites collide.

    d. Removes any sprite in `sprite_list` that is overlapping `sprite`.

9. What is special about a sprite's `update()` function?

    a. It is called automatically each time through the game loop.

    b. It is called automatically when the code calls `update()` on any list that sprite is in.

    c. There is no special significance to that function.

10. What is the proper command to add a sprite to an instance of `pygame.sprite.Group()` pointed to by a `sprite_list`?

    a. `sprite_list.append(my_sprite)`

    b. `sprite_list.add(my_sprite)`

    c. `sprite_list.insert(my_sprite)`

11. If the screen is 600 wide and 400 tall, where will this sprite be moved?

    ```
    mysprite.rect.x = 600
    mysprite.rect.y = 400
    ```

    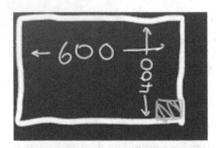

    a.

    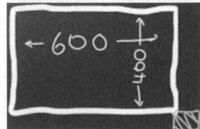

    b.

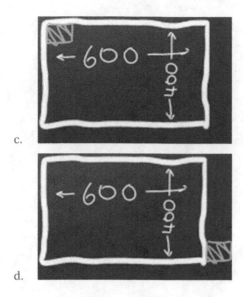

c.

d.

Exercise

Check the appendix for the exercise "Sprite Collecting" that goes along with this chapter.

CHAPTER 15

■ ■ ■

Libraries and Modules

A *library* is a collection of code for functions and classes. Often, these libraries are written by someone else and brought into the project so that the programmer does not have to reinvent the wheel. In Python the term used to describe a library of code is *module*.

By using import pygame and import random, the programs created so far have already used modules. A library can be made up of multiple modules that can be imported. Often a library only has one module, so these words can sometimes be used interchangeably.

Modules are often organized into groups of similar functionality. In this class, programs have already used functions from the math module, the random module, and the pygame library. Modules can be organized so that individual modules contain other modules. For example, the pygame module contains submodules for pygame.draw, pygame.image, and pygame.mouse.

Modules are not loaded unless the program asks them to. This saves time and computer memory. This chapter shows how to create a module and how to import and use that module.

Why Create a Library?

There are three major reasons for a programmer to create his or her own libraries:

1. It breaks the code into smaller, easier to use parts.

2. It allows multiple people to work on a program at the same time.

3. The code written can be easily shared with other programmers.

Some of the programs already created in this book have started to get rather long. By separating a large program into several smaller programs, it is easier to manage the code. For example, in the prior chapter's sprite example, a programmer could move the sprite class into a separate file. In a complex program, each sprite might be contained in its own file.

If multiple programmers work on the same project, it is nearly impossible to do so if all the code is in one file. However, by breaking the program into multiple pieces, it becomes easier. One programmer could work on developing an Orc sprite class. Another programmer could work on the Goblin sprite class. Since the sprites are in separate files, the programmers do not run into conflict.

Modern programmers rarely build programs from scratch. Often programs are built from parts of other programs that share the same functionality. If one programmer creates code that can handle a mortgage application form, then that code will ideally go into a library. Then any other program that needs to manage a mortgage application form at that bank can call on that library.

Creating Your Own Module/Library File:

In this example we will break apart a short program into multiple files. Here we have a function in a file named test.py and a call to that function:

```
# Foo function
def foo():
    print("foo!")

# Foo call
foo()
```

Yes, this program is not too long to be in one file. But if both the function and the main program code were long, it would be different. If we had several functions, each 100 lines long, it would be time consuming to manage that large of a file. But for this example we will keep the code short for clarity.

We can move the foo function out of this file. Then this file would be left with only the main program code. (In this example there is no reason to separate them, aside from learning how to do so.)

To do this, create a new file and copy the foo function into it. Save the new file with the name my_functions.py. The file must be saved to the same directory as test.py.

```
# Foo function
def foo():
    print("foo!")

# Foo call that doesn't work
foo()
```

Unfortunately it isn't as simple as this. The file `test.py` does not know to go and look at the `my_functions.py` file and import it. We have to add the command to import it:

```
# Import the my_functions.py file
import my_functions

# Foo call that still doesn't work
foo()
```

That still doesn't work. What are we missing? Just like when we import pygame, we have to put the package name in front of the function. Like this:

```
# Import the my_functions.py file
import my_functions

# Foo call that does work
my_functions.foo()
```

This works because `my_functions.` is prepended to the function call.

Namespace

A program might have two library files that need to be used. What if the libraries had functions that were named the same? What if there were two functions named `print_report`—one that printed grades and one that printed an account statement? For instance:

```
def print_report():
    print("Student Grade Report:" )

def print_report():
    print("Financial Report:" )
```

How do you get a program to specify which function to call? Well, that is pretty easy. You specify the *namespace*. The namespace is the work that appears before the function name in the code below:

```
import student_functions
import financial_functions

student_functions.print_report()
financial_functions.print_report()
```

So now we can see why this might be needed. But what if you don't have name collisions? Typing in a namespace each and every time can be tiresome. You can get around this by importing the library into the *local namespace*. The local namespace is a list of functions, variables, and classes that you don't have to prepend with a namespace. Going back to the `foo` example, let's remove the original import and replace it with a new type of import:

```
# import foo
from my_functions import *

foo()
```

This works even without my_functions. prepended to the function call. The asterisk is a wildcard that will import all functions from my_functions. A programmer could import individual ones if desired by specifying the function name.

Third Party Libraries

When working with Python, it is possible to use many libraries that are built into Python. Take a look at all the libraries that are available here:

http://docs.python.org/3/py-modindex.html

It is possible to download and install other libraries. There are libraries that work with the Web, complex numbers, databases, and more.

- Pygame: The library used to create games.

    http://www.pygame.org/docs/

- wxPython: Create GUI programs, with windows, menus, and more.

    http://www.wxpython.org/

- pydot: Generate complex directed and nondirected graphs.

    http://code.google.com/p/pydot/

- NumPy: Sophisticated library for working with matrices.

    http://numpy.scipy.org/

A wonderful list of Python libraries and links to installers for them is available here: http://www.lfd.uci.edu/~gohlke/pythonlibs/

Going through lists of libraries that are available can help you brainstorm what types of programs you can create. Most programming involves assembling large parts, rather than writing everything from scratch.

Review

Multiple Choice Quiz

1. What is a library?

    a. A collection of functions and/or classes that can be imported into a project.

    b. A store where you can buy code from other developers.

    c. Any code that has not been written by a developer.

    d. A .pyc file.

2. Why would a person create a library?

    a. It provides an easy way for developers to share code between projects and other developers.

    b. It makes the code run faster.

    c. It makes the code smaller.

    d. Libraries are something to be avoided by developers.

3. Why does the following code not work?

The first file:

```
def foo():
    print("foo!")
```

And the second file:

```
import my_functions

foo()
```

a. The program should read my_functions.foo()

b. The program should read import my_functions.py

c. The program should read import foo

d. The program should read from foo import my_functions

4. What is the proper code to import the math library into the local namespace?

a. from math import *

b. import math

c. import local

d. from math import local

e. import math into local

5. What does the asterisk represent in the following line of code:

```
from my_functions import *
```

a. Wildcard. Import every function in the my_functions module.

b. It represents the local namespace.

c. My God, it's full of stars!

Short Answer Worksheet

1. What is a Python library?

2. What are some of the reasons why a programmer would want to create his/her own library file?

3. There are two ways to import library files in Python. Give an example of each.

4. How do calls to functions and classes differ depending on how the library is imported?

5. Can library files import other library files?

6. What is a namespace?

Exercise

Check the appendix for the exercise "Moving Sprites" that goes along with this chapter.

CHAPTER 16

■■■

Searching

Searching is an important and very common operation that computers do all the time. Searches are used every time someone does a ctrl-f for "find," when a user uses "type-to" to quickly select an item, or when a web server pulls information about a customer to present a customized web page with the customer's order.

There are a lot of ways to search for data. Google has based an entire multibillion dollar company on this fact. This chapter introduces the two simplest methods for searching: the *linear search* and the *binary search*.

Reading from a File

Before discussing how to search we need to learn how to read data from a file. Reading in a data set from a file is *way* more fun than typing it in by hand each time.

Let's say we need to create a program that will allow us to quickly find the name of a super villain. To start with, our program needs a database of super villains. To download this data set, download and save this file:

```
http://ProgramArcadeGames.com/chapters/16_searching/super_villains.txt
```

These are random names generated by the nine.frenchboys.net web site. Save this file and remember which directory you saved it to.

In the same directory as super_villains.txt, create, save, and run the following python program:

```python
file = open("super_villains.txt")

for line in file:
    print(line)
```

There is only one new command in this code open. Because it is a built-in function like print, there is no need for an import. Full details on this function can be found in https://docs.python.org/3/library/functions.html#open, but at this point the documentation for that command is so technical it might not even be worth looking at.

The above program has two problems with it, but it provides a simple example of reading in a file. Line 1 opens a file and gets it ready to be read. The name of the file is in between the quotes. The new variable file is an object that represents the file being read. Line 3 shows how a normal for loop may be used to read through a file line by line. Think of file as a list of lines, and the new variable line will be set to each of those lines as the program runs through the loop.

Try running the program. One of the problems with it is that the text is printed double-spaced. The reason for this is that each line pulled out of the file and stored in the variable line includes the carriage return as part of the string. Remember the carriage return and line feed introduced back in Chapter 1? The print statement adds yet another carriage return and the result is double-spaced output.

The second problem is that the file is opened, but not closed. This problem isn't as obvious as the double-spacing issue, but it is important. The Windows operating system can only open so many files at once. A file can normally only be opened by one program at a time. Leaving a file open will limit what other programs can do with the file and take up system resources. It is necessary to close the file to let Windows know the program is no longer working with that file. In this case it is not too important because once any program is done running, the Windows will automatically close any files left open. But since it is a bad habit to program like that, let's update the code:

```python
file = open("super_villains.txt")

for line in file:
    line = line.strip()
    print(line)

file.close()
```

The listing above works better. It has two new additions. On line 4 is a call to the `strip` method built into every `String` class. This function returns a new string without the trailing spaces and carriage returns of the original string. The method does not alter the original string but instead creates a new one. This line of code would not work:

```
line.strip()
```

If the programmer wants the original variable to reference the new string, she must assign it to the new returned string as shown on line 4.

The second addition is on line 7. This closes the file so that the operating system doesn't have to go around later and clean up open files after the program ends.

Reading into an Array

It is useful to read in the contents of a file to an array so that the program can do processing on it later. This can easily be done in python with the following code:

```
# Read in a file from disk and put it in an array.
file = open("super_villains.txt")

name_list = []
for line in file:
    line = line.strip()
    name_list.append(line)

file.close()
```

This combines the new pattern of how to read a file, along with the previously learned pattern of how to create an empty array and append to it as new data comes in, which was shown back in Chapter 8. To verify the file was read into the array correctly, a programmer could print the length of the array:

```
print( "There were",len(name_list),"names in the file.")
```

Or the programmer could bring the entire contents of the array:

```
for name in name_list:
    print(name)
```

Go ahead and make sure you can read in the file before continuing on to the different searches.

Linear Search

If a program has a set of data in an array, how can it go about finding where a specific element is? This can be done one of two ways. The first method is to use a *linear search*. This starts at the first element and keeps comparing elements until it finds the desired element (or runs out of elements.)

Linear Search Algorithm

```
# --- Linear search
key = "Morgiana the Shrew"

i = 0
while i < len(name_list) and name_list[i] != key:
    i += 1

if i < len(name_list):
    print( "The name is at position", i)
else:
    print( "The name was not in the list." )
```

The linear search is rather simple. Line 2 sets up an increment variable that will keep track of exactly where in the list the program needs to check next. The first element that needs to be checked is zero, so i is set to zero.

The next line is a bit more complex. The computer needs to keep looping until one of two things happens. It finds the element, or it runs out of elements. The first comparison sees if the current element we are checking is less than the length of the list. If so, we can keep looping. The second comparison sees if the current element in the name list is equal to the name we are searching for.

This check to see if the program has run out of elements *must occur first*. Otherwise the program will check against a non-existent element, which will cause an error.

Line 4 simply moves to the next element if the conditions to keep searching are met in line 3.

At the end of the loop, the program checks to see if the end of the list was reached on line 6. Remember, a list of n elements is numbered 0 to n-1. Therefore if i is equal to the length of the list, the end has been reached. If it is less, we found the element.

Variations on the Linear Search

Variations on the linear search can be used to create several common algorithms. For example, say we had a list of aliens. We might want to check this group of aliens to see if one of the aliens is green. Or are all the aliens green? Which aliens are green?

To begin with, we'd need to define our alien:

```
class Alien:
    """ Class that defines an alien"""
    def __init__(self, color, weight):
        """ Constructor. Set name and color"""
        self.color = color
        self.weight = weight
```

Then we'd need to create a function to check and see if it has the property that we are looking for. In this case, is it green? We'll assume the color is a text string, and we'll convert it to uppercase to eliminate case sensitivity.

```python
def has_property(my_alien):
    """ Check to see if an item has a property.
    In this case, is the alien green? """
    if my_alien.color.upper() == "GREEN":
        return True
    else:
        return False
```

Does at Least One Item Have a Property?

Is at least one alien green? We can check. The basic algorithm behind this check:

```python
def check_if_one_item_has_property_v1(my_list):
    """ Return true if at least one item has a
    property. """
    i = 0
    while i < len(my_list) and not has_property(my_list[i]):
        i += 1

    if i < len(my_list):
        # Found an item with the property
        return True
    else:
        # There is no item with the property
        return False
```

This could also be done with a for loop. In this case, the loop will exit early by using a return once the item has been found. The code is shorter, but not every programmer would prefer it. Some programmers feel that loops should not be prematurely ended with a return or break statement. It all goes to personal preference—or the personal preference of the person that is footing the bill.

```python
def check_if_one_item_has_property_v2(my_list):
    """ Return true if at least one item has a
    property. Works the same as v1, but less code. """
    for item in my_list:
        if has_property(item):
            return True
    return False
```

Do All Items Have a Property?

Are all aliens green? This code is very similar to the prior example. Spot the difference and see if you can figure out the reason behind the change.

```python
def check_if_all_items_have_property(my_list):
    """ Return true if at ALL items have a property. """
    for item in my_list:
        if not has_property(item):
            return False
    return True
```

Create a List with All Items Matching a Property

What if you wanted a list of aliens that are green? This is a combination of our prior code and the code to append items to a list that we learned about back in Chapter 7.

```python
def get_matching_items(list):
    """ Build a brand new list that holds all the items
    that match our property. """
    matching_list = []
    for item in list:
        if has_property(item):
            matching_list.append(item)
    return matching_list
```

How would you run all these in a test? The code above can be combined with this code to run:

```python
alien_list = []
alien_list.append(Alien("Green", 42))
alien_list.append(Alien("Red", 40))
alien_list.append(Alien("Blue", 41))
alien_list.append(Alien("Purple", 40))

result = check_if_one_item_has_property_v1(alien_list)
print("Result of test check_if_one_item_has_property_v1:", result)

result = check_if_one_item_has_property_v2(alien_list)
print("Result of test check_if_one_item_has_property_v2:", result)

result = check_if_all_items_have_property(alien_list)
print("Result of test check_if_all_items_have_property:", result)

result = get_matching_items(alien_list)
print("Number of items returned from test get_matching_items:", len(result))
```

For a full working example see:

programarcadegames.com/python_examples/show_file.php?file=property_check_examples.py

These common algorithms can be used as part of a solution to a larger problem, such as finding all the addresses in a list of customers that aren't valid.

Binary Search

A faster way to search a list is possible with the *binary search*. The process of a binary search can be described by using the classic number guessing game "guess a number between 1 and 100" as an example. To make it easier to understand the process, let's modify the game to be "guess a number between 1 and 128." The number range is inclusive, meaning both 1 and 128 are possibilities.

If a person were to use the linear search as a method to guess the secret number, the game would be rather long and boring.

```
Guess a number 1 to 128: 1
Too low.
Guess a number 1 to 128: 2
Too low.
Guess a number 1 to 128: 3
Too low.
....
Guess a number 1 to 128: 93
Too low.
Guess a number 1 to 128: 94
Correct!
```

Most people will use a binary search to find the number. Here is an example of playing the game using a binary search:

```
Guess a number 1 to 128: 64
Too low.
Guess a number 1 to 128: 96
Too high.
Guess a number 1 to 128: 80
Too low.
Guess a number 1 to 128: 88
Too low.
Guess a number 1 to 128: 92
Too low.
Guess a number 1 to 128: 94
Correct!
```

Each time through the rounds of the number guessing game, the guesser is able to eliminate one-half of the problem space by getting a high or low as a result of the guess.

In a binary search, it is necessary to track an upper and a lower bound of the list that the answer can be in. The computer or number guessing human picks the midpoint of those elements. Revisiting the example:

A lower bound of 1, upper bound of 128, midpoint of $\frac{1+128}{2} = 64.5$.

```
Guess a number 1 to 128: 64
Too low.
```

A lower bound of 65, upper bound of 128, midpoint of $\dfrac{65+128}{2} = 96.5$.

```
Guess a number 1 to 128: 96
Too high.
```

A lower bound of 65, upper bound of 95, midpoint of $\dfrac{65+95}{2} = 80$.

```
Guess a number 1 to 128: 80
Too low.
```

A lower bound of 81, upper bound of 95, midpoint of $\dfrac{81+95}{2} = 88$.

```
Guess a number 1 to 128: 88
Too low.
```

A lower bound of 89, upper bound of 95, midpoint of $\dfrac{89+95}{2} = 92$.

```
Guess a number 1 to 128: 92
Too low.
```

A lower bound of 93, upper bound of 95, midpoint of $\dfrac{93+95}{2} = 94$.

```
Guess a number 1 to 128: 94
Correct!
```

A binary search requires significantly fewer guesses. Worst case, it can guess a number between 1 and 128 in 7 guesses. One more guess raises the limit to 256. Nine guesses can get a number between 1 and 512. With just 32 guesses, a person can get a number between 1 and 4.2 billion.

To figure out how large the list can be given a certain number of guesses, the formula works out like n=x^g where n is the size of the list and g is the number of guesses. For example:

```
2⁷=128 (7 guesses can handle 128 different numbers)
2⁸=256
2⁹=512
2³²=4,294,967,296
```

If you have the problem size, we can figure out the number of guesses using the *log* function. Specifically, *log base 2*. If you don't specify a base, most people will assume you mean the natural log with a base of e ≈ 2.71828, which is not what we want. For example, using log base 2 to find how many guesses:

```
log₂ 128 = 7
log₂ 65,536 = 16
```

Enough math! Where is the code? The code to do a binary search is more complex than a linear search:

```
# --- Binary search
key = "Morgiana the Shrew";
lower_bound = 0
upper_bound = len(name_list)-1
found = False
```

```
# Loop until we find the item, or our upper/lower bounds meet
while lower_bound <= upper_bound and not found:

    # Find the middle position
    middle_pos = (lower_bound + upper_bound) // 2

    # Figure out if we:
    # move up the lower bound, or
    # move down the upper bound, or
    # we found what we are looking for
    if name_list[middle_pos] < key:
        lower_bound = middle_pos + 1
    elif name_list[middle_pos] > key:
        upper_bound = middle_pos - 1
    else:
        found = True

if found:
    print( "The name is at position", middle_pos)
else:
    print( "The name was not in the list." )
```

Since lists start at element zero, line 3 sets the lower bound to zero. Line 4 sets the upper bound to the length of the list minus one. So for a list of 100 elements the lower bound will be 0 and the upper bound 99.

The Boolean variable on line 5 will be used to let the while loop know that the element has been found.

Line 6 checks to see if the element has been found or if we've run out of elements. If we've run out of elements, the lower bound will end up equalling the upper bound.

Line 7 finds the middle position. It is possible to get a middle position of something like 64.5. It isn't possible to look up position 64.5. (Although J. K. Rowling was rather clever in enough coming up with Platform $9\frac{3}{4}$, that doesn't work here.) The best way of handling this is to use the // operator first introduced way back in Chapter 6. This is similar to the / operator, but will only return integer results. For example, 11 // 2 would give 5 as an answer, rather than 5.5.

Starting at line 8, the program checks to see if the guess is high, low, or correct. If the guess is low, the lower bound is moved up to just past the guess. If the guess is too high, the upper bound is moved just below the guess. If the answer has been found, found is set to True ending the search.

With the a list of 100 elements, a person can reasonably guess that on average with the linear search, a program will have to check 50 of them before finding the element. With the binary search, on average you'll still need to do about 7 guesses. In an advanced algorithms course you can find the exact formula. For this course, just assume average and worst cases are the same.

Review

Multiple Choice Quiz

1. Before reading from a file, a program must:

    a. Open it with the open command.

    b. Initialize it with the init command.

    c. Reset the file with a reset command.

2. In order to read in each line of the file a program should:

   a. Use a `for` loop

   b. Use the `read_all_lines` command.

   c. Access each line in an array.

3. What will happen if a program fails to close a file after reading it?

   a. The file will be marked as busy and will be inaccessible until the program ends.

   b. The file will not be able to be used until the computer restarts.

   c. The programmer will get a call from his mother reminding him that he forgot to close his that file, *again*.

   d. Nothing, it doesn't really matter if you don't close the file.

4. What processing usually needs to be done on a line after it has been read in?

   a. The carriage return and/or line feed need to be stripped of the end of the line.

   b. The line needs to be converted to uppercase.

   c. The line needs to be converted from a string of integers to a string of letters.

   d. The dilithium crystals must be recalibrated before use.

5. What is wrong with this linear search?

```
i = 0
while my_list[i] != key and i < len(my_list):
i += 1
```

   a. The loop needs to check to see if we ran out of list items before checking to see if the item is equal to the key.

   b. The first check should be == not !=.

   c. The second check should be <= not <.

   d. The second check should be > not <.

6. After this code runs, what is the proper way to tell if the item was found or not?

```
i = 0
while i < len(my_list) and my_list[i] != key:
i += 1
```

   a. `if i == len(my_list):`

   b. `if my_list[i] != key:`

   c. `if my_list[i] == key:`

   d. `if i > len(my_list):`

7. A binary search starts looking:

   a. In the middle of the list.

   b. At the beginning of the list.

   c. At the end of the list.

   d. At a random spot in the list.

8. Using a binary search, a list of 128 elements takes at most how many times through the search loop?

   a. 7

   b. 64

   c. 128

   d. 1

9. In a binary search, how do you know if an element is not in the list and the search should stop?

   a. The lower bound is equal or greater than the upper bound.

   b. After every item has been checked.

   c. When the key is not equal to the middle element.

   d. When i is greater than or equal to the list length.

10. If the key is less than the middle element, the search should:

   a. Move the upper bound down to the middle element.

   b. Move the lower bound up to the middle element.

Short Answer Worksheet Linear Search Review

Answer the following, assuming a program uses the linear search:

1. If a list has *n* elements, in the *best* case how many elements would the computer need to check before it found the desired element?

2. If a list has *n* elements, in the *worst* case how many elements would the computer need to check before it found the desired element? (Remember, give your answer in terms of n.)

3. If a list has *n* elements, how many elements need to be checked to determine that the desired element does not exist in the list?

4. If a list has *n* elements, what would the *average* number of elements be that the computer would need to check before it found the desired element?

5. Take the example linear search code and put it in a function called linear_ search. Take in the list along with the desired element as parameters. Return the position of the element, or -1 if it was not found. Once you've written the function, try it out with the following code to see if it works:

```
# --- Put your definition for linear_search right below:

# --- Now if the function works, all these tests should pass:

my_list = [4, 3, 2, 1, 5, 7, 6]

r = linear_search(my_list, 3)
if r == 1:
    print("Test A passed")
else:
    print("Test A failed")

r = linear_search(my_list, 2)
if r == 2:
    print("Test B passed")
else:
    print("Test B failed")

r = linear_search(my_list, 10)
if r == -1:
    print("Test C passed")
else:
    print("Test C failed")
```

Binary Search Review

Answer the following, assuming a program uses the binary search and that the search list is in order:

1. If a list has *n* elements, in the *best* case how many elements would the computer need to check before it found the desired element?

2. If a list has *n* elements, in the *worst* case how many elements would the computer need to check before it found the desired element?

3. If a list has *n* elements, how many elements need to be checked to determine that the desired element does not exist in the list?

4. If a list has *n* elements, what would the *average* number of elements be that the computer would need to check before it found the desired element?

5. Take the example binary search code and put it in a function named binary_search. Take in the list along with the desired element as parameters. Return the position of the element, or -1 if it was not found. Once you've written the function, try it out with the following code to see if it works:

```
# --- Put your definition for binary_search right below:

# --- Now if the function works, all these tests should pass:

my_list = [0, 3, 5, 12, 18, 50, 70, 78]

r = binary_search(my_list, 3)
if r == 1:
    print("Test A passed")
else:
    print("Test A failed")

r = binary_search(my_list, 2)
if r == 2:
    print("Test B passed")
else:
    print("Test B failed")

r = binary_search(my_list, 10)
if r == -1:
    print("Test C passed")
else:
    print("Test C failed")
```

Challenge Question

1. Does the following function correctly detect whether a list contains at least one positive element? Write code to try it out. Explain why it does work or why it does not work. Come up with working code.

```
def detect_positive(list):
    for element in list:
        if element > 0:
            return True
        else:
            return False
```

Exercise

Check the appendix for the exercise "Spell Check" that goes along with this chapter.

CHAPTER 17

■ ■ ■

Array-Backed Grids

Games like minesweeper, tic-tac-toe, and many types of adventure games keep data for the game in a grid of numbers. For example, a tic-tac-toe board:

	O	O
	X	
X		

...can use a grid of numbers to represent the empty spots, the O's, and the X's like this:

0	2	2
0	1	0
1	0	0

This grid of numbers can also be called a *two-dimensional array* or a *matrix*. (Finally, we get to learn about The Matrix.) The values of the numbers in the grid represent what should be displayed at each board location. In the prior example, 0 represents a spot where no one has played, a 1 represents an X, and a 2 represents an O.

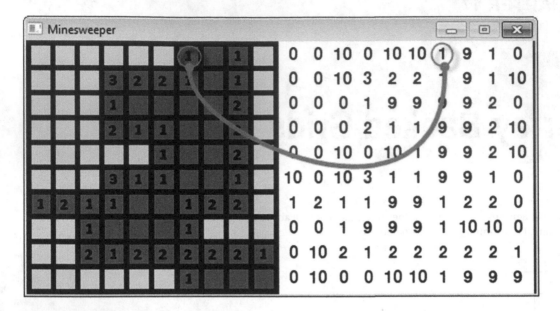

Minesweeper game, showing the backing grid of numbers

The figure above is an example from the classic minesweeper game. This example has been modified to show both the classic display on the left, and the grid of numbers used to display the board on the right.

The number 10 represents a mine, the number 0 represents a space that has not been clicked, and the number 9 represents a cleared space. The numbers 1 to 8 represent how many mines are within the surrounding 8 squares, and is only filled in when the user clicks on the square.

Minesweeper can actually have two grids: one for the regular display, and a completely separate grid of numbers that will track if the user has placed flags on the board marking where she thinks the mines are.

Classic adventure game maps are created using a tiled map editor. These are huge grids where each location is simply a number representing the type of terrain that goes there. The terrain could be things such as dirt, a road, a path, green grass, brown grass, and so forth. Programs like Tiled Qt shown in the next figure allow a developer to easily make these maps and write the grid to disk.

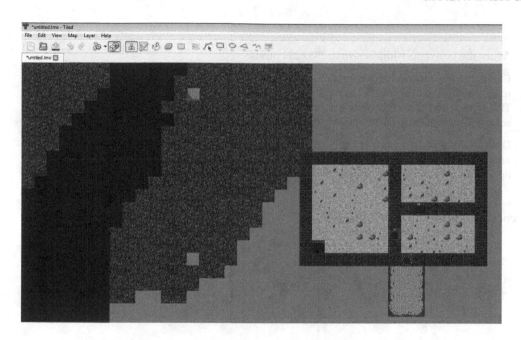

Using Qt Tiles to create an adventure map

Adventure games also use multiple grids of numbers, just like minesweeper has a grid for the mines and a separate grid for the flags. One grid, or layer, in the adventure game represents terrain you can walk on; another for things you can't walk on like walls and trees; a layer for things that can instantly kill you, like lava or bottomless pits; one for objects that can be picked up and moved around; and yet another layer for initial placement of monsters.

Maps like these can be loaded in a Python program, but unfortunately a full description of how to manage is beyond the scope of this book. Projects like `https://github.com/bitcraft/PyTMX` provide some of the code needed to load these maps.

Application

Enough talk, let's write some code. This example will create a grid that will trigger if we display a white or green block. We can change the grid value and make it green by clicking on it. This is a first step to a grid-based game like minesweeper, battleship, connect four, etc.

Go to the example code page and download the base template file: `ProgramArcadeGames.com/python_examples/f.php?file=pygame_base_template.py`.

Starting with the blank template file, attempt to re-create this program following the instructions here. The final program is at the end of this chapter, but don't skip ahead and copy it! If you do that you'll have learned nothing. Anyone can copy and paste the code, but if you can re-create this program, you have skills that people are willing to pay for. If you can only copy and paste, you've wasted your time here.

Drawing the Grid

1. Adjust the program's window size to 255×255 pixels.

2. Create variables named width, height, and margin. Set the width and height to 20. This will represent how large each grid location is. Set the margin to 5. This represents the margin between each grid location and the edges of the screen. Create these variables before the main program loop.

3. Draw a white box in the upper left corner. Draw the box drawn using the height and width variables created earlier. (Feel free to adjust the colors.) When you get done your program's window should look like the next figure.

Step 3

4. Use a for loop to draw 10 boxes in a row. Use column for the variable name in the for loop. The output will look like one long box until we add in the margin between boxes. See the next figure.

Step 4

5. Adjust the drawing of the rectangle to add in the margin variable. Now there should be gaps between the rectangles. See the next figure.

Step 5

6. Add the margin before drawing the rectangles, in addition to between each rectangle. This should keep the box from appearing right next to the window edge. See the next figure.

Step 6

7. Add another `for` loop that also will loop for each row. Call the variable in this `for` loop `row`. Now we should have a full grid of boxes. See the next figure.

Step 7

Populating the Grid

Now we need to create a two-dimensional array. Creating a two-dimensional array in Python is, unfortunately, not as easy as it is in some other computer languages. There are some libraries that can be downloaded for Python that make it easy, but for this example they will not be used.

1. To create a two-dimensional array and set an example, use the code below:

```
# --- Create grid of numbers
# Create an empty list
grid = []
# Loop for each row
for row in range(10):
    # For each row, create a list that will
    # represent an entire row
    grid.append([])
    # Loop for each column
    for column in range(10):
        # Add a the number zero to the current row
        grid[row].append(0)
```

A much shorter example is below, but this example uses some odd parts of Python that I don't bother to explain in this book:

```
grid = [[0 for x in range(10)] for y in range(10)]
```

Use one of these two examples and place the code to create our array ahead of your main program loop.

2. Set an example location in the array to 1.

Two-dimensional arrays are usually represented addressed by first their row and then the column. This is called a row-major storage. Most languages use row-major storage, with the exception of Fortran and MATLAB. Fortran and MATLAB use column-major storage.

```
# Set row 1, column 5 to one
grid[1][5] = 1
```

Place this code somewhere ahead of your main program loop.

3. Select the color of the rectangle based on the value of a variable named color. Do this by first finding the line of code where the rectangle is drawn. Ahead of it, create a variable named color and set it equal to white. Then replace the white color in the rectangle declaration with the color variable.

4. Select the color based on the value in the grid. After setting color to white, place an if statement that looks at the value in grid[row][column] and changes the color to green if the grid value is equal to 1. There should now be one green square. See the following figure.

Step 11

5.   Print "click" to the screen if the user clicks the mouse button. See
     bitmapped_graphics.py for example code of how to detect a mouse click.

6.   Print the mouse coordinates when the user clicks the mouse. See move_mouse.py
     for an example on getting the position of the mouse. See the next figure.

```
76 *Python Shell*

File   Edit   Shell   Debug   Options   Window:

Python 3.1.2  (r312:79149, Mar 21
win32
Type "copyright", "credits" or "
>>> ============================
>>>
Click: (63, 38)
Click: (107, 98)
Click: (20, 16)
|
```

Step 13

7. Convert the mouse coordinates into grid coordinates. Print those instead. Remember to use the width and height of each grid location combined with the margin. It will be necessary to convert the final value to an integer. This can be done by using int *or* by using the integer division operator // instead of the normal division operator /. See the next figure.

```
7% *Python Shell*

File   Edit   Shell   Debug   Options   Windows

Python 3.1.2 (r312:79149, Mar 21
win32
Type "copyright", "credits" or "
>>> ============================
>>>
Row: 0 Column: 2
Row: 2 Column: 3
Row: 2 Column: 1
Row: 1 Column: 4
```

Step 14

8. Set the grid location at the row/column clicked to 1. See the next figure.

Step 15

Final Program

```
"""
 Example program to show using an array to back a grid on-screen.

 Sample Python/Pygame Programs
http://programarcadegames.com/

 Explanation video: http://youtu.be/mdTeqiWyFnc
"""
import pygame

# Define some colors
BLACK = (0, 0, 0)
WHITE = (255, 255, 255)
GREEN = (0, 255, 0)
RED = (255, 0, 0)

# This sets the WIDTH and HEIGHT of each grid location
WIDTH = 20
HEIGHT = 20

# This sets the margin between each cell
MARGIN = 5

# Create a 2 dimensional array. A two dimensional
# array is simply a list of lists.
grid = []
for row in range(10):
    # Add an empty array that will hold each cell
    # in this row
    grid.append([])
    for column in range(10):
        grid[row].append(0)  # Append a cell

# Set row 1, cell 5 to one. (Remember rows and
# column numbers start at zero.)
grid[1][5] = 1

# Initialize pygame
pygame.init()

# Set the HEIGHT and WIDTH of the screen
WINDOW_SIZE = [255, 255]
screen = pygame.display.set_mode(WINDOW_SIZE)

# Set title of screen
pygame.display.set_caption("Array Backed Grid")

# Loop until the user clicks the close button.
done = False
```

```
# Used to manage how fast the screen updates
clock = pygame.time.Clock()

# -------- Main Program Loop -----------
while not done:
    for event in pygame.event.get():  # User did something
        if event.type == pygame.QUIT:  # If user clicked close
            done = True  # Flag that we are done so we exit this loop
        elif event.type == pygame.MOUSEBUTTONDOWN:
            # User clicks the mouse. Get the position
            pos = pygame.mouse.get_pos()
            # Change the x/y screen coordinates to grid coordinates
            column = pos[0] // (WIDTH + MARGIN)
            row = pos[1] // (HEIGHT + MARGIN)
            # Set that location to zero
            grid[row][column] = 1
            print("Click ", pos, "Grid coordinates: ", row, column)

    # Set the screen background
    screen.fill(BLACK)

    # Draw the grid
    for row in range(10):
        for column in range(10):
            color = WHITE
            if grid[row][column] == 1:
                color = GREEN
            pygame.draw.rect(screen,
                             color,
                             [(MARGIN + WIDTH) * column + MARGIN,
                              (MARGIN + HEIGHT) * row + MARGIN,
                              WIDTH,
                              HEIGHT])

    # Limit to 60 frames per second
    clock.tick(60)

    # Go ahead and update the screen with what we've drawn.
    pygame.display.flip()

# Be IDLE friendly. If you forget this line, the program will 'hang'
# on exit.
pygame.quit()
```

and start work on your own video game!

Review

Multiple Choice Quiz

1. In computer science, a grid of numbers is called a:

   a. Two-dimensional array

   b. Bingo board

   c. One-dimensional array

   d. Two-dimensional board

2. To print the value of the top left corner of a 10x10 two-dimensional array, the current code would be:

   a. `print(my_array[0][0])`

   b. `print(my_array[1][1])`

   c. `print(my_array[0,0])`

   d. `print(my_array[1,1])`

3. To store a 10 into an x, y position on the grid of (0, 5), what is the correct code?

   a. `my_array[5][0] = 10`

   b. `my_array[0][5] = 10`

   c. `[0][5] = 10`

   d. `my_array = 10`

   e. `my_array[10] = (0,5)`

   f. `print( my_arrayp[1,1] )`

4. To process an entire two-dimensional array, a program needs:

   a. Two nested for loops: one for each row, one for each element in the row.

   b. Two sequential for loops: one for each row, one for each element in the row.

   c. One for loop to process every element.

   d. A function for each element in the grid.

   e. Two nested classes: one for each row, one for each element.

5. In the chapter example, how does the program find which grid location was clicked on with the mouse?

   a. Divide coordinates by the size of each grid location (including the margin).

   b. Subtract the margin, divide by grid size.

   c. Subtract the grid size.

   d. Divide the grid size by the x and y coordinates.

Short Answer Worksheet

1. Start with the final program. Modify it so that rather than just changing the block the user clicks on, it also changes the blocks of the squares next to the user's click. If the user clicks on an edge, make sure the program doesn't crash and still handles the click appropriately.

2. Write a celebrity-finding function.

   Start with a function check_celebrity that takes an *n* by *n* matrix named grid as a parameter.

   The grid location grid[i][j] = 1 if person i knows person j

   and grid[i][j] = 0 otherwise.

   (Assume that grid[i][i] = 1 for every i, since every person knows him/herself.)

   A celebrity is a person who is known by everyone and does not know anyone besides him/herself.

   Write a function that given the matrix grid, prints all the celebrities.
   For example, in the following grid person 2 is a celebrity:

   ```
        0  1  2  3
      --------------
   0 |  1  1  1  0
   1 |  0  1  1  0
   2 |  0  0  1  0
   3 |  1  0  1  1
   ```

   In the next example, no one is a celebrity:

   ```
        0  1  2  3  4
      ----------------
   0 |  1  1  1  0  1
   1 |  0  1  1  0  1
   2 |  0  0  1  0  0
   3 |  1  0  1  1  1
   4 |  1  0  0  1  1
   ```

   Remember: A matrix can be represented as a list of lists, where each sublist is a row of the matrix. For example, the first matrix can be represented as:

   grid = [[1, 1, 1, 0], [0, 1, 1, 0], [0, 0, 1, 0], [1, 0, 1, 1]]

Or you can use multiple lines to define the grid:

```
grid = [ [1, 1, 1, 0],
         [0, 1, 1, 0],
         [0, 0, 1, 0],
         [1, 0, 1, 1] ]
```

You can test your function with code like the following test cases:

```
print("Test 1, Should show #2 is a celebrity.")
grid = [ [1, 1, 1, 0],
         [0, 1, 1, 0],
         [0, 0, 1, 0],
         [1, 0, 1, 1] ]

check_celebrity(grid)

print("Test 2, Should show no one is a celebrity.")
grid = [ [1, 1, 1, 0, 1],
         [0, 1, 1, 0, 1],
         [0, 0, 1, 0, 0],
         [1, 0, 0, 1, 1],
         [1, 0, 0, 1, 1] ]

check_celebrity(grid)

print("Test 3, Should show #2 is a celebrity.")
grid = [ [1, 1, 1, 0, 1],
         [0, 1, 1, 0, 1],
         [0, 0, 1, 0, 0],
         [0, 0, 1, 0, 1],
         [1, 0, 1, 1, 1] ]

check_celebrity(grid)

print("Test 4, Should show no one is a celebrity.")
grid = [ [1, 1, 1, 0, 1],
         [0, 1, 1, 0, 1],
         [1, 0, 1, 0, 0],
         [0, 0, 1, 0, 1],
         [1, 0, 1, 1, 1] ]

check_celebrity(grid)
```

Sorting

Binary searches only work on lists that are in order. So how do programs get a list in order? How does a program sort a list of items when the user clicks a column heading or otherwise needs something sorted?

There are several algorithms that do this. The two easiest algorithms for sorting are the *selection sort* and the *insertion sort*. Other sorting algorithms exist as well, such as the shell, merge, heap, and quick sorts.

The best way to get an idea on how these sorts work is to watch them. To see common sorting algorithms in action visit this excellent web site:

http://www.sorting-algorithms.com

Each sort has advantages and disadvantages. Some sort a list quickly if the list is almost in order to begin with. Some sort a list quickly if the list is in a completely random order. Other lists sort fast but take more memory. Understanding how sorts work is important in selecting the proper sort for your program.

Swapping Values

Before learning to sort, we need to learn how to swap values between two variables. This is a common operation in many sorting algorithms. Suppose a program has a list that looks like the following:

```
my_list = [15,57,14,33,72,79,26,56,42,40]
```

The developer wants to swap positions 0 and 2, which contain the numbers 15 and 14 respectively. See the following figure.

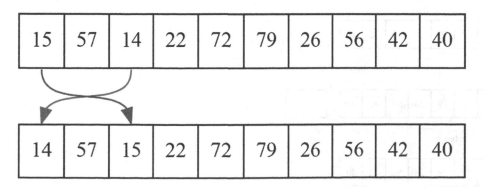

Swapping values in an array

A first attempt at writing this code might look something like this:

```
my_list[0] = my_list[2]
my_list[2] = my_list[0]
```

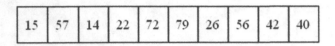

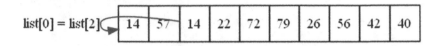

Incorrect attempt to swap array values

Look at the figure above to get an idea on what would happen. This clearly does not work. The first assignment list[0] = list[2] causes the value 15 that exists in position 0 to be overwritten with the 14 in position 2 and irretrievably lost. The next line with list[2] = list[0] just copies the 14 back to cell 2, which already has a 14.

To fix this problem, swapping values in an array should be done in three steps. It is necessary to create a temporary variable to hold a value during the swap operation. See the next figure. The code to do the swap looks like the following:

```
temp = my_list[0]
my_list[0] = my_list[2]
my_list[2] = temp
```

The first line copies the value of position 0 into the temp variable. This allows the code to write over position 0 with the value in position 2 without data being lost. The final line takes the old value of position 0, currently held in the temp variable, and places it in position 2.

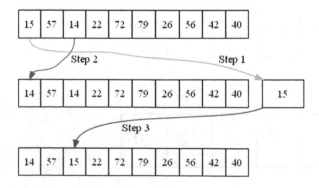

Correct method to swap array values

Selection Sort

The selection begins by looking at element 0. Then code next scans the rest of the list from element 1 to n-1 to find the smallest number. The smallest number is swapped into element 0. The code then moves on to element 1, then 2, and so forth. Graphically, the sort looks like the following figure.

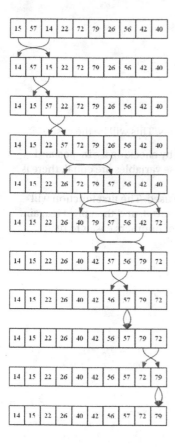

Selection Sort

The code for a selection sort involves two nested loops. The outside loop tracks the current position that the code wants to swap the smallest value into. The inside loop starts at the current location and scans to the right in search of the smallest value. When it finds the smallest value, the swap takes place.

```
def selection_sort(my_list):

    """ Sort a list using the selection sort """

    # Loop through the entire array
    for cur_pos in range(len(my_list)):
        # Find the position that has the smallest number
        # Start with the current position
        min_pos = cur_pos
```

```
        # Scan left to right (end of the list)
        for scan_pos in range(cur_pos + 1, len(my_list)):

            # Is this position smallest?
            if my_list[scan_pos] < my_list[min_pos]:

                # It is, mark this position as the smallest
                min_pos = scan_pos

        # Swap the two values
        temp = my_list[min_pos]
        my_list[min_pos] = my_list[cur_pos]
        my_list[cur_pos] = temp
```

The outside loop will always run n times. The inside loop will run $\frac{n}{2}$ times. This will be the case regardless if the list is in order or not. The loops' efficiency may be improved by checking if min_pos and cur_pos are equal before the code does the swap at the end of the sort. If those variables are equal, there is no need to do those three lines.

In order to test the selection sort code above, the following code may be used. The first function will print out the list. The next code will create a list of random numbers, print it, sort it, and then print it again. On line 3 the print statement right-aligns the numbers to make the column of numbers easier to read. Formatting print statements will be covered in Chapter 21.

```
# Before this code, paste the selection sort and import random

def print_list(my_list):
    for item in my_list:
        print("{:3}".format(item), end="")
    print()

# Create a list of random numbers
my_list = []
for i in range(10):
    my_list.append(random.randrange(100))

# Try out the sort
print_list(my_list)
selection_sort(my_list)
print_list(my_list)
```

See an animation of the selection sort at:

```
http://www.sorting-algorithms.com/selection-sort
```

For a truly unique visualization of the selection sort, search YouTube for "selection sort dance" or use this link:

```
http://youtu.be/Ns4TPTC8whw
```

Insertion Sort

The insertion sort is similar to the selection sort in how the outer loop works. The insertion sort starts at the left side of the array and works to the right side. The difference is that the insertion sort does not select the smallest element and put it into place; the insertion sort selects the next element to the right of what was already sorted. Then it slides up each larger element until it gets to the correct location to insert. Graphically, it looks like the next figure.

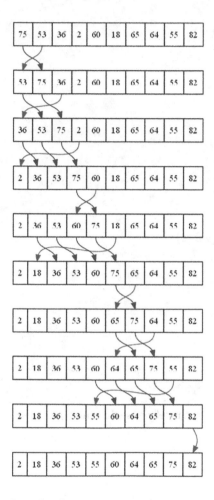

Insertion Sort

The insertion sort breaks the list into two sections: the sorted half and the unsorted half. In each round of the outside loop, the algorithm will grab the next unsorted element and insert it into the list.

In the code below, the key_pos marks the boundary between the sorted and unsorted portions of the list. The algorithm scans to the left of key_pos using the variable scan_pos. Note that in the insertion short, scan_pos goes down to the left, rather than up to the right. Each cell location that is larger than key_value gets moved up (to the right) one location.

When the loop finds a location smaller than key_value, it stops and puts key_value to the left of it.

The outside loop with an insertion sort will run n times. The inside loop will run an average of $\frac{n}{2}$ times if the loop is randomly shuffled. If the loop is close to a sorted loop already, then the inside loop does not run very much, and the sort time is closer to n.

```python
def insertion_sort(my_list):

    """ Sort a list using the insertion sort """

    # Start at the second element (pos 1).
    # Use this element to insert into the
    # list.
    for key_pos in range(1, len(my_list)):

        # Get the value of the element to insert
        key_value = my_list[key_pos]

        # Scan from right to the left (start of list)
        scan_pos = key_pos - 1

        # Loop each element, moving them up until
        # we reach the position the
        while (scan_pos >= 0) and (my_list[scan_pos] > key_value):
            my_list[scan_pos + 1] = my_list[scan_pos]
            scan_pos = scan_pos - 1

        # Everything's been moved out of the way, insert
        # the key into the correct location
        my_list[scan_pos + 1] = key_value
```

See an animation of the insertion sort at:

```
http://www.sorting-algorithms.com/insertion-sort
```

For another dance interpretation, search YouTube for "insertion sort dance" or use this link:

```
http://youtu.be/ROalU37913U
```

Review

Multiple Choice Quiz

1. How many lines of code are normally used to swap two values?

    a. 3

    b. 2

    c. 4

    d. 5

2. What is key in writing code to properly swap two values?

    a. Using the swap operator.

    b. Make sure you use the == operator rather than the = operator.

    c. Using a variable to temporarily hold one of the values while swapping.

3. In the selection sort, what does the outside loop do?

    a. Selects the next element that we will be placing the smallest remaining value into.

    b. Finds the smallest value in the list.

    c. Counts the number of items in the list.

4. In the selection sort, what does the inside loop do?

    a. Selects the next element that we will be placing the smallest remaining value into.

    b. Finds the smallest value in the list.

    c. Counts the number of items in the list.

5. In the insertion sort, what does the outside loop do?

    a. Slides an element into a sorted position.

    b. Selects the next element to be slid into a sorted position.

    c. Finds the smallest value in the list.

6. In the insertion sort, what does the inside loop do?

    a. Slides an element into a sorted position.

    b. Selects the next element to be slid into a sorted position.

    c. Finds the smallest value in the list.

7. If the selection sort and insertion sort run in n^2 time, what is n?

    a. The number of lines of code.

    b. The number of elements to sort.

    c. The time it takes to sort in milliseconds.

    d. The number of lines of code.

    e. The size of each element.

8. If the selection sort and insertion sort run in n² time, what does that mean if I have a problem size of 100 (n = 100) and increase it by 10 times to n = 1000?

    a. The 1,000 elements will take about 1,000 times longer to sort than a list of 100 elements.

    b. The 1,000 elements will take about 100 times longer to sort than a list of 100 elements.

    c. The 1,000 elements will take about 10 times longer to sort than a list of 100 elements.

    d. The 1,000 elements will take about 4 times longer to sort than a list of 100 elements.

    e. The 1,000 elements will take about 2 times longer to sort than a list of 100 elements.

9. What type of list does the insertion sort work particularly well on?

    a. A list that already close to being in order.

    b. A list that is in reverse order.

    c. A randomly sorted list.

Short Answer Worksheet

1. Write code to swap the values 25 and 40.

    ```
    my_list = [55, 41, 52, 68, 45, 27, 40, 25, 37, 26]
    ```

2. Write code to swap the values 2 and 27.

    ```
    my_list = [27, 32, 18,  2, 11, 57, 14, 38, 19, 91]
    ```

3. Why does the following code not work?

    ```
    my_list = [70, 32, 98, 88, 92, 36, 81, 83, 87, 66]
    temp = list[0]
    my_list[1] = list[0]
    my_list[0] = temp
    ```

4. Show how the following numbers can be sorted using the selection sort. Show the numbers after each iteration of the outer loop, similar to what is shown earlier in the chapter where we showed how the numbers move around. I am not looking for a copy of the code to do the sort.

    97 74 8 98 47 62 12 11 0 60

5. Show how the following numbers can be sorted using the selection sort:

    74 92 18 47 40 58 0 36 29 25

6. Show how the following numbers can be sorted using the insertion sort. Note: The 0 will not be immediately sorted into place. If you think it should, go back and review how the insertion sort works again.

    74   92   18   47   40   58   0   36   29   25

7. Show how the following numbers can be sorted using the insertion sort:

    37   11   14   50   24   7   17   88   99   9

8. Explain what min_pos does in the selection sort.

9. Explain what cur_pos does in the selection sort.

10. Explain what scan_pos does in the selection sort.

11. Explain what key_pos and key_value are in the insertion sort.

12. Explain scan_pos in the insertion sort.

13. Look at the example sort program in the examples section here:

    http://ProgramArcadeGames.com/python_examples/f.php?file=sorting_examples.py

    Modify the sorts to print the number of times the inside loop is run and the number of times the outside loop is run. Modify the program to work with a list of 100. Paste the code you used here. Run the program and list the numbers you got here. (Don't forget this part!)

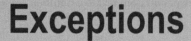

Exceptions

When something goes wrong with your program, do you want to keep the user from seeing a red Python error message? Do you want to keep your program from hanging? If so, then you need *exceptions*.

Exceptions are used to handle abnormal conditions that can occur during the execution of code. Exceptions are often used with file and network operations. This allows code to gracefully handle running out of disk space, network errors, or permission errors.

Vocabulary

There are several terms and phrases used while working with exceptions. Here are the most common:

- *Exception*: This term could mean one of two things. First, the condition that results in abnormal program flow. Or it could be used to refer to an object that represents the data condition. Each exception has an object that holds information about it.

- *Exception handling*: The process of handling an exception to normal program flow.

- *Catch block* or *exception block*: Code that handles an abnormal condition is said to catch the exception.

- *Throw* or *raise*: When an abnormal condition to the program flow has been detected, an instance of an exception object is created. It is then thrown or raised to code that will catch it.

- *Unhandled exception* or *Uncaught exception*: An exception that is thrown but never caught. This usually results in an error and the program ending or crashing.

- *Try block*: A set of code that might have an exception thrown in it.

Most programming languages use the terms throw and catch. Unfortunately Python doesn't. Python uses raise and exception. We introduce the throw/catch vocabulary here because they are the most prevalent terms in the industry.

Exception Handling

The code for handling exceptions is simple. See the example below:

```
# Divide by zero
try:
    x = 5 / 0
except:
    print("Error dividing by zero")
```

On line 2 is the try statement. Every indented line below it is part of the try block. There may be no *un*indented code below the try block that doesn't start with an except statement. The try statement defines a section of code that the code will attempt to execute.

If there is any exception that occurs during the processing of the code the execution will immediately jump to the catch block. That block of code is indented under the except statement on line 4. This code is responsible for handling the error.

A program may use exceptions to catch errors that occur during a conversion from text to a number. For example:

```
# Invalid number conversion
try:
    x = int("fred")
except:
    print("Error converting fred to a number")
```

An exception will be thrown on line 3 because "fred" cannot be converted to an integer. The code on line 5 will print out an error message.

Below is an expanded version on this example. It error checks a user's input to make sure an integer is entered. If the user doesn't enter an integer, the program will keep asking for one. The code uses exception handling to capture a possible conversion error that can occur on line 5. If the user enters something other than an integer, an exception is thrown when the conversion to a number occurs on line 5. The code on line 6 that sets number_entered to True will not be run if there is an exception on line 5.

```
number_entered = False
while not number_entered:
    number_string = input("Enter an integer: ")
    try:
        n = int(number_string)
        number_entered = True
    except:
        print("Error, invalid integer")
```

Files are particularly prone to errors during operations with them. A disk could fill up, a user could delete a file while it is being written, it could be moved, or a USB drive could be pulled out mid-operation. These types of errors may also be easily captured by using exception handling.

```
# Error opening file
try:
    my_file = open("myfile.txt")
except:
    print("Error opening file")
```

Multiple types of errors may be captured and processed differently. It can be useful to provide a more exact error message to the user than a simple "an error has occurred."

In the code below, different types of errors can occur inside the try block. By placing IOError after except, only errors regarding Input and Output (IO) will be handled by that code. Likewise the next except block only handles errors around converting values because of the ValueError, and the next block covers division by zero errors. The last exception handling occurs on the last two lines. Since that except block does not include a particular type of error, it will handle any error not covered by the prior except blocks above. The catch-all except must always be last.

```
# Multiple errors
try:
    my_file = open("myfile.txt")
    my_line = my_file.readline()
    my_int = int(s.strip())
    my_calculated_value = 101 / my_int
except IOError:
    print("I/O error")
except ValueError:
    print("Could not convert data to an integer.")
except ZeroDivisionError:
    print("Division by zero error")
except:
    print("Unexpected error")
```

A list of built-in exceptions is available from this web address: http://docs.python.org/library/exceptions.html

Example: Saving High Score

This shows how to save a high score between games. The score is stored in a file called high_score.txt.

```
"""
Show how to use exceptions to save a high score for a game.

Sample Python/Pygame Programs
http://programarcadegames.com/
"""


def get_high_score():
    # Default high score
    high_score = 0

    # Try to read the high score from a file
    try:
        high_score_file = open("high_score.txt", "r")
        high_score = int(high_score_file.read())
        high_score_file.close()
        print("The high score is", high_score)
    except IOError:
        # Error reading file, no high score
        print("There is no high score yet.")
    except ValueError:
        # There's a file there, but we don't understand the number.
        print("I'm confused. Starting with no high score.")

    return high_score
```

```python
def save_high_score(new_high_score):
    try:
        # Write the file to disk
        high_score_file = open("high_score.txt", "w")
        high_score_file.write(str(new_high_score))
        high_score_file.close()
    except IOError:
        # Hm, can't write it.
        print("Unable to save the high score.")

def main():
    """ Main program is here. """
    # Get the high score
    high_score = get_high_score()

    # Get the score from the current game
    current_score = 0
    try:
        # Ask the user for his/her score
        current_score = int(input("What is your score? "))
    except ValueError:
        # Error, can't turn what they typed into a number
        print("I don't understand what you typed.")

    # See if we have a new high score
    if current_score > high_score:
        # We do! Save to disk
        print("Yea! New high score!")
        save_high_score(current_score)
    else:
        print("Better luck next time.")

# Call the main function, start up the game
if __name__ == "__main__":
    main()
```

Exception Objects

More information about an error can be pulled from the *exception object*. This object can be retrieved while catching an error using the as keyword. For example:

```python
try:
    x = 5 / 0
except ZeroDivisionError as e:
    print(e)
```

The e variable points to more information about the exception that can be printed out. More can be done with exceptions objects, but unfortunately that is beyond the scope of this chapter. Check the Python documentation online for more information about the exception object.

Exception Generating

Exceptions may be generated with the `raise` command. For example:

```
# Generating exceptions
def get_input():
    user_input = input("Enter something: ")
    if len(user_input) == 0:
        raise IOError("User entered nothing")

getInput()
```

Try taking the code above, and add exception handling for the IOError raised.

It is also possible to create custom exceptions, but that is also beyond the scope of this book. Curious readers may learn more by going to:

```
http://docs.python.org/tutorial/errors.html#raising-exceptions
```

Proper Exception Use

Exceptions should not be used when `if` statements can just as easily handle the condition. Normal code should not raise exceptions when running the happy path scenario. Well-constructed try/catch code is easy to follow, but code involving many exceptions and jumps in code to different handlers can be a nightmare to debug. (Once I was assigned the task of debugging code that read an XML document. It generated dozens of exceptions for each line of the file it read. It was incredibly slow and error prone. That code should have never generated a single exception in the normal course of reading a file).

Review

Multiple Choice Quiz

1. What is an exception?

    a. Something that results in abnormal program flow.

    b. An `if` statement that is `False`.

    c. Code that handles an unexpected condition in the program.

    d. Paramore thinks you are the only one.

2. What is a `catch` or `exception` block?

    a. Something computers play in the back yard.

    b. Code that may cause an error that needs to be handled.

    c. Code that handles an unexpected condition in the program.

    d. A block with 22 lines in it.

3. What is a try block?

    a. Something that results in abnormal program flow.

    b. An if statement that is False.

    c. Code that handles an unexpected condition in the program.

    d. There is no try block, only do or not do blocks.

    e. Code that may cause an error that needs to be handled.

4. What will print for x?

    ```
    try:
            x = 5/0
            y = 10
    except:
            print("Error")
    print(x)
    ```

    a. 5/0

    b. Infinity

    c. 5

    d. 0 because the error has been caught.

    e. x will not print, there is an error.

5. What does the keyword raise do?

    a. Checks for errors.

    b. Brings code back to life after it has been executed.

    c. Generates a new exception that will be handled by a try block.

    d. Generates a new exception that will be handled by an except block.

6. What will print for y?

    ```
    try:
            x = 5/0
            y = 10
    except:
            print("Error")
    print(y)
    ```

    a. 10

    b. Infinity

    c. 5

    d. 10 because the error has been caught.

    e. y will not print, there is an error.

7. What is e?

```
try:
        x = 5 / 0
except ZeroDivisionError as e:
        print(e)
```

   a. 5

   b. 0

   c. An object that stores data about the error.

   d. A class that stores data about the error.

   e. A library for exception handling.

Short Answer Worksheet

1. Define the following terms in your own words. Don't just copy/paste from the book:

   • Exception

   • Exception Handling

   • Try block

   • Catch block

   • Unhandled exception

   • Throw

2. Show how to modify the following code so that an error is printed if the number conversion is not successful. Modify this code; don't just copy the example from the text. No need to ask again if the conversion is unsuccessful.

```
user_input_string = input("Enter a number:")
user_value = int(user_input_string)
```

3. What will the following code output? Predict, and then run the code to see if you are correct. Write your prediction here and if you are right. If you aren't, make sure you understand why. (Make sure to write both the prediction, and the actual results. If the program raises an error, list that fact for this and the next problem as well.)

```
x = 5
y = 0
print("A")
try:
    print("B")
    a = x / y
    print("C")
except:
    print("D")
print("E")
print(a)
```

4. What will the following code output? Predict, and then run the code to see if you are correct. Write your prediction here and if you are right. If you aren't, make sure you understand why.

```
x = 5
y = 10
print("A")
try:
    print("B")
    a = x / y
    print("C")
except:
    print("D")
print("E")
print(a)
```

CHAPTER 20

■ ■ ■

Recursion

A child couldn't sleep, so her mother told her a story about a little frog,
 who couldn't sleep, so the frog's mother told her a story about a little bear,
  who couldn't sleep, so the bear's mother told her a story about a little weasel...
   who fell asleep.
   ...and the little bear fell asleep;
   ...and the little frog fell asleep;
   ...and the child fell asleep.

(Source: `http://everything2.com/title/recursion`)

Recursion is an object or process that is defined in terms of itself. Mathematical patterns such as factorials and the Fibonacci series are recursive. Documents that can contain other documents, which themselves can contain other documents, are recursive. Fractal images and even certain biological processes are recursive in how they work.

Where Is Recursion Used?

Documents, such as web pages, are naturally recursive. For example, the next figure shows a web document.

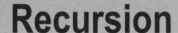

Web Page Title
Content for web page goes here Copyright © Info

Web page

That web document can be contained in a box, which can help layout the page as shown in the following figure.

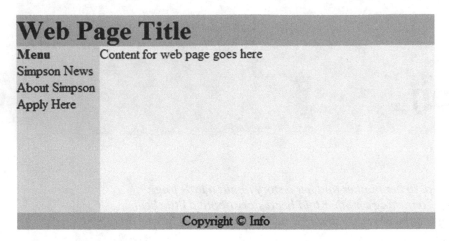

Web page with tables

This works *recursively*. Each box can contain a web page, which can have a box, which could contain another web page as shown in the figure.

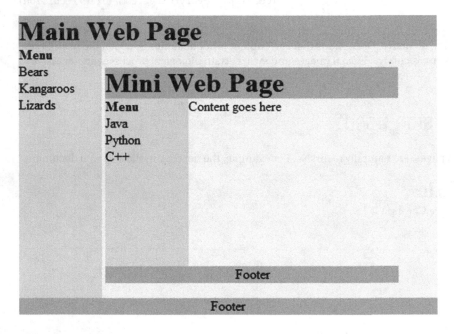

Web page with recursion

Recursive functions are often used with advanced searching and sorting algorithms. We'll show some of that here, and if you decide to learn about data structures, you will see a lot more of it.

Even if a person does not become a programmer, understanding the concept of recursive systems is important. If there is a business need for recursive table structures, documents, or something else, it is important to know how to specify this to the programmer up front.

For example, a person might specify that a web program for recipes needs the ability to support ingredients and directions. A person familiar with recursion might state that each ingredient could itself be recipes with other ingredients (that could be recipes.) The second system is considerably more powerful.

How Is Recursion Coded?

In prior chapters, we have used functions that call other functions. For example:

```python
def f():
    g()
    print("f")

def g():
    print("g")

f()
```

It is also possible for a function to call itself. A function that calls itself is using a concept called *recursion*. For example:

```python
def f():
    print("Hello")
    f()

f()
```

The example above will print Hello and then call the f() function again. Which will cause another Hello to be printed out and another call to the f() function. This will continue until the computer runs out of something called *stack space*. When this happens, Python will output a long error that ends with:

```
RuntimeError: maximum recursion depth exceeded
```

The computer is telling you, the programmer, that you have gone too far down the rabbit hole.

Controlling Recursion Depth

To successfully use recursion, there needs to be a way to prevent the function from endlessly calling itself over and over again. The example below counts how many times it has been called and uses an if statement to exit once the function has called itself 10 times.

```python
def f(level):
    # Pring the level we are at
    print("Recursion call, level",level)
    # If we haven't reached level ten…
    if level < 10:
        # Call this function again
        # and add one to the level
        f(level+1)
```

```
# Start the recursive calls at level 1
f(1)

Recursion call, level 1
Recursion call, level 2
Recursion call, level 3
Recursion call, level 4
Recursion call, level 5
Recursion call, level 6
Recursion call, level 7
Recursion call, level 8
Recursion call, level 9
Recursion call, level 10
```

Recursion Factorial Calculation

Any code that can be done recursively can be done without using recursion. Some programmers feel that the recursive code is easier to understand.

Calculating the factorial of a number is a classic example of using recursion. Factorials are useful in probability and statistics. For example:

$$10! = 10 \cdot 9 \cdot 8 \cdot 7 \cdot 6 \cdot 5 \cdot 4 \cdot 3 \cdot 2 \cdot 1$$

Recursively, this can be described as:

$$n! = \begin{cases} 1 & \text{if } n = 0, \\ n \cdot (n-1)! & \text{if } n > 0. \end{cases}$$

Below are two example functions that calculate n!. The first one is non-recursive; the second one is recursive.

```python
# This program calculates a factorial
# WITHOUT using recursion
def factorial_nonrecursive(n):
    answer = 1
    for i in range(2, n + 1):
        answer = answer * i
    return answer

# This program calculates a factorial
# WITH recursion
def factorial_recursive(n):
    if n <= 1:
        return 1
    else:
        return n * factorial_recursive(n - 1)
```

The functions do nothing by themselves. Below is an example where we put it all together. This example also adds some print statements inside the function so we can see what is happening.

```
# This program calculates a factorial
# WITHOUT using recursion

def factorial_nonrecursive(n):
    answer = 1
    for i in range(2, n + 1):
        print(i, "*", answer, "=", i * answer)
        answer = answer * i
    return answer

print("I can calculate a factorial!")
user_input = input("Enter a number:")
n = int(user_input)
answer = factorial_nonrecursive(n)
print(answer)

# This program calculates a factorial
# WITH recursion

def factorial_recursive(n):
    if n == 1:
        return n
    else:
        x = factorial_recursive(n - 1)
        print( n, "*", x, "=", n * x )
        return n * x

print("I can calculate a factorial!")
user_input = input("Enter a number:")
n = int(user_input)
answer = factorial_recursive(n)
print(answer)

I can calculate a factorial!
Enter a number:7
2 * 1 = 2
3 * 2 = 6
4 * 6 = 24
5 * 24 = 120
6 * 120 = 720
7 * 720 = 5040
5040
I can calculate a factorial!
```

```
Enter a number:7
2 * 1 = 2
3 * 2 = 6
4 * 6 = 24
5 * 24 = 120
6 * 120 = 720
7 * 720 = 5040
5040
```

Recursive Rectangles

Recursion is great to work with structured documents that are themselves recursive. For example, a web document can have a table divided into rows and columns to help with layout. One row might be the header, another row the main body, and finally the footer. Inside a table cell might be another table. And inside of that can exist yet another table.

Another example is e-mail. It is possible to attach another person's e-mail to your own e-mail. But that e-mail could have another e-mail attached to it and so on.

Can we visually see recursion in action in one of our pygame programs? Yes! Figure shows an example program that draws a rectangle and recursively keeps drawing rectangles inside of it. Each rectangle is 20% smaller than the parent rectangle. Look at the code. Pay close attention to the recursive call in the recursive_draw function.

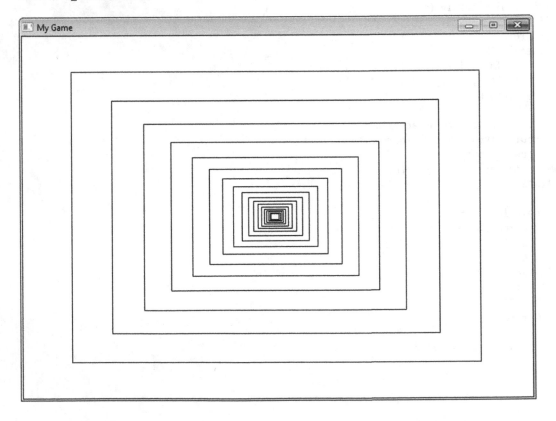

Recursive Rectangles

```
"""
 Recursively draw rectangles.

 Sample Python/Pygame Programs
 http://programarcadegames.com/
"""
import pygame

# Colors
BLACK = (0, 0, 0)
WHITE = (255, 255, 255)


def recursive_draw(x, y, width, height):
    """ Recursive rectangle function. """
    pygame.draw.rect(screen, BLACK,
                     [x, y, width, height],
                     1)

    # Is the rectangle wide enough to draw again?
    if(width > 14):
        # Scale down
        x += width * .1
        y += height * .1
        width *= .8
        height *= .8
        # Recursively draw again
        recursive_draw(x, y, width, height)

pygame.init()

# Set the height and width of the screen
size = [700, 500]
screen = pygame.display.set_mode(size)

pygame.display.set_caption("My Game")

# Loop until the user clicks the close button.
done = False

# Used to manage how fast the screen updates
clock = pygame.time.Clock()
```

```
# -------- Main Program Loop -----------
while not done:
    for event in pygame.event.get():
        if event.type == pygame.QUIT:
            done = True

    # Set the screen background
    screen.fill(WHITE)

    # ALL CODE TO DRAW SHOULD GO BELOW THIS COMMENT
    recursive_draw(0, 0, 700, 500)
    # ALL CODE TO DRAW SHOULD GO ABOVE THIS COMMENT

    # Go ahead and update the screen with what we've drawn.
    pygame.display.flip()

    # Limit to 60 frames per second
    clock.tick(60)

# Be IDLE friendly. If you forget this line, the program will 'hang'
# on exit.
pygame.quit()
```

Fractals

Fractals are defined recursively. Here is a very simple fractal, showing how it changes depending on how deep the recursion goes.

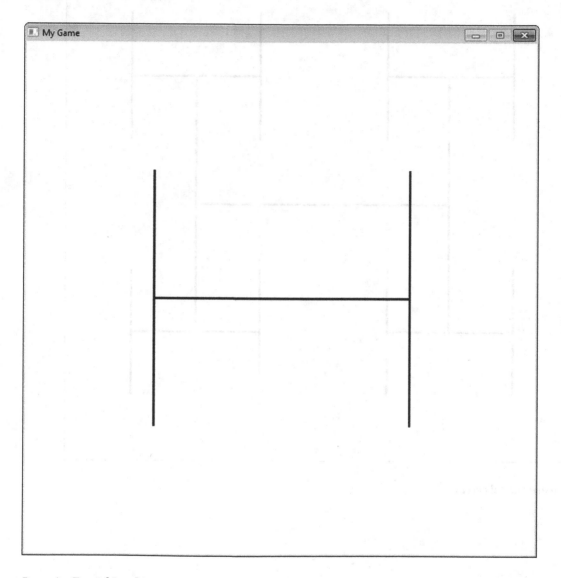

Recursive Fractal Level 0

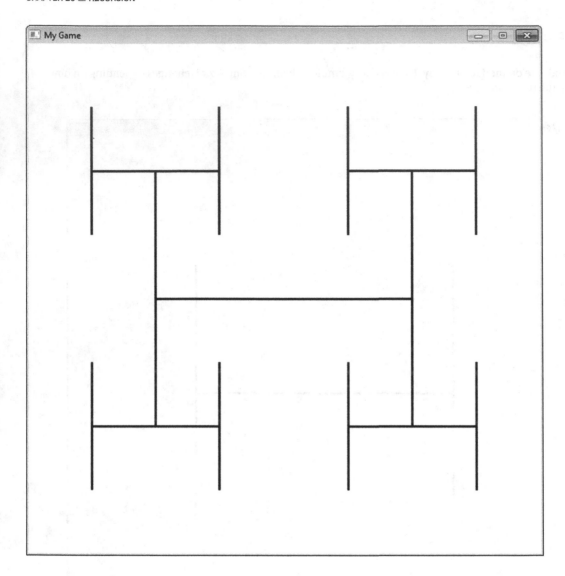

Recursive Fractal Level 1

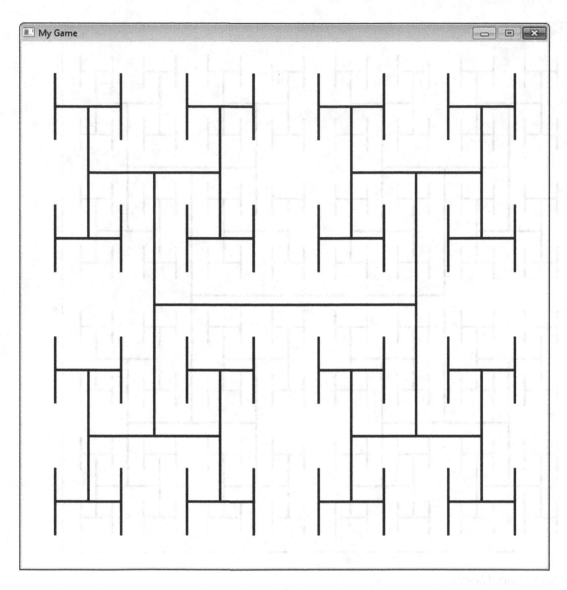

Recursive Fractal Level 2

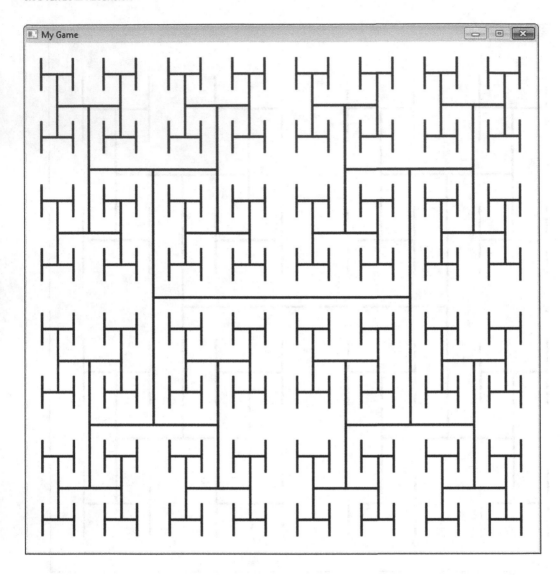

Recursive Fractal Level 3

```
"""
 Sample fractal using recursion.

 Sample Python/Pygame Programs
 http://programarcadegames.com/
"""

import pygame

# Define some colors
black = (0, 0, 0)
white = (255, 255, 255)
```

```
green = (0, 255, 0)
red = (255, 0, 0)

def recursive_draw(x, y, width, height, count):
    # Draw the rectangle
    # pygame.draw.rect(screen,black,[x,y,width,height],1)
    pygame.draw.line(screen,
                     black,
                     [x + width*.25, height // 2 + y],
                     [x + width*.75, height // 2 + y],
                     3)
    pygame.draw.line(screen,
                     black,
                     [x + width * .25, (height * .5) // 2 + y],
                     [x + width * .25,  (height * 1.5) // 2 + y],
                     3)
    pygame.draw.line(screen,
                     black,
                     [x + width * .75, (height * .5) // 2 + y],
                     [x + width * .75, (height * 1.5) // 2 + y],
                     3)

    if count > 0:
        count -= 1
        # Top left
        recursive_draw(x, y, width // 2, height // 2, count)
        # Top right
        recursive_draw(x + width // 2, y, width // 2, height // 2, count)
        # Bottom left
        recursive_draw(x, y + width // 2, width // 2, height // 2, count)
        # Bottom right
        recursive_draw(x + width // 2, y + width // 2, width // 2, height // 2, count)

pygame.init()

# Set the height and width of the screen
size = [700, 700]
screen = pygame.display.set_mode(size)

pygame.display.set_caption("My Game")

# Loop until the user clicks the close button.
done = False

# Used to manage how fast the screen updates
clock = pygame.time.Clock()
```

```
# -------- Main Program Loop -----------
while not done:
    for event in pygame.event.get():
        if event.type == pygame.QUIT:
            done = True

    # Set the screen background
    screen.fill(white)

    # ALL CODE TO DRAW SHOULD GO BELOW THIS COMMENT
    fractal_level = 3
    recursive_draw(0, 0, 700, 700, fractal_level)
    # ALL CODE TO DRAW SHOULD GO ABOVE THIS COMMENT

    # Go ahead and update the screen with what we've drawn.
    pygame.display.flip()

    # Limit to 20 frames per second
    clock.tick(20)

# Be IDLE friendly. If you forget this line, the program will 'hang'
# on exit.
pygame.quit()
```

Recursive Binary Search

Recursion can be also be used to perform a binary search. Here is a non-recursive binary search from Chapter 16:

```
def binary_search_nonrecursive(search_list, key):
    lower_bound = 0
    upper_bound = len(search_list) - 1
    found = False
    while lower_bound < upper_bound and found == False:
        middle_pos = (lower_bound + upper_bound) // 2
        if search_list[middle_pos] < key:
            lower_bound = middle_pos + 1
        elif list[middle_pos] > key:
            upper_bound = middle_pos
        else:
            found = True

    if found:
        print( "The name is at position",middle_pos)
    else:
        print( "The name was not in the list." )

binary_search_nonrecursive(name_list,"Morgiana the Shrew")
```

This same binary search written in a recursive manner:

```
def binary_search_recursive(search_list, key, lower_bound, upper_bound):
    middle_pos = (lower_bound + upper_bound) // 2
    if search_list[middle_pos] < key:
        binary_search_recursive(search_list,
                                key,
                                middle_pos + 1,
                                upper_bound)
    elif search_list[middle_pos] > key:
        binary_search_recursive(search_list,
                                key,
                                lower_bound,
                                middle_pos )
    else:
        print("Found at position", middle_pos)


lower_bound = 0
upper_bound = len(name_list) - 1
binary_search_recursive(name_list,
                        "Morgiana the Shrew",
                        lower_bound,
                        upper_bound)
```

Review

Short Answer Worksheet

1. "To understand recursion, one must first understand recursion." Explain the joke.

2. Two mirrors face each other. Explain how their reflections demonstrate the property of recursion.

3. Explain how Multi-Level Marketing uses recursion.

4. Explain how the sweep function in the classic minesweeper game could be done with recursion.

5. Explain how finding your way out of a maze could be done with recursion.

6. Use the Chrome browser and create your own screenshot at:

    http://juliamap.googlelabs.com

    Use your mouse and mouse wheel to zoom into an interesting part of the fractal.

7. Write a recursive function f(n) that takes in a value *n* and returns the value for f, given the definition below.

$$f_n = \begin{cases} 6 & \text{if } n = 1, \\ \frac{1}{2} f_{n-1} + 4 & \text{if } n > 1. \end{cases}$$

Then write a for loop that prints out the answers for values of n from 1 to 10. It should look like:

```
n= 1 , a= 6
n= 2 , a= 7.0
n= 3 , a= 7.5
n= 4 , a= 7.75
n= 5 , a= 7.875
n= 6 , a= 7.9375
n= 7 , a= 7.96875
n= 8 , a= 7.984375
n= 9 , a= 7.9921875
n= 10 , a= 7.99609375
```

The function should not have a print statement inside it, nor a loop. The for loop that is written should be outside the function and call the function to get the results and print them.

Write recursive code that will print out the first 10 terms of the sequence below.

$$f_n = \begin{cases} 1 & \textit{if } n = 1 \\ 1 & \textit{if } n = 2 \\ f(n-1) + f(n-2) & \textit{if } n > 2 \end{cases}$$

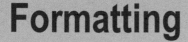

Formatting

Here is a quick table for reference when doing text formatting. For a detailed explanation of how text formatting works, keep reading.

Number	Format	Output	Description
3.1415926	{:.2f}	3.14	2 decimal places
3.1415926	{:+.2f}	+3.14	2 decimal places with sign
-1	{:+.2f}	-1.00	2 decimal places with sign
3.1415926	{:.0f}	3	No decimal places (will round)
5	{:0>2d}	05	Pad with zeros on the left
1000000	{:,}	1,000,000	Number format with comma separator
0.25	{:.2%}	25.00%	Format percentage
1000000000	{:.2e}	1.00e+09	Exponent notation
11	{:>10d}	11	Right aligned
11	{:<10d}	11	Left aligned
11	{:^10d}	11	Center aligned

Decimal Numbers

Try running the following program, which prints out several random numbers.

```
import random

for i in range(10):
    x = random.randrange(20)
    print(x)
```

The output is left justified and numbers look terrible:

```
16
13
2
0
```

```
10
3
18
1
14
5
```

We can use string formatting to make the list of numbers look better by right justifying them. The first step is to use the `format` command on the string. See below:

```
import random

for i in range(10):
    x = random.randrange(20)
    print("{}".format(x) )
```

This gets our program closer to right justify the number, but we aren't quite there yet. See how the string ends with `.format(x)`. All strings are actually instances of a class named `String`. That class has methods that can be called. One of them is `format`.

The `format` function will not print out the curly braces {} but instead replaces them with the value in `x`. The output (below) looks just like what we had before.

```
7
15
4
12
3
8
7
15
12
8
```

To right justify, we add more information about how to format the number between the curly braces {}:

```
import random

for i in range(10):
    x = random.randrange(20)
    print("{:2}".format(x) )
```

The output:

```
 7
15
 4
12
 3
 8
 7
15
12
 8
```

This is better; we have right-justified numbers! But how does it work? The :2 that we added isn't exactly intuitive.

Here's the breakdown: The { } tells the computer we are going to format a number. After the : inside the curly braces will be formatting information. In this case we give it a 2 to specify a *field width* of two characters. The field width value tells the computer to try to fit the number into a field two characters wide. By default, it will try to right justify numbers and left justify text.

Even better, the program no longer needs to call str( ) to convert the number to a string. Leave the string conversions out.

What if you had large numbers? Let's make bigger random numbers:

```
import random

for i in range(10):
    x = random.randrange(100000)
    print("{:6}".format(x) )
```

This gives output that is right justified but still doesn't look good:

```
18394
72242
97508
21583
11508
76064
88756
77413
 7930
81095
```

Where are the commas? This list would look better with separators between each three digits. Take a look at the next example to see how they are added in:

```
import random

for i in range(10):
    x = random.randrange(100000)
    print("{:6,}".format(x) )
```

The output:

```
65,732
30,248
13,802
17,177
 3,584
 7,598
21,672
82,900
72,838
48,557
```

We added a comma after the field width specifier, and now our numbers have commas. That comma must go *after* the field width specifier, not before. Commas are included in calculating the field width. For example, 1,024 has a field width of 5, not 4.

We can print multiple values and combine the values with text. Run the code below.

```
x = 5
y = 66
z = 777
print("A - '{}' B - '{}' C - '{}'".format(x, y, z))
```

The program will substitute numbers in for the curly braces, and still print out all of the other text in the string:

```
A - '5' B - '66' C - '777'
```

If there are three sets of curly braces, the computer will expect three values to be listed in the format command. The first value given will replace the first curly brace.

Sometimes we may want to print the same value twice. Or show them in a different order than how they were fed into the format function.

```
x = 5
y = 66
z = 777
print("C - '{2}' A - '{0}' B - '{1}' C again - '{2}'".format(x, y, z))
```

See that by placing a number in the curly braces, we can specify which parameter passed into the format function we want printed out. Parameters are numbered starting at 0, so x is considered parameter 0.

We can still specify formatting information after a colon. For example:

```
x = 5
y = 66
z = 777
print("C - '{2:4}' A - '{0:4}' B - '{1:4}' C again - '{2:4}'".format(x, y, z))
```

We can see that the code above will show the values right justified with a field width of 4:

```
C - ' 777' A - '   5' B - '  66' C again - ' 777'
```

Strings

Let's look at how to format strings.

The following list looks terrible.

```
my_fruit = ["Apples","Oranges","Grapes","Pears"]
my_calories = [4, 300, 70, 30]

for i in range(4):
    print(my_fruit[i], "are", my_calories[i], "calories.")
```

The output:

```
Apples are 4 calories.
Oranges are 300 calories.
Grapes are 70 calories.
Pears are 30 calories.
```

Now try it using the format command. Note how we can put additional text and more than one value into the same line.

```
my_fruit = ["Apples", "Oranges", "Grapes", "Pears"]
my_calories = [4, 300, 70, 30]

for i in range(4):
    print("{:7} are {:3} calories.".format(my_fruit[i],my_calories[i]) )
```

The output:

```
Apples  are   4 calories.
Oranges are 300 calories.
Grapes  are  70 calories.
Pears   are  30 calories.
```

That's pretty cool, and it looks the way we want it. But what if we didn't want the numbers right justified and the text left justified? We can use < and > characters like the following example:

```
my_fruit = ["Apples", "Oranges", "Grapes", "Pears"]
my_calories = [4, 300, 70, 30]

for i in range(4):
    print("{:>7} are {:<3} calories.".format(my_fruit[i],my_calories[i]) )
```

The output:

```
 Apples are 4   calories.
Oranges are 300 calories.
 Grapes are 70  calories.
  Pears are 30  calories.
```

Leading Zeros

This produces output that isn't right:

```
for hours in range(1,13):
    for minutes in range(0,60):
        print("Time {}:{}".format(hours, minutes))
```

The not-very-good output:

```
Time 8:56
Time 8:57
Time 8:58
Time 8:59
Time 9:0
Time 9:1
Time 9:2
```

We need to use leading zeros for displaying numbers in clocks. Rather than specify a 2 for the field width, instead use 02. This will pad the field with zeros rather than spaces.

```
for hours in range(1,13):
    for minutes in range(0,60):
        print("Time {:02}:{:02}".format(hours, minutes))
```

The output:

```
Time 08:56
Time 08:57
Time 08:58
Time 08:59
Time 09:00
Time 09:01
Time 09:02
```

Floating-Point Numbers

We can also control floating-point output. Examine the following code and its output:

```
x = 0.1
y = 123.456789
print("{:.1}  {:.1}".format(x,y) )
print("{:.2}  {:.2}".format(x,y) )
print("{:.3}  {:.3}".format(x,y) )
print("{:.4}  {:.4}".format(x,y) )
print("{:.5}  {:.5}".format(x,y) )
print("{:.6}  {:.6}".format(x,y) )
print()
print("{:.1f}  {:.1f}".format(x,y) )
print("{:.2f}  {:.2f}".format(x,y) )
print("{:.3f}  {:.3f}".format(x,y) )
print("{:.4f}  {:.4f}".format(x,y) )
print("{:.5f}  {:.5f}".format(x,y) )
print("{:.6f}  {:.6f}".format(x,y) )
```

And here's the output for that code:

```
0.1   1e+02
0.1   1.2e+02
0.1   1.23e+02
0.1   123.5
0.1   123.46
0.1   123.457

0.1   123.5
0.10   123.46
0.100   123.457
0.1000   123.4568
0.10000   123.45679
0.100000   123.456789
```

A format of .2 means to display the number with two digits of precision. Unfortunately this means if we display the number 123, which has three significant numbers rather than rounding it we get the number in scientific notation: 1.2e+02.

A format of .2f (note the f) means to display the number with two digits after the decimal point. So the number 1 would display as 1.00 and the number 1.5555 would display as 1.56.

A program can also specify a field width character:

```
x = 0.1
y = 123.456789
print("'{:10.1}'   '{:10.1}'".format(x,y) )
print("'{:10.2}'   '{:10.2}'".format(x,y) )
print("'{:10.3}'   '{:10.3}'".format(x,y) )
print("'{:10.4}'   '{:10.4}'".format(x,y) )
print("'{:10.5}'   '{:10.5}'".format(x,y) )
print("'{:10.6}'   '{:10.6}'".format(x,y) )
print()
print("'{:10.1f}'   '{:10.1f}'".format(x,y) )
print("'{:10.2f}'   '{:10.2f}'".format(x,y) )
print("'{:10.3f}'   '{:10.3f}'".format(x,y) )
print("'{:10.4f}'   '{:10.4f}'".format(x,y) )
print("'{:10.5f}'   '{:10.5f}'".format(x,y) )
print("'{:10.6f}'   '{:10.6f}'".format(x,y) )
```

The format 10.2f does not mean 10 digits before the decimal and 2 after. It means a total field width of 10. So there will be 7 digits before the decimal, the decimal which counts as 1 more, and 2 digits after.

```
'        0.1'   '     1e+02'
'        0.1'   '   1.2e+02'
'        0.1'   '  1.23e+02'
'        0.1'   '     123.5'
'        0.1'   '    123.46'
'        0.1'   '   123.457'
```

341

```
'     0.1'  '     123.5'
'    0.10'  '    123.46'
'   0.100'  '   123.457'
'  0.1000'  '  123.4568'
' 0.10000'  ' 123.45679'
'0.100000'  '123.456789'
```

Printing Dollars and Cents

If you want to print a floating-point number for cost, you use an f. See below:

```
cost1  = 3.07
tax1   = cost1 * 0.06
total1 = cost1 + tax1

print("Cost:  ${0:5.2f}".format(cost1) )
print("Tax:   {0:5.2f}".format(tax1) )
print("------------")
print("Total: ${0:5.2f}".format(total1) )
```

Remember! It would be easy to think that %5.2f would mean 5 digits, a decimal, followed by 2 digits. But it does not. It means a total field width of 8, including the decimal and the 2 digits after. Here's the output:

```
Cost:  $ 3.07
Tax:      0.18
------------
Total: $ 3.25
```

Danger! The above code has a mistake that is very common when working with financial transactions. Can you spot it? Try spotting it with the expanded code example below:

```
cost1  = 3.07
tax1   = cost1 * 0.06
total1 = cost1 + tax1

print("Cost:  ${0:5.2f}".format(cost1) )
print("Tax:   {0:5.2f}".format(tax1) )
print("------------")
print("Total: ${0:5.2f}".format(total1) )

cost2  = 5.07
tax2   = cost2 * 0.06
total2 = cost2 + tax2

print()
print("Cost:  ${0:5.2f}".format(cost2) )
print("Tax:   {0:5.2f}".format(tax2) )
print("------------")
print("Total: ${0:5.2f}".format(total2) )
```

```
print()
grand_total = total1 + total2
print("Grand total: ${0:5.2f}".format(grand_total) )
```

Here's the output:

```
Cost:  $ 3.07
Tax:      0.18
------------
Total: $ 3.25

Cost:  $ 5.07
Tax:      0.30
------------
Total: $ 5.37

Grand total: $ 8.63
```

Spot the mistake? You have to watch out for rounding errors! Look at that example; it seems like the total should be $ 8.62 but it isn't.

Print formatting doesn't change the number, only what is output! If we changed the print formatting to include three digits after the decimal the reason for the error becomes more apparent:

```
Cost:  $3.070
Tax:     0.184
------------
Total: $3.254

Cost:  $5.070
Tax:     0.304
------------
Total: $5.374

Grand total: $8.628
```

Again, formatting for the display does not change the number. Use the round command to change the value and truly round. See below:

```
cost1 = 3.07
tax1 = round(cost1 * 0.06, 2)
total1 = cost1 + tax1

print("Cost:  ${0:5.2f}".format(cost1) )
print("Tax:    {0:5.2f}".format(tax1) )
print("------------")
print("Total: ${0:5.2f}".format(total1) )

cost2 = 5.07
tax2 = round(cost2 * 0.06,2)
total2 = cost2 + tax2
```

```
print()
print("Cost:   ${0:5.2f}".format(cost2) )
print("Tax:     {0:5.2f}".format(tax2) )
print("------------")
print("Total: ${0:5.2f}".format(total2) )

print()
grand_total = total1 + total2
print("Grand total: ${0:5.2f}".format(grand_total) )
```

Output:

```
Cost:   $ 3.07
Tax:       0.18
------------
Total: $ 3.25

Cost:   $ 5.07
Tax:       0.30
------------
Total: $ 5.37

Grand total: $ 8.62
```

The round command controls how many digits after the decimal we round to. It returns the rounded value but does not change the original value. See below:

```
x = 1234.5678
print(round(x, 2))
print(round(x, 1))
print(round(x, 0))
print(round(x, -1))
print(round(x, -2))
```

See below to figure out how feeding the round() function values like -2 for the digits after the decimal affects the output:

```
1234.57
1234.6
1235.0
1230.0
1200.0
```

Use in Pygame

We don't just have to format strings for print statements. The example timer.py uses string formatting and blits the resulting text to the screen to make an on-screen timer:

```python
# Use python string formatting to format in leading zeros
output_string = "Time: {0:02}:{1:02}".format(minutes,seconds)

# Blit to the screen
text = font.render(output_string, True, BLACK)
screen.blit(text, [250, 250])
```

Review

Short Answer Worksheet

1. Take the following program:

    ```python
    score = 41237
    highscore = 1023407

    print("Score:      " + str(score) )
    print("High score: " + str(highscore) )
    ```

    Which right now outputs:

    ```
    Score:      41237
    High score: 1023407
    ```

    Use print formatting so that the output instead looks like:

    ```
    Score:          41,237
    High score:  1,023,407
    ```

    Make sure the print formatting works for any integer from zero to nine million.

2. Create a program that loops from 1 to 20 and lists the decimal equivalent of their inverse. Use print formatting to exactly match the following output:

    ```
    1/1  = 1.0
    1/2  = 0.5
    1/3  = 0.333
    1/4  = 0.25
    1/5  = 0.2
    1/6  = 0.167
    1/7  = 0.143
    1/8  = 0.125
    1/9  = 0.111
    1/10 = 0.1
    1/11 = 0.0909
    ```

```
1/12 = 0.0833
1/13 = 0.0769
1/14 = 0.0714
1/15 = 0.0667
1/16 = 0.0625
1/17 = 0.0588
1/18 = 0.0556
1/19 = 0.0526
1/20 = 0.05
```

3. Write a recursive function that will calculate the Fibonacci series, and use output formatting. Your result should look like:

```
 1 -          0
 2 -          1
 3 -          1
 4 -          2
 5 -          3
 6 -          5
 7 -          8
 8 -         13
 9 -         21
10 -         34
11 -         55
12 -         89
13 -        144
14 -        233
15 -        377
16 -        610
17 -        987
18 -      1,597
19 -      2,584
20 -      4,181
21 -      6,765
22 -     10,946
23 -     17,711
24 -     28,657
25 -     46,368
26 -     75,025
27 -    121,393
28 -    196,418
29 -    317,811
30 -    514,229
31 -    832,040
32 -  1,346,269
33 -  2,178,309
34 -  3,524,578
35 -  5,702,887
```

4. Why does the problem above run so slow? How could it be made to run faster?

CHAPTER 22

■ ■ ■

Exercises

Exercise 1: Custom Calculators

Exercise 2: Create-a-Quiz

Exercise 3: Camel

Exercise 4: Create-a-Picture

Exercise 5: Loopy Lab

Exercise 6: Adventure!

Exercise 7: Animation

Exercise 8: Functions

Exercise 9: Functions and User Control

Exercise 10: Bit-Mapped Graphics, Sound Effects, and Music

Exercise 11: Classes and Graphics

Exercise 12: Sprite Collecting

Exercise 13: Moving Sprites

Exercise 14: Spell Check

Exercise 15: Final Exercise

Exercise 1: Custom Calculators

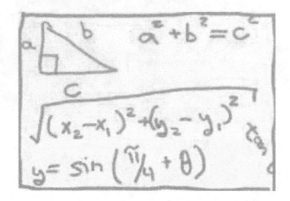

In this exercise we'll create three custom calculator programs. To help create these exercises check the code in Chapter 2. In particular, the example program at the end of that chapter provides a good template for the code needed in this exercise.

Make sure you can write out simple programs like what is assigned in this exercise. Be able to do it from memory as well as on paper. These programs follow a very common pattern in computing:

1. Take in data

2. Perform calculations

3. Output data

Programs take in data from sources such as databases, 3D models, game controllers, keyboards, and the Internet. They perform calculations and output the result. Sometimes we even do this in a loop thousands of times a second.

It is a good idea to do the calculations separate from the output of the data. While it is possible to do the calculation inside the print statement, it is better to do the calculation, store it in a variable, and then output it later. This way calculations and output aren't mixed together.

When writing programs it is a good idea to use blank lines to separate logical groupings of code. For example, place a blank line between the input statements, the calculation, and the output statement. Also, add comments to your program labeling these sections.

For this exercise you will create three short programs:

Program A

Create a program that asks the user for a temperature in Fahrenheit, and then prints the temperature in Celsius. Search the Internet for the correct calculation. Look at Chapter 2 for the miles-per-gallon example to get an idea of what should be done.

Sample run:

```
Enter temperature in Fahrenheit: 32
The temperature in Celsius: 0.0
```

Sample run:

```
Enter temperature in Fahrenheit: 72
The temperature in Celsius: 22.2222222222
```

The numbers from this program won't be formatted nicely. That is OK. But if it bothers you, look ahead to Chapter 21 and see how to make your output look great!

Program B

Create a new program that will ask the user for the information needed to find the area of a trapezoid, and then print the area. The formula for the area of a trapezoid is:

$$A = \frac{1}{2}(x_1 + x_2)h$$

Sample run:

```
Area of a trapezoid
Enter the height of the trapezoid: 5
Enter the length of the bottom base: 10
Enter the length of the top base: 7
The area is: 42.5
```

Program C

Create your own original problem and have the user plug in the variables. If you are not in the mood for anything original, choose an equation from this list:

Area of a circle	$A = \pi r^2$
Area of an ellipse	$A = \pi r_1 r_2$
Area of an equilateral triangle	$A = \dfrac{h^2 \sqrt{3}}{3}$
Volume of a cone	$V = \dfrac{\pi r^2 h}{3}$
Volume of a sphere	$V = \dfrac{4 \pi r^3}{3}$
Area of an arbitrary triangle	$A = \dfrac{1}{2} ab \, \sin C$

When done, check to make certain your variable names begin with a lowercase letter and that you are using blank lines between logical groupings of the code. (Between input, calculations, and output in this case.)

Exercise 2: Create-a-Quiz

Now is your chance to write your *own* quiz. Use these quizzes to filter job applicants, weed out potential mates, or just plain have a chance to sit on the other side of the desk and make, rather than take, the quiz.

This exercise applies the material used in Chapter 4 on using if statements. It also requires a bit of Chapter 2 because the program must calculate a percentage.

Description

This is the list of features your quiz needs to have:

1. Create your own quiz with five or more questions. You can ask questions that require:

    -   a number as an answer (e.g., What is 1+1?)

    -   text (e.g. What is Harry Potter's last name?)

    -   a selection (Which of these choices are correct? A, B, or C?)

2. If you have the user enter non-numeric answers, think and cover the different ways a user could enter a correct answer. For example, if the answer is "a," would "A" also be acceptable? See Chapter 4 for a reminder on how to do this.

3. Let the user know if they get the question correct. Print a message depending on the user's answer.

4. You need to keep track of how many questions they get correct.

5. At the end of the program print the percentage of questions the user gets right.

Keep the following in mind when creating the program:

1. Variable names should start with a lowercase letter. Uppercase letters work, but it is not considered proper. (Right, you didn't realize that programming was going to be like English Tea Time, did you?)

2. To create a running total of the number correct, create a variable to store this score. Set it to zero. With an `if` statement, add one to the variable each time the user gets a correct answer. (How do you know if they got it correct? Remember that if you are printing out "correct" then you have already done that part. Just add a line there to add one to the number correct.) If you don't remember how to add one to a variable, go back and review Chapter 2.

3. Treat true/false questions like multiple choice questions; just compare to "True" or "False." Don't try to do `if a:` we'll implement `if` statements like that later on in the class, but this isn't the place.

4. Calculate the percentage by using a formula at the end of the game. Don't just add 20% for each question the user gets correct. If you add 20% each time, then you have to change the program 5 places if you add a 6th question. With a formula, you only need 1 change.

5. To print a blank line so that all the questions don't run into each other, use the following code:

   ```
   print()
   ```

6. Remember the program can print multiple items on one line. This can be useful when printing the user's score at the end.

   ```
   print("The value in x is", x)
   ```

7. Separate out your code by using blank lines to group sections together. For example, put a blank line between the code for each question.

8. Sometimes it makes sense to reuse variables. Rather than having a different variable to hold the user's answer for each question, you could reuse the same one.

9. Use descriptive variable names. `x` is a terrible variable name. Instead use something like `number_correct`.

Example Run

Here's an example from my program:

```
Quiz time!

How many books are there in the Harry Potter series? 7
Correct!

What is 3*(2-1)? 3
Correct!

What is 3*2-1? 5
Correct!
```

```
Who sings Black Horse and the Cherry Tree?
1. Kelly Clarkson
2. K.T. Tunstall
3. Hillary Duff
4. Bon Jovi
? 2
Correct!

Who is on the front of a one dollar bill
1. George Washington
2. Abraham Lincoln
3. John Adams
4. Thomas Jefferson
? 2
No.

Congratulations, you got 4 answers right.
That is a score of 80.0 percent.
```

Exercise 3: Camel

Description of the Camel Game

The idea for Camel originally came from the Heath Users Group and was published in More BASIC Computer Games in 1979.

352

The idea is to ride your camel across the desert while being chased. You need to manage your thirst, how tired the camel is, and how far ahead of the natives you are.

This is one of the first games I programmed on the Apple //e. The game is flexible. I've known people to create Star Wars themed versions of this game where you need to ride a wampa across Hoth. It is easy to add sandstorms and other random events to the game to make it more interesting.

Sample Run of Camel

Here is a sample run of the game:

```
Welcome to Camel!
You have stolen a camel to make your way across the great Mobi desert.
The natives want their camel back and are chasing you down! Survive your
desert trek and outrun the natives.

A. Drink from your canteen.
B. Ahead moderate speed.
C. Ahead full speed.
D. Stop and rest.
E. Status check.
Q. Quit.
Your choice? C

You traveled 12 miles.

A. Drink from your canteen.
B. Ahead moderate speed.
C. Ahead full speed.
D. Stop and rest.
E. Status check.
Q. Quit.
Your choice? C

You traveled 17 miles.

A. Drink from your canteen.
B. Ahead moderate speed.
C. Ahead full speed.
D. Stop and rest.
E. Status check.
Q. Quit.
Your choice? e

Miles traveled:  29
Drinks in canteen:  3
The natives are 31 miles behind you.
```

```
A. Drink from your canteen.
B. Ahead moderate speed.
C. Ahead full speed.
D. Stop and rest.
E. Status check.
Q. Quit.
Your choice? b

You traveled 6 miles.

...and so on until...

A. Drink from your canteen.
B. Ahead moderate speed.
C. Ahead full speed.
D. Stop and rest.
E. Status check.
Q. Quit.
Your choice? C

You traveled 12 miles.
The natives are getting close!

A. Drink from your canteen.
B. Ahead moderate speed.
C. Ahead full speed.
D. Stop and rest.
E. Status check.
Q. Quit.
Your choice? C

You traveled 11 miles.
The natives are getting close!
You made it across the desert! You won!
```

Programming Guide

Here are the steps to complete this exercise. Feel free to modify and add to the exercise. Try the game with friends and family.

1. Create a new program and print the instructions to the screen. Do this with multiple `print` statements. Don't use one `print` statement and multiple \n characters to jam everything on one line.

   ```
   Welcome to Camel!
   You have stolen a camel to make your way across the great Mobi desert.
   The natives want their camel back and are chasing you down! Survive your
   desert trek and out run the natives.
   ```

2. Create a Boolean variable called done and set to False.

3. Create a while loop that will keep looping while done is False.

4. Inside the loop, print out the following:

   A. Drink from your canteen.
   B. Ahead moderate speed.
   C. Ahead full speed.
   D. Stop for the night.
   E. Status check.
   Q. Quit.

5. Ask the user for their choice. Make sure to add a space before the quote so the user input doesn't run into your text.

6. If the user's choice is Q, then set done to True. By doing something like user_choice.upper() instead of just user_choice in your if statement you can make it case insensitive.

7. Test and make sure that you can quit out of the game.

8. Before your main program loop, create variables for miles traveled, thirst, and camel tiredness. Set these to zero.

9. Create a variable for the distance the natives have traveled and set it to -20. (Twenty miles back.)

10. Create and set an initial number of drinks in the canteen.

11. Add an elif in your main program loop and see if the user is asking for status. If so, print out something like this:

    Miles traveled: 0
    Drinks in canteen: 3
    The natives are 10 miles behind you.

12. Add an elif in your main program loop and handle if the user wants to stop for the night. If the user does, reset the camel's tiredness to zero. Print that the camel is happy, and move the natives up a random amount from 7 to 14 or so.

13. Add an elif in your main program loop and handle if the user wants to go ahead full speed. If the user does, go forward a random amount between 10 and 20 inclusive. Print how many miles the user traveled. Add 1 to thirst. Add a random 1 to 3 to camel tiredness. Move the natives up 7 to 14 miles.

14. Add an elif in your main program loop and handle if the user wants to go ahead moderate speed. If the user does, go forward a random amount between 5 and 12 inclusive. Print how many miles the user traveled. Add 1 to thirst. Add 1 to camel tiredness. Move the natives up 7 to 14 miles.

15. Add an elif in your main program loop and handle if the user wants to go ahead drink from the canteen. If the user does, make sure there are drinks in the canteen. If there are, subtract one drink and set the player's thirst to zero. Otherwise print an error.

16. In the loop, print "You are thirsty." if the user's thirst is above 4.

17. Print "You died of thirst!" if the user's thirst is above 6. Set done to true. Make sure you create your code so that the program doesn't print *both* "You are thirsty" and "You died of thirst!" Use `elif` as appropriate.

18. Print "Your camel is getting tired." if the camel's tiredness is above 5.

19. Print "Your camel is dead." if the camel's tiredness is above 8. Like the prior steps, print one or the other. It is a good idea to include a check with the done variable so that you don't print that your camel is getting tired after you died of thirst.

20. If the natives have caught up, print that they caught the player and end the game.

21. Else if the natives are less than 15 miles behind, print "The natives are getting close!"

22. If the user has traveled 200 miles across the desert, print that they won and end the game. Make sure they aren't dead before declaring them a winner.

23. Add a one-in-twenty chance of finding an oasis. Print that the user found it, refill the canteen, reset player thirst, and rest the camel.

24. Play the game and tune the numbers so it is challenging but not impossible. Fix any bugs you find.

Hints

- Remember that it is good idea to put blank lines between logical groupings of code in your program. For example, but a blank line after the instructions and between each user command.

- It is considered better style to use `while not done:` instead of `while done == False:`

- To prevent bad message combinations, such as printing "You died of thirst." and "You found an oasis!" on the same turn, use the and operator. Such as, `if not done and thirst > 4:`

Exercise 4: Create-a-Picture

Description

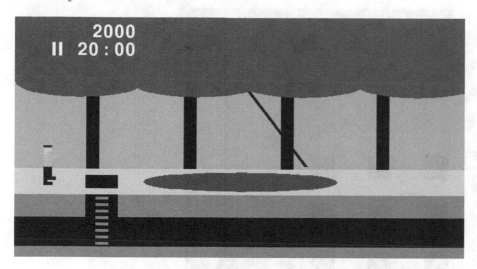

Your assignment: Draw a pretty picture. The goal of this exercise is to get practice using functions, using for loops, and introduce computer graphics.

To practice all your new skills:

- Have an image with multiple colors.

- Make a coherent picture. Don't just make abstract art with random shapes. That's not challenging.

- Try out several types of graphical functions (e.g., circles, rectangles, lines, etc.).

- Use a while or for loop to create a repeating pattern. Do not just redraw the same thing in the same location 10 times. Actually use that index variable as an offset to displace what you are drawing. Remember that you can contain multiple drawing commands in a loop, so you can draw multiple train cars for example.

For a template program to modify, look at the following example programs:

ProgramArcadeGames.com/python_examples/f.php?file=pygame_base_template.py
ProgramArcadeGames.com/python_examples/f.php?file=simple_graphics_demo.py

See Chapter 6 for an explanation of the template. For official documentation on the draw module:

http://www.pygame.org/docs/ref/draw.html

To select new colors, either use

http://www.colorpicker.com/

or open up the Windows Paint program and click on "Edit Colors." Copy the values for Red, Green, and Blue. Do not worry about colors for hue, Saturation, or Brilliance.

Please use comments and blank lines to make it easy to follow your program. If you have 5 lines that draw a robot, group them together with blank lines above and below. Then add a comment at the top telling the reader what you are drawing.

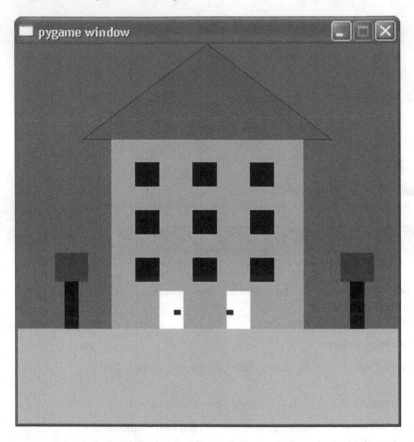

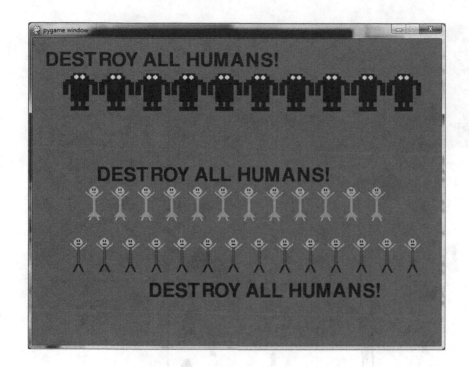

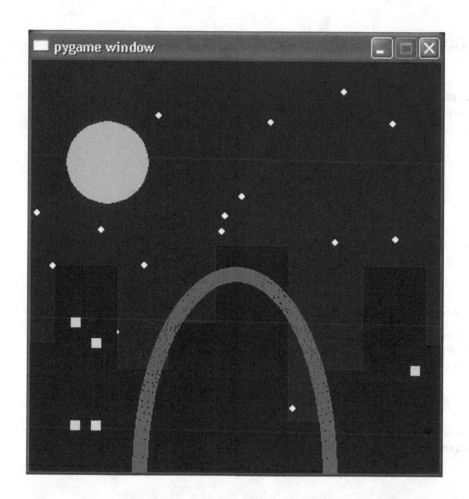

Exercise 5: Loopy Lab

Part 1

Write a Python program that will print the following:

```
10
11 12
13 14 15
16 17 18 19
20 21 22 23 24
25 26 27 28 29 30
31 32 33 34 35 36 37
38 39 40 41 42 43 44 45
46 47 48 49 50 51 52 53 54
```

Tips for Part 1

- Generate the output for part one using two for loops, one nested.

- Create a separate variable to store numbers that will be printed. Don't use the variables that you created in your for loops. This will be a third variable that starts at 10 and goes up one each time.

Part 2

Create a big box out of *n* rows of little o's for any desired size n. Use an input statement to allow the user to enter the value for n and then print the properly sized box.

```
E.g. n = 3
oooooo
o    o
oooooo

E.g. n = 8
oooooooooooooooo
o              o
o              o
o              o
o              o
o              o
o              o
oooooooooooooooo
```

Part 3

Print the following for any positive integer n. Use an input statement to allow the user to enter the value for n and then print the properly sized box.

E.g. n = 3

```
1 3 5 5 3 1
3 5     5 3
5         5
5         5
3 5     5 3
1 3 5 5 3 1
```

E.g. n = 5

```
1 3 5 7 9 9 7 5 3 1
3 5 7 9     9 7 5 3
5 7 9         9 7 5
7 9             9 7
9                 9
9                 9
7 9             9 7
5 7 9         9 7 5
3 5 7 9     9 7 5 3
1 3 5 7 9 9 7 5 3 1
```

Don't worry about handling the spacing for multi-digit numbers. Chapter 21 covers this if you want to look ahead, but it isn't needed.

This part of the exercise is difficult. Skip to part 4 if you aren't interested in the challenge.

Part 4

Start with the pygame template code:

ProgramArcadeGames.com/python_examples/f.php?file=pygame_base_template.py

Use nested for loops to draw small green rectangles. Make the image look like the following figure.

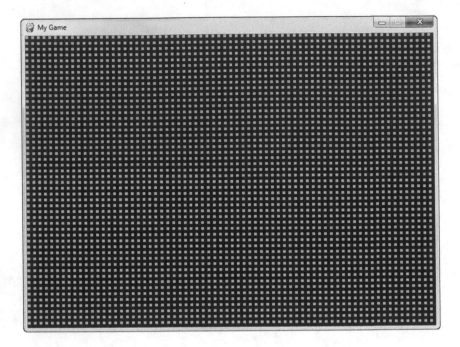

Pygame Grid

Do not create the grid by drawing lines; use a grid created by rectangles.

If this is too boring, create a similar grid of something else. It is OK to change the color, size, and type of shape drawn. Just get used to using nested for loops to generate a grid.

Sometimes people feel the need to add a zero to the offset in this program. Remind yourself, adding zero to a number is kind of silly.

Exercise 6: Adventure!

Description of the Adventure Game

One of the first games I ever played was a text adventure called Colossal Cave Adventure. You can play the game online to get an idea what text adventure games are like. Arguably the most famous of this genre of game is the Zork series.

The first "large" program I created myself was a text adventure. It is easy to start an adventure like this. It is also a great way to practice using lists. Our game for this exercise will involve a list of rooms that can be navigated by going north, east, south, or west. Each room will be a list with the room description, and then what rooms are in each of the directions. See the section below for a sample run:

Sample Run

```
You are in a dusty castle room.
Passages lead to the north and south.
What direction? n

You are in the armory.
There is a room off to the south.
What direction? s

You are in a dusty castle room.
Passages lead to the north and south.
What direction? s
```

```
You are in a torch-lit hallway.
There are rooms to the east and west.
What direction? e

You are in a bedroom. A window overlooks the castle courtyard.
A hallway is to the west.
What direction? w

You are in a torch-lit hallway.
There are rooms to the east and west.
What direction? w

You are in the kitchen. It looks like a roast is being made for supper.
A hallway is to the east.
What direction? w

Can't go that way.
You are in the kitchen. It looks like a roast is being made for supper.
A hallway is to the east.
What direction?
```

Creating Your Dungeon

Before you start, sketch out the dungeon that you want to create. It might look something like this:

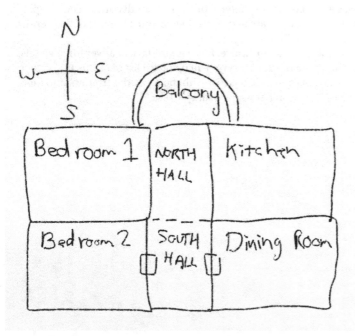

Next, number all of the rooms starting at zero.

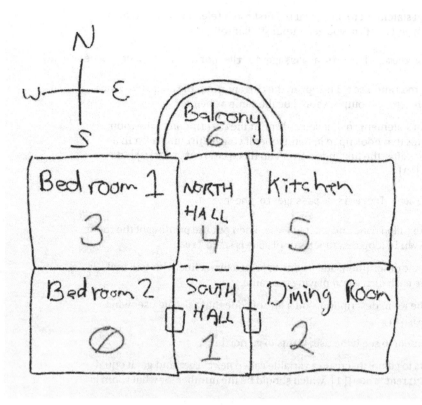

Use this sketch to figure out how all the rooms connect. For example, room 0 connects to room 3 to the north, room 1 to the east, and no room to the south and west.

Step-by-step Instructions

1. Create an empty array called room_list.

2. Create a variable called room. Set it equal to an array with five elements. For the first element, create a string with a description of your first room. The last four elements will be the number of the next room if the user goes north, east, south, or west. Look at your sketch to see what numbers to use. Use None if no room hooks up in that direction. (Do not put None in quotes. It is a special value that represents no value.)

3. Append this room to the room list.

4. Repeat the prior two steps for each room you want to create. Just reuse the room variable.

5. Create a variable called current_room. Set it to zero.

6. Print the room_list variable. Run the program. You should see a really long list of every room in your adventure. (If you are using an IDE like Wing, don't leave it scrolled way off to the right.)

7. Adjust your print statement to only print the first room (element zero) in the list. Run the program and confirm you get output similar to:

```
['You are in a room. There is a passage to the north.', 1, None, None, None]
```

8. Using current_room and room_list, print the current room the user is in. Since your first room is zero, the output should be the same as before.

9. Change the print statement so that you only print the description of the room, and not the rooms that hook up to it. Remember if you are printing a list in a list the index goes after the first index. Don't do this: [current_room[0]], do [current_room][0]

```
You are in a room. There is a passage to the north.
```

10. Create a variable called done and set it to False. Then put the printing of the room description in a while loop that repeats until done is set to True.

11. Before printing the description, add a code to print a blank line. This will make it visually separate each turn when playing the game.

12. After printing the room description, add a line of code that asks the user what direction they wish to go.

13. Add an if statement to see if the user wants to go north.

14. If the user wants to go north, create a variable called next_room and get it equal to room_list[current_room][1], which should be the number for what room is to the north.

15. Add another if statement to see if the next room is equal to None. If it is, print "You can't go that way." Otherwise set current_room equal to next_room.

16. Test your program. Can you go north to a new room?

17. Add elif statements to handle east, south, and west. Add an else statement to let the user know the program doesn't understand what she typed.

18. Add several rooms, at least five. It may be necessary to draw out the rooms and room numbers to keep everything straight. Test out the game. You can use \n or triple quotes if you have a multiline room description.

19. Optional: Add a quit command. Make sure that the program works for upper and lower case directions. Have the program work if the user types in "north" or "n."

Spend a little time to make this game interesting. Don't simply create an "East room" and a "West room." That's boring.

Also spend a little time to double-check spelling and grammar. Without a word processor checking your writing, it is important to be careful.

Use \n to add carriage returns in your descriptions so they don't print all on one line. Don't put spaces around the \n, or the spaces will print.

What I like about this program is how easy it is to expand into a full game. Using all eight cardinal directions (including "NorthWest"), along with "up" and "down" is rather easy. Managing an inventory of objects that can exist in rooms, be picked up, and dropped is also a matter of keeping lists.

Expanding this program into a full game is one of the two options for the final exercise.

Exercise 7: Animation

Requirements

Modify the prior Create-a-Picture exercise, or start a new one.
Animate the image. Try one or more of the following:

- Move an item across the screen.

- Move an item back and forth.

- Move up/down/diagonally.

- Move in circles.

- Have a person wave their arms.

- Create a stoplight that changes colors.

Remember, the more flair the better! Have fun with this exercise, and take time to see what you can do.

Exercise 8: Functions

Write this as all one program. The entire thing should be able to run straight through.
There are several parts to this program. Here is a description of each part:

1. Write a function called min3 that will take three numbers as parameters and
    return the smallest value. If more than one number tied for smallest, still return
    that smallest number. Use a proper if/elif/else chain. Once you've finished
    writing your function, copy/paste the following code and make sure that it runs
    against the function you created:

    ```
    print(min3(4, 7, 5))
    print(min3(4, 5, 5))
    print(min3(4, 4, 4))
    print(min3(-2, -6, -100))
    print(min3("Z", "B", "A"))
    ```

    You should get this result:

    ```
    4
    4
    4
    -100
    A
    ```

    The function should return the value, not print the value. Also, while there is a
    min function built into Python, don't use it. Please use if statements and practice
    creating it yourself. Leave the testing statements in the program so the instructor
    can check the program. If you also get None to print out, then chances are you are
    using print instead of return in your function.

2. Write a function called box that will output boxes given a height and width. Once you've finished writing your function, copy and paste the following code after it and make sure it works with the function you wrote:

```
box(7,5)  # Print a box 7 high, 5 across
print()   # Blank line
box(3,2)  # Print a box 3 high, 2 across
print()   # Blank line
box(3,10) # Print a box 3 high, 10 across
```

You should get the following results from the sample code:

```
*****
*****
*****
*****
*****
*****
*****

**
**
**

*********
*********
*********
```

Go back and look at Chapter 7 if you've forgotten how to do this.

3. Write a function called find that will take a list of numbers, my_list, along with one other number, key. Have it search the list for the value contained in key. Each time your function finds the key value, print the array position of the key. You will need to juggle three variables: one for the list, one for the key, and one for the position of where you are in the list.

This code will look similar to the Chapter 8 code for iterating though a list using the range and len functions. Start with that code and modify the print to show each element and its position. Then instead of just printing each number, add an if statement to only print the ones we care about.

Copy/paste this code to test it:

```
my_list = [36, 31, 79, 96, 36, 91, 77, 33, 19, 3, 34, 12, 70, 12, 54, 98, 86, 11, 17, 17]

find(my_list, 12)
find(my_list, 91)
find(my_list, 80)
```

...check for this output:

```
Found 12 at position 11
Found 12 at position 13
Found 91 at position 5
```

Use a for loop with an index variable and a range. Inside the loop use an if statement. The function can be written in about four lines of code.

4. Write one program that has the following:

- Functions:

    - Write a function named create_list that takes in a list size and returns a list of random numbers from 1-6 (i.e., calling create_list(5) should return 5 random numbers from 1-6. (Remember, Chapter 8 has code showing how to do something similar, creating a list out of five numbers the user enters. Here, you need to create random numbers rather than asking the user.)

      To test, use this code against the function you wrote:

      ```
      my_list = create_list(5)
      print(my_list)
      ```

      And you should get output of five random elements that looks something like:

      ```
      [2,5,1,6,3]
      ```

    - Write a function called count_list that takes in a list and a number. Have the function return the number of times the specified number appears in the list.

      To test, use this code against the function you wrote:

      ```
      count = count_list([1,2,3,3,3,3,4,2,1],3)
      print(count)
      ```

      And you should get output something like:

      ```
      3
      ```

    - Write a function called average_list that returns the average of the list passed into it.

      To test, use this code against the function you wrote:

      ```
      avg = average_list([1,2,3])
      print(avg)
      ```

      And you should get output something like:

      ```
      2
      ```

- Now that the functions have been created, use them all in a main program that will:

  - Create a list of 10,000 random numbers from 1 to 6. This should take one line of code. Use the function you created earlier in the exercise.)

  - Print the count of 1 through 6. (That is, print the number of times 1 appears in the 10,000. And then do the same for 2–6.)

  - Print the average of all 10,000 random numbers.

Exercise 9: User Control

This exercise gives you a chance to practice drawing an object with a function and allowing the user to control it.

Create one program that has the following:

1. Create at least two different functions that draw an object to the screen. For example, draw_bird and draw_tree. Do not draw a stick figure; we did that one already. Create your own unique item. If you created your own object in the create-a-picture exercise feel free to adapt it to this exercise.

2. In Chapter 11, we talked about moving graphics with the keyboard, a game controller, and the mouse. Pick two of those and use them to control two different items on the screen.

3. In the case of the game controller and the keyboard, make sure to add checks so that your object does not move offscreen and get lost.

Exercise 10: Bitmapped Graphics and User Control

Create a graphics-based program. You can start a new program or continue with a prior exercise. This is the checklist for completing this exercise:

- Make sure this program is created in its own directory. Use an empty directory you already have, or create a new one.

- Incorporate at least one function that draws an item on the screen. The function should take position data that specifies where to draw the item. (Note: You will also need to pass a reference to the "screen." Another note: this is difficult to do with images loaded from a file. I recommend doing this only with regular drawing commands.)

- Add the ability to control an item via mouse, keyboard, or game controller.

- Include some kind of bit-mapped graphics. Do not include bit-mapped graphics as part of your "draw with a function." That won't work well until we've learned a bit more.

- Include sound. You could make a sound when the user clicks the mouse, hits a key, moves to a certain location, etc. If the sound is problematic, try using the program Audacity to load the sound, and then export it as an .ogg file.

- If you send this program to someone, make sure you send all the files. It is easy to forget to add the images and sound files.

Example Code:

`ProgramArcadeGames.com/index.php?chapter=example_code`

Sounds and bitmaps you can use:

`opengameart.org`

It is OK to use code from prior exercises, such as Exercise 5.

Exercise 11: Classes and Graphics

Graphics provide an excellent opportunity to use classes. Each graphic object can be represented by an *object*. Each type of graphic object can be represented by a *class*. An object's location, speed, and color can be stored in *attributes*.

Instructions

1. Start a new program with:

    `ProgramArcadeGames.com/python_examples/f.php?file=pygame_base_template.py`

2. Right after the default colors are defined in the example program, create a class called `Rectangle`.

    • Add x and y attributes, which will be used for storing the object's position.

    • Create a `draw` method. Have the method create a green 10×10 rectangle at the location stored in x and y. Don't forget to use `self.` before the variables. The method will need to take in a reference to `screen` so that the `pygame.draw.rect` function can draw the rectangle to the correct screen.

3. Before the program loop, create a variable called `my_object` and set it equal to a new instance of `Rectangle`.

4. Inside the main program loop, call `my_object`'s `draw()` method.

5. Checkpoint: Make sure your program works, and the output looks like this figure.

Rectangle in top left corner

6. Right after the program creates the instance of Rectangle, set the x and y values to something new, like 100, 200. Run the program again to make sure it works and the rectangle moves to the new coordinates.

7. Add attributes to the class for height and width. Draw the rectangle using these new attributes. Run the program and make sure it works.

8. Get the object to move:

   • Add attributes for change_x and change_y.

   • Create a new method called move(), that adjusts x and y based on change_x and change_y. (Note that the move method will not need screen as a parameter because it doesn't draw anything to the screen.)

   • Set my_object's change_x and change_y to values, like 2 and 2.

   • Call the move() method in the main program loop.

   • Test to make sure the object moves.

9. Randomize the object

- Import the random library
- Set the x location to a random number between 0 and 700. You can do this in the loop where you create the object, or it can be done in the __init__ method.
- Set the y location to a random number between 0 and 500.
- Set the height and width to a random number between 20 and 70.
- Set the change_x and change_y to random numbers between -3 and 3.
- Test and make sure it looks like this figure.

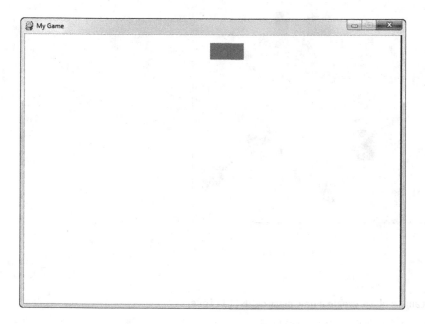

Rectangle in random spot

10. Create and display a list of objects

- Before the code that creates the my_object, create an empty list, called my_list
- Create a for loop that loops 10 times.
- Put the code that creates my_object into the for loop
- Append my_object to my_list.
- Inside the main program loop, loop through each item of my_list.

- Call the draw and move methods for each item of the list.

  - Make sure that the code calls the draw method of the element pulled out by the for loop, don't just use my_object.draw(). This is one of the most common mistakes.

- Test and see if your program looks like the next figure.

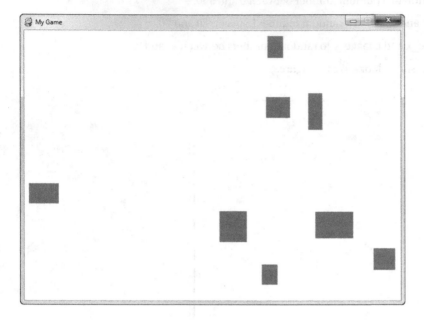

Ten rectangles

11. Use inheritance

    - After the Rectangle class, create a new class called Ellipse.

    - Set Rectangle to be the parent class of Ellipse.

    - You do NOT need to create a new ___init___; we will just inherit the parent class's method.

    - Create a new draw method that draws an ellipse instead of a rectangle.

    - Create a new for loop that adds 10 instances of Ellipse to my_list in addition to the 10 rectangles. (Just use two separate for loops.)

    - Make sure you don't create a new list; just add them to the same my_list.

    - Since both rectangles and ellipses were added to the same list, you only need one loop to go through the list and draw both. Don't make the mistake of having two loops, one for rectangles and one for ellipses. It doesn't work that way.

    - Test and see if your program looks like this next figure.

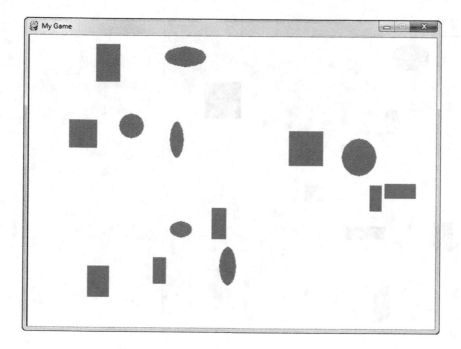

Rectangles and ellipses

12.   Make it more colorful

  •   Adjust the program, so that color is an attribute of Rectangle.

  •   Draw the rectangles and ellipses using the new color.

  •   In the for loops, set the shapes to random colors. Remember, colors are
      specified by three numbers in a list, so you need a list of three random numbers
      (r, g, b).

  •   Test and see if your program looks like the next figure.

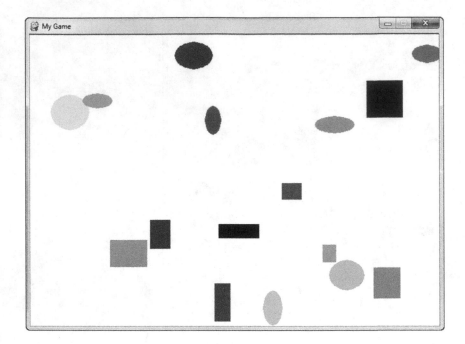

Colorful shapes

13. Try it with more than 10 items of each type. This next figure shows 1,000 shapes.

14. You are done! Turn in your program.

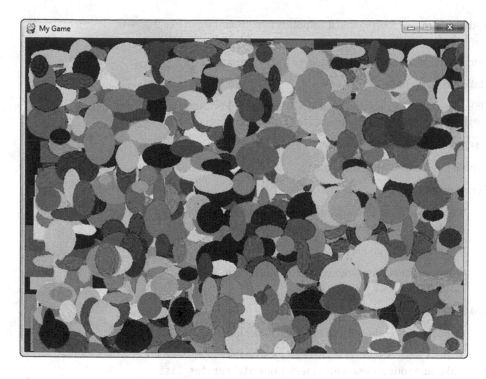

Shapes gone crazy

Exercise 12: Sprite Collecting

This exercise practices using pygame sprites as described in Chapter 14.

1. Make sure this program is created in its own directory.

2. Start with the following program:

   ProgramArcadeGames.com/python_examples/f.php?file=sprite_collect_blocks.py

3. Update the comments at the beginning to reflect that it is now your program, not mine.

4. Modify it so the player moves with the keyboard rather than the mouse. Take a look at the move_sprite_keyboard_smooth.py program also available on the example page:

   ProgramArcadeGames.com/python_examples/f.php?file=move_sprite_keyboard_smooth.py

   • Out of this file, you will need to grab the Player class and move it to your own program. Do not get rid of the Block class. You will have both the Block and Player class in your program.

   • Right now, your player is an instance of Block. You will need to change it so that you create an instance of Player. Note that the constructor for Player takes different parameters than Block.

- Update your event loop so that it responds to keyboard input like this new example does.

- Remove the code that moves the player with the mouse.

- Make the player blue.

- Make sure there is exactly one call to `all_sprites_list.update()` in your main program loop. This will call the `update()` method in every sprite.

- Test and make sure it works now.

5. Create both good sprites and bad sprites

   - Good Sprites

     - Where you create 50 blocks now, instead of adding them to a list called `block_list`, add them to a list called `good_block_list`.

     - Make the blocks green.

     - Where you check for block collisions in the main loop, update the check so it uses `good_block_list`.

   - Bad Sprites

     - Duplicate this code and add 50 more blocks to a new list called `bad_block_list`.

     - Make sure your program only creates one `all_sprites_list`.

     - Don't re-create the list right before you add bad blocks or the player.

     - Make the blocks red.

     - Duplicate that code and check against `bad_block_list`. Decrease the score instead of increasing it.

     - Test and make sure it is working.

   - Use graphics to signify good/bad sprites as shown in the `sprite_collect_graphic.py` example file. Failure to use graphics is only a two-point penalty.

6. Rather than simply use `print` to display the score on the console, display the score on the graphics window. Go back to the end of Chapter 6 and look up the section on drawing text.

7. Add sound effects for when the user hits good blocks, or bad blocks. Here are a couple from `OpenGameArt.org`:

   `ProgramArcadeGames.com/labs/sprite_collecting/good_block.wav`
   `ProgramArcadeGames.com/labs/sprite_collecting/bad_block.wav`

8. Looking back at how we made a sound to begin with, we triggered the sound with a mouse click event. We won't be doing that here. Find the code that you already have that detects when a collision occurs. Play the sound when you have a collision. Also, remember that when you load a sound, it needs to be done before the main loop, but after the `pygame.init()` command.

9. Add a check and make sure the player doesn't slide off the end of the screen. This check should go in the update method of the Player class. There should be four if statement checks, one for each border. If the player's x and y get outside the bounds of the screen, reset the player back inside the screen. Do not modify change_x or change_y. That doesn't work for player-controlled objects. Don't forget to check the right and bottom borders; they are easy to get wrong.

10. Download a wav or ogg file and have it play a sound if the user tries to slide off the screen. Here's one sound you can use:

    ProgramArcadeGames.com/labs/sprite_collecting/bump.wav

11. Check to make sure the bump sound doesn't continually play when the user is at the edge of the screen. If it does, the program is checking the edge incorrectly.

12. If you send your program to anyone, remember they will need all the files, not just the Python program.

Exercise 13: Sprite Moving

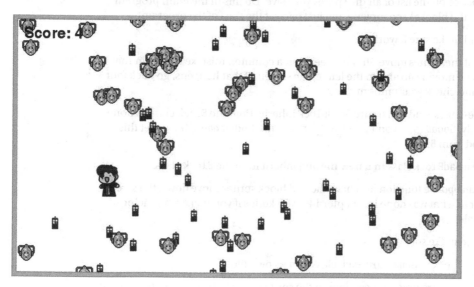

This exercise practices uses pygame sprites as described in Chapter 14 and separates the classes into different files as described in Chapter 15.

1. Make sure this program is created in its own directory.

2. Start with a copy of the program you wrote for Exercise 12: Sprite Collecting. Copy those files into the directory for this exercise.

3. Move the Block class into a new file. Many people get confused between the name of the library file, the name of the class, and the variable that points to the instance of the object. Library files should be all lowercase. I'd recommend calling your new file that you put the Block class into block_library.py.

4. Make sure your program runs like before. Adjust `import` statements as needed. Remember that you prepend the library name to the class, not the variable that points to the instance of the class. For example: `my_dog = dog_library.Dog()` and NOT `dog_library.my_dog = Dog()` because `Dog` is what is in the library, not `my_dog`.

5. Define a `GoodBlock` class **in a new file**, and inherit from your `Block` class. I'd recommend using the file name `goodblock_library.py` to keep with the pattern we set up before. Remember, define the class. Don't create an instance of it. Your `for` loop that creates the instances does not move.

6. Add a new `update` method. (You probably don't need a new `__init__` method.) Make the good block randomly move up, down, left or right each update. (Change `self.rect.x` and `self.rect.y` randomly each time the `update` function is called. Not to a completely new number, but add a random number from -3 to 3 or so. Remember that `random.randrange(-3,3)` does not generate a random number from -3 to 3.)

7. Change your `for` loop so that it creates instances of the `GoodBlock` class and not your old regular `Block` class.

8. Call `update` on the list of all the sprites you have. Do this in the main program loop so the blocks keep moving, not just once at the start of the program.

9. Test and make sure it works.

10. It is ok if the sprites move off the screen, but a common mistake results in the sprites all moving up and to the left off the screen. If that happens, go back four steps and check your random range.

11. Double-check, and make sure `GoodBlock` inherits from the `Block` class. If done correctly, `GoodBlock` won't need an `__init__` method because it will get this method from `Block`.

12. Create a `BadBlock` class **in a new file** and inherit from the `Block` class.

13. Make an `update` function and have the bad block sprites move down the screen, similar to what was done in Chapter 14. Extra kudos if you make a bouncing rectangle.

14. Test, and make sure it works.

15. Double-check to make sure each class is in its own file.

16. If you have extra time, you can look at the sprite examples section on the web site and see how to get sprites to bounce or move in circles.

Exercise 14: Spell Check

This exercise shows how to create a spell checker. To prepare for the exercise, go to:

`ProgramArcadeGames.com/index.php?chapter=examples` list

...and download the files listed below. The files are also in the "Searching and Sorting Examples" section.

- `AliceInWonderLand.txt` - Text of "Alice In Wonderland"
- `AliceInWonderLand200.txt` - First chapter of "Alice In Wonderland"
- `dictionary.txt` - A list of words

Requirements

Write a single program in Python that checks the spelling of the first chapter of "Alice In Wonderland." First use a linear search, then use a binary search. Print the line number along with the word that does not exist in the dictionary.

Follow the steps below carefully. If you don't know how to accomplish one step, ask before moving on to the next step.

Steps to Complete:

1. If you work off the BitBucket template, skip ahead to step 6.
2. Find or create a directory for your project.
3. Download the dictionary to the directory.
4. Download first 200 lines of Alice In Wonderland to your directory.
5. Start a Python file for your project.
6. It is necessary to split apart the words in the story so that they may be checked individually. It is also necessary to remove extra punctuation and white space. Unfortunately, there is not any good way of doing this with what the book has covered so far. The code to do this is short, but a full explanation is beyond the scope of this class. Include the following function in your program. Remember, function definitions should go at the top of your program just after the imports. We'll call this function in a later step.

```
import re

# This function takes in a line of text and returns
# a list of words in the line.
def split_line(line):
    return re.findall('[A-Za-z]+(?:\'[A-Za-z]+)?',line)
```

This code uses a *regular expression* to split the text apart. Regular expressions are very powerful and relatively easy to learn. To learn more about regular expressions, see:

http://en.wikipedia.org/wiki/Regular_expression

7. Read the file dictionary.txt into an array. Go back to the chapter on Searching, or see the searching_example.py for example code on how to do this. This does *not* have anything to do with the import command, libraries, or modules. Don't call the dictionary word_list or something generic because that will be confusing. Call it dictionary_list or something similar.

8. Close the file.

9. Print --- Linear Search ---

10. Open the file AliceInWonderLand200.txt

11. We are *not* going to read the story into a list. Do not create a new list here like you did with the dictionary.

12. Start a for loop to iterate through each line.

13. Call the split_line function to split apart the line of text in the story that was just read in. Store the list that the function returns in a new variable named words. Remember, just calling the function won't do anything useful. You need to assign a variable equal (words) to the result. If you've forgotten now to capture the return value from a function, flip back to the functions chapter to find it.

14. Start a nested for loop to iterate through each word in the words list. This should be inside the for loop that runs through each line in the file. (One loop for each line, another loop for each word in the line.)

15. Using a linear search, check the current word against the words in the dictionary. Check the chapter on searching or the searching_example.py for example code on how to do this. The linear search is just three lines long. When comparing to the word to the other words in the dictionary, convert the word to uppercase. In your while loop just use word.upper() instead of word for the key. This linear search will exist inside the for loop created in the prior step. We are looping through each word in the dictionary, looking for the current word in the line that we just read in.

16. If the word was not found, print the word. Don't print anything if you do find the word; that would just be annoying.

17. Close the file.

18. Make sure the program runs successfully before moving onto the next step.

19. Create a new variable that will track the line number that you are on. Print this line number along with the misspelled from the prior step.

20. Make sure the program runs successfully before moving onto the next step.

21. Print --- Binary Search ---

22. The linear search takes quite a while to run. To temporarily disable it, it may be commented out by using three quotes before and after that block of code. Ask if you are unsure how to do this.

23. Repeat the same pattern of code as before, but this time use a binary search. Much of the code from the linear search may be copied, and it is only necessary to replace the lines of code that represent the linear search with the binary search.

24. Note the speed difference between the two searches.

25. Make sure the linear search is re-enabled, if it was disabled while working on the binary search.

26. Upload the final program or check in the final program.

Example Run

```
--- Linear Search ---
Line 3   possible misspelled word: Lewis
Line 3   possible misspelled word: Carroll
Line 46  possible misspelled word: labelled
Line 46  possible misspelled word: MARMALADE
Line 58  possible misspelled word: centre
Line 59  possible misspelled word: learnt
Line 69  possible misspelled word: Antipathies
Line 73  possible misspelled word: curtsey
Line 73  possible misspelled word: CURTSEYING
Line 79  possible misspelled word: Dinah'll
Line 80  possible misspelled word: Dinah
Line 81  possible misspelled word: Dinah
Line 89  possible misspelled word: Dinah
Line 89  possible misspelled word: Dinah
Line 149  possible misspelled word: flavour
Line 150  possible misspelled word: toffee
Line 186  possible misspelled word: croquet
--- Binary Search ---
Line 3   possible misspelled word: Lewis
Line 3   possible misspelled word: Carroll
Line 46  possible misspelled word: labelled
Line 46  possible misspelled word: MARMALADE
Line 58  possible misspelled word: centre
Line 59  possible misspelled word: learnt
Line 69  possible misspelled word: Antipathies
Line 73  possible misspelled word: curtsey
Line 73  possible misspelled word: CURTSEYING
Line 79  possible misspelled word: Dinah'll
Line 80  possible misspelled word: Dinah
Line 81  possible misspelled word: Dinah
Line 89  possible misspelled word: Dinah
Line 89  possible misspelled word: Dinah
```

```
Line 149   possible misspelled word: flavour
Line 150   possible misspelled word: toffee
Line 186   possible misspelled word: croquet
```

Exercise 15: Final Exercise

There are two options for the final exercise: A "video game option" and a "text adventure option."

Video Game Option

This is it! This is your chance to use your creativity and really show off what you can create in your own game.

This final exercise is divided into three parts. Each part raises the bar on what your game needs to be able to do.

Requirements for Part 1:

- Open up a screen.
- Set up the items to be drawn on the screen.
- Provide some sort of rudimentary player movement via mouse, keyboard, or game controller.

Tips:

- If your program will involve things running into each other, start by using sprites. Do not start by using drawing commands and expect to add in sprites later. It won't work and you'll need to start over from scratch. This will be sad.
- If you are coding a program like minesweeper or connect four, do **not** use sprites. Since collision detection is not needed, there is no need to mess with sprites.
- Under "longer game examples" I have two programs that show how to create pong or breakout style games. Don't just turn these in as Part 1 though; you'll need to add a lot before it really qualifies.
- OpenGameArt.org has a lot of images and sounds you can use royalty-free.
- Kenney.nl has many images and sounds as well.

Requirements for Part 2:

For Final Exercise Part 2, your game should be mostly functional. A person should be able to sit down and play the game for a few minutes and have it feel like a real game. Here are some things you might want to add:

- Be able to collide with objects.
- Players can lose the game if something bad happens.
- Onscreen score.
- Some initial sound effects.
- Movement of other characters in the screen.
- The ability to click on mines or empty spots.

Requirements for Part 3:

For the final part, add in the last polish for your game. Here are some things you might want to add:

- Multiple levels
- Sounds
- Multiple "lives"
- Title and instruction screens
- Background music
- Heat-seeking missiles
- Hidden doors
- A "sweep" action in a minesweeper game or the ability to place "flags"

Text Adventure Option

Not interested in a video game? Continue your work from the "Adventure!" game.

Requirements for Part 1:

1. Rather than have each room be a list of [description, north, east, south, west], create a Room class. The class should have a constructor that takes in (description, north, east, south, west) and sets fields for the description and all of the directions. Get the program working with the new class.

2. Expand the game so that a person can travel up and down. Also expand it so the person can travel northwest, southwest, northeast, and southeast.

3. Create another class for Object. Give the object fields for name, description, and current room. For example, you might have a name of "key," a description of "This is a rusty key that looks like it would fit in an old lock. It has not been used in a long time." The current room number would be 3 if the key was in room 3. If the player is carrying the key then the current room for the object will be -1.

4. Create a list for objects, and add several objects to the list. The code for this will be very similar to the list of rooms that you created and added to the list of rooms.

5. After printing the description of the room, have the program search the entire list of objects, and print if the room of the object matches the room the player is in. For example, if current_room == current_object.room then print: "There is a key here."

6. Test your game and make sure it works.

Requirements for Part 2:

1. Add the ability to pick up an object. If the user types get key then:

    1. Split the user input so you split out and just have a variable equal to "key."

    2. Search the list until you find an object that matches what the user is trying to pick up.

    3. If the object isn't found, or if the object isn't in the current room, print an error.

    4. If the object is found and it is in the current room, then set the object's room number to -1.

2. Add the ability to drop an object.

3. Add a command for "inventory" that will print every object who's room number is equal to -1.

4. Add the ability to use the objects. For example "use key" or "swing sword" or "feed bear."

Requirements for Part 3:

Expand the game some more. Try some of these ideas:

1. Create a file format that allows you to load the rooms and objects from a file rather than write code for it.

2. Have monsters with hit points.

3. Split the code up into multiple files for better organization.

4. Remove globals using a main function as shown at the end of the chapter about functions.

5. Have objects with limited use. Like a bow that only has so many arrows.

6. Have creatures with limited health, and weapons that cause random damage and have a random chance to hit.

Index

■ A

Adventure game
    description, 365
    dungeon creation, 366–367
    instructions, 367–368
    maps, 288–289
Animation, 369
    background color, 137–138
    code, 140
    direction and speed, 139
    initialization, 138
    Pixel Aspect Ratio, 138
    rectangle, 138, 140
    square, 141
Apple Macintosh computers, 36
Apple text screen, 83
Arc, 96
Array-Backed Grids
    adventure games, 289
    application, 289
    color, 293
    color variable, 293
    for loop, 290, 292
    Fortran and MATLAB, 293
    grid on-screen, 296–297
    margin variable, 291
    minesweeper, 288
    move_mouse.py, 294
    program's window size, 290
    two-dimensional array, 293
    width, height and margin, 290
Arrays, 131

■ B

Binary number system, 34
Binary Search
    Boolean variable, 281
    guesser, 279

Bitmapped graphics, 372
    background image, 206–208
    JPEG compression artifacts, 210
    new folder, 205–206
    player image, 208
    program, 211–212
    sounds, 210–211
    spaceship, solid black background, 209
Blank Window, 90, 92
Blender, 145

■ C

Camel game
    description, 352
    program, 354–356
Cartesian coordinate system
    ASCII art, 84
    graphics, 82
    lower-right quadrant, 85
    rudimentary graphics, 83
    spaceware text screen, 84
    text-based, 82
    text screen, 83
Catch block, 311
Classes
    address, 218–219, 221, 223
    adventure game, data, 217
    Ball class, 225–226
    character, 218
    constructors, 231–232
    Dog class, 223–224
    and graphics
        inheritance, 376
        move(), 374
        my_list, 375
        my_object, 373
    inheritance
        boat, 233–234
        child classes, 234

Classes (*cont.*)
    constructors, 236
    Person (), 236
    relationships, 237
  references
    functions, 229–230
    Person() class, 226–227
    variables, 228
  static *vs.* instance variables, 237–238
Colors, 85–86
Compilers, 36
Computer language
  Altair 8800, 33
  assembly language, 35
  binary number system, 34
  CLI, 37
  compiler, 34, 36
  data and computer instructions, 34
  definition, computers, 33
  disadvantage, 36
  hexadecimal codes, 34
  history of, 37
  interpreters, 36–37
  JVM, 37
  linkers, 36
  Python, 37
  source code in program, 36
  Tiobe keeps track, 37
  VES, 37
Counting by numbers other than one, 65
Custom calculator
  program, 348–349
  kinetic energy, 11

■ D

3D Animation, 145–146
Decimal numbers
  field width, characters, 337
  format command, 336, 338
  random numbers, 335–336
  str(), 337
  string formatting, 336

■ E

Ellipse, 95
Event processing loop, 88–89
Exception object, 314
Exceptions
  generating, 315
  handling, 311–312
  if statements, 315
  object, 314
  score saving, 313
  terms and phrases, 311
  uncaught exception, 311

■ F

File extensions, 9
Floating-point number, 74
For loops
  Boolean variable, 71
  code, 68–69
  legal variable name, 63
  print statement, 63
  range function, 63
  starting and ending number, 64
Formatting
  Dollars and Cents, printing, 342–344
  floating point numbers, 340–342
  leading zeros, 340
  Pygame, 345
  strings, 338
Fractals, recursive
  coding, 330–332
  level 0, 327
  level 1, 328
  level 2, 329
  level 3, 330
Frame of the game, 89–90
Frames-per-second (FPS), 60
Functions
  box, 370
  calling functions, 160
  create_list, 371
  definition, 154
  docstrings, 158
  draw_tree(), 154
  examples, 161–165
  global variables, 160–161
  min3, 369
  mudball game, 165–167
  parameters, 154–155
  pass-by-copy, 159
  pygame, 179
  return statement, 156
  snowman, 180
  stick figure, 181, 183–185
  variable scope, 158
  volume_cylinder, 156–157

■ G

Game controller. *See* Joystick
1GL language, 34
2GL language, 34
Graphics
  bitmapped graphics, 92
  blank window, 81
  command, 90
  drawing command, 90
  drawing lines, 93
  full-screen games, 87

loops and offsets, 93–94
program listing, 99–101
rectangle drawing, 95
set_mode, 87
text, 97–98
Guessing game
calculator program, 61
FPS rate, 60
FSP video games, 60
game loop, 61
graphics, 59
loop the loop, 62
Python, 62
while loop, 62

■ H

Hexadecimal codes, 34

■ I

Increment operators, 70–71
Insertion sort, 305–306
Integrated Development
    Environment (IDLE), 2
Interpreter, 37

■ J

Joystick
calls program, 196–200
center (0,0), 193
down (0,1), 195
down left (-1,1), 195
down right (1,1), 195
floating-point values, 192
left (-1,0), 195
right (1,0), 195
up (0,-1), 194
up left (-1,-1), 194
up right (1,-1), 194

■ K

Keyboard, 187–191

■ L

Libraries and modules, 267
multiple files, 268
multiple programmers, 268
namespace, 269
package name, 269
third party libraries, 270
Linear search
algorithm, 276
property, 278
variations, 276–277

Linkers, 36
Linux computers, 36
Lists
addition, 125
array, 122
data type, 123
grocery lists, 122
ice cube trays, 123
IDLE's command line, 122
index, 122
iteration, 124
location, 123
modification, 126
Python, 121
type function, 121
value, 123
Local namespace, 269
Looping
alignment, 112
code, 111
end character, 108
index variables, 110
nested, 109–110
print statement, 107–108
rectangle, 109
spaces addition, 113
video explanations, 107

■ M

Mac installation, 3–6
Make games and get paid, 9–10
McDonald's applications, 10
Mouse, 186–187

■ N

Nesting loops, 66
Number guessing game, 279

■ O

Optional wing IDE, 7–9

■ P

Picture creation
functions and loops, 357
Windows Paint program, 357
Polygon drawing, 96
Printing
assignment operator, 16–18
comments, 15–16
custom equation calculators, 21–25
escape codes, 14–15
mathematical expression, 13
multiple items, 13
operators, 19–20

Printing (*cont.*)
    order of operations, 20
    text, 12
    trig functions, 20
    variables, 18–19
Pygame, 1
Pygame module, 267
Pygame library, 247, 249
    graphics, 85
    pygame.py file, 85
Python, 1, 87

Q

Quiz
    description, 350–351
    program, 351
Quiz games
    mixing the = and == operators, 43
    Boolean variables, 44, 46
    case insensitive comparisons, 48
    Else and Else If, 46–47
    equal/not, 43
    flowchart, 42
    greater than/less than numbers, 42–43
    if statements, 41, 47–48, 50–51
    indentation, 43
    multiple text possibilities, 48
    using And/Or, 44

R

Random numbers
    import statement, 74
    range function, 74
random.py, 74
Rectangle, 95
Recursion
    factorial calculation, 322–324
    fractal (*see* Fractals, recursive)
    functions, 320–321
    if statement, 321
    rectangles, 324–326
    recursive binary search, 332–333
    recursive_draw function, 324
    stack space, 321
    web page, 319–320
Recursive binary search, 332–333
"Running total" code pattern, 66–67

S

Screen flipping, 90
Searching
    binary search, 273
    empty array, 275
    linear search, 273

Secret code
    Unicode chart, 128
    UTF-8 value, 129–130
Selection sort, 303–304
Send feedback, 10
Side scrolling platformer, 259
Snow animation
    code explanation, 141–143
    Program Listing, 143, 145
Sorting
    insertion, 305–306
    selection, 303–304
    swapping values, 301–302
Source code, 36
Spell checker, 383–385
Sprites
    and collisions, 248
    bitmapped graphic, 250
    Block class, 249
    Game Class, 254
    moving, 253
    platformer, 258
    program loop, 252–253
    Pygame library, 247
    random library, 249
    red block, 251
    sheets, 262
    shooting things, 255
    snake/centipede type, 260
    walls, 256
Sprite sheet platformer, 262
Starting Python, 2
Strings, 127–128

T

Terminal window, 3
Text adventure option, 387–388
Tic-tac-toe board, 287
Two-dimensional array, 287
Try block, 311

U

Unix installation, 6

V

Video game option, 386–387

W, X, Y, Z

While loops
    increment variable, 70
    program, 72–73
    programmer, 72
Windows installation, 1–2

Printed in the United States
By Bookmasters